Advance praise for *Christmas Unwrapped*...

"The destructive pathology of consumerism is all about us and plain to see. Christmas, by our cultural standards, exposes that pathology and pushes it to its most visible distorting extremity. This fine book—with its historical perspective, acute social analysis, and keen sensitivity to the human crisis among us—is sure to illuminate the deathly choices so easily made among us, all in the name of caring religious celebration! Beyond illumination, the book invites sober alternatives, thus an important read."

— WALTER BRUEGGEMANN, Columbia Theological Seminary

"*Christmas Unwrapped* suggests that the most popular holiday of the year is no longer, if it ever was, a religious holiday. It is, rather, a celebration of consumer capitalism as a religion. Examinations of the original event as narrated in the Christian gospels, Santa Claus as an American icon, and the most loved Christmas movies, illuminate the Christmas we 'buy into' as a cultural artifact with strong political and social effects. These essays, consistently insightful, often informative and amusing, and frequently frightening, effectively identify reasons for the widespread discomfort, criticism, and resistance to the practice of Christmas. This collection is not only a good read, but is also a must-read."

— MARGARET MILES, The Graduate Theological Union, Berkeley

Christmas
Unwrapped

CONSUMERISM, CHRIST, AND CULTURE

**EDITED BY
RICHARD HORSLEY AND JAMES TRACY**

TRINITY PRESS INTERNATIONAL
Harrisburg, Pennsylvania

Trinity Press International, P.O. Box 1321, Harrisburg, PA 17105
Trinity Press International is a division of The Morehouse Group.

Cover art: Christmas scene, Timothy Hursley/SuperStock.
Cover design: Jim Booth

Library of Congress Cataloging-in-Publication Data

Christmas unwrapped: consumerism, Christ, and culture / edited by Richard Horsley and James Tracy.
    p. cm.
   Includes bibliographical references and index.
   ISBN 1-56338-319-5 (alk. paper)
   1. Christmas – United States. 2. Christmas – Economic aspects – United States.
3. Consumption (Economics) – United States. 4. Christmas in motion pictures.
5. United States – Social life and customs. I. Horsley, Richard A.   II. Tracy, James, 1961-
GT4986.A1 C477 2001
394.2663'0973 – dc21

                          00-064839

Printed in the United States of America

01   02   03   04   05   06   10   9   8   7   6   5   4   3   2   1

Contents

Part 4:
THEORETICAL AND THEOLOGICAL REFLECTIONS

Introduction

James Tracy

For most Americans, the word "Christmas" conjures up a collection of pleasant images. Christmas in our associations is, as Scrooge's nephew says, "a good time; a kind, forgiving, charitable, pleasant time; the only time I know of, in the long calendar of the year, when men and women seem by one consent to open up their shut-up hearts freely, and to think of people below them as if they really were fellow-passengers to the grave, and not another race of creatures bound on other journeys."

Christmas summons images of family gathered around a decorated tree, of music and light and the comforting smell of a special dinner cooking on a snowy winter day. Carolers at the door, sleigh rides, chestnuts roasting on an open fire, and sugar plums also come into play, although almost no one today experiences any of these. Memories shimmering with the sheen of childhood magic emerge of Santa Claus as the mysterious impish distributor of presents found on Christmas morn under the tree.

These images are appealing—and powerful. They offer a Yuletide in which people greet their fellows warmly in a seasonal harbor from an otherwise cold society, a light-filled and entertaining respite from the gray of winter, a time when we are given gifts and when values are realigned into their proper chain of being—with family and friendship taking their proper place at the top of our lives' hierarchy. These are wholesome, deeply resonant symbols of the values we hold dear and of a world for which we yearn.

But is this the Christmas we actually experience? How many people standing in line at the malls would say that their Christmas season is replete with warmth, affection, and neighborliness? In fact, Christmas is experienced by most adults as a time of intensified stress. They feel obliged to go through the motions of preparation for what they have been socialized to believe are Yuletide necessities, spending large portions of their income on obligatory gifts and long hours of increasingly limited leisure time fighting for parking spaces—in the process, piling up debt that may take months to repay.

The Currier and Ives or Dickensian Christmas that is sought never actually existed. It is little wonder, then, that the frenzied activity supposed to culminate in such a Christmas instead delivers disappointment as its denouement. The result is often "holiday blues" and even severe depression. Americans are bombarded with a flurry of marketing imagery that leads them on an annual consumerist chase after a chimera.

1

It has become commonplace for religious and other pundits to decry what they consider the poisoning of the Christmas well with untoward commercialism. Such jeremiads usually call for a return to the "original meaning" of Christmas, either as a Christian celebration of Jesus' birth or as a spiritual celebration of "family values." However well-intentioned, these critiques fall wide of the mark, in no small measure because they at least implicitly posit a golden age of Christmas observance from which we have fallen. In short, they assume that Christmas was once a religious holiday into which the marketplace has insinuated itself.

This assumption is historically inaccurate and analytically anemic. The fact is that the Christmas festival has never—since its inception—been particularly spiritual. It has, of course, accrued different meanings in varied times and contexts, some of which will be touched upon. In the context of modern America, though, it is certainly not the case that the marketplace has co-opted a Christian celebration to increase sales; it is far more accurate and illuminating to recognize Christmas today as the religious expression of consumer capitalism. In other words, Christmas is not an autonomous subject that has been victimized by the rise of modern advertising. Rather, it is but one face (the religious facet) of that multiheaded hydra that has become America's cultural hegemon—namely, consumer capitalism.

Many hundreds of books have been written about Christmas. Surprisingly, though, it was not until the publication of Stephen Nissenbaum's *The Battle for Christmas: A Cultural History of America's Most Cherished Holiday*[1] that a historian of the first water rigorously applied the tools of contemporary social science to a trenchant examination of the historical emergence of the many meanings and appropriations of Christmas in America. Nissenbaum's analysis has, in fact, been germinal for this book. Most of the contributors to this volume in one way or another use Nissenbaum's impressive work as the starting point for their own analyses. For this reason, it is sensible to provide here—for those who have not read *The Battle for Christmas*—a brief overview of Nissenbaum's insights that have most informed the essays in this volume.

Christmas, Nissenbaum demonstrates, never had an immaculate conception. As the Roman Empire was being christianized, church leaders placed a thin Christian veneer over the traditional and ineradicable pagan celebration around the time of the winter solstice. While there was absolutely no scriptural basis for celebrating the birth of Jesus, this proved a convenient vehicle by which the church could appropriate so deeply entrenched a pagan holiday. Many pagan elements persisted, of course, in the now-Christian holiday. These included remnants of Roman paganism, as well as subsequent accretions of northern European paganism when Christendom spread.

By the Middle Ages and well into the early modern period in Europe, Christmas was a peasant celebration marked by excess, carnality, and, significantly, at least momentary "social inversion" (8). Christmas, according to Nissenbaum, "once occasioned a kind of behavior that would be shocking today: It was a time of heavy drinking when the rules that governed people's behavior were momentarily abandoned in favor of an unrestrained 'carnival,' a kind of December Mardi Gras" (x).

Christmas as practiced in England in the seventeenth century so offended the Puritans that in 1659 the General Court of the Massachusetts Bay Colony outlawed its observance. "In New England," Nissenbaum notes, "for the first two centuries of white settlement most people did not celebrate Christmas. In fact, the holiday was systematically suppressed by Puritans during the colonial period and largely ignored by their descendants. It was actually *illegal* to celebrate Christmas in Massachusetts between 1659 and 1681 (the fine was five shillings)" (3, Nissenbaum's italics).

Anyone familiar with the Puritans' sensibilities will readily understand why they took offense to a celebration for which there was "no biblical or historical reason to place the birth of Jesus on December 25" (4), which was marked by excessive public drinking and gluttony, and which often included ribald, even lewd, activities such as "mumming" (cross-dressing that was associated with overt sexual frolics) (7).

Of equal concern for the Puritan establishment was the fact that English norms treated Christmas festivity as "an occasion when the social hierarchy itself was symbolically turned upside down, in a gesture that inverted designated roles of gender, age, and class" (8). Christmas occasioned "the mockery of established authority, aggressive begging (often involving the threat of doing harm), and even the invasion of wealthy homes" (5).

The quaint and harmless carolers that Scrooge sends to flight merely by angrily picking up his ruler were not so easily dismissed in the medieval and early modern eras. The peasants were wont to go "wassailing" in a seasonal mood of social inversion, entering unbidden into the homes of their socioeconomic superiors with demands for favors and treats ("give us some figgy pudding; we won't go until we get some"). The wealthier homeowner fully understood that failure to provide his unwelcome guests with sweets would quickly sour the visit.

As with so many Puritan experiments, the attempt to simply stamp out these Christmas traditions failed. As the late Roman-era church leaders understood, it is easier to appropriate than to eradicate such popular traditions. By the early national period, when American cities became more populous and impersonal, these behaviors, according to Nissenbaum, "had become even more threatening, combining carnival rowdiness with urban gang violence and Christmas-season riots" (x–xi). This led New York's elites to pursue the domestication of Christmas. Nissenbaum attributes this endeavor to a circle of literati that included Clement Moore and Washington Irving, "a small group of antiquarian-minded New York gentlemen—men who knew one another and were members of a distinct social set. Collectively, those men became known as the Knickerbockers.... [They] felt that they belonged to a patrician class whose authority was under siege" (64–65).

As a means of social control and in concert with emergent middle-class sensibilities, the Knickerbockers sought to transfer Christmas merrymaking from the public realm to the domestic sphere, in the process transforming holiday treating from a class-based demand of gifts from elites ("was-sailing") to a family-centered giving of gifts by parents to children. As Nissenbaum states, "age replaced class as the axis along which the Christmas gift exchange took place" (109). The great stroke of genius that effected this successful appropriation, Nissenbaum argues, was the creation of Santa Claus as though he were a venerable Dutch tradition. Santa Claus was, in fact, an "invented tradition" who, "far from being a creature of ancient Dutch folklore...was essentially devised by a group of non-Dutch New Yorkers in the early nineteenth century" (x). The major literary vehicle for disseminating this new notion of a domesticated Christmas symbolically focused on Santa Claus as the bringer of gifts to children in their homes was, of course, Clement Moore's poem, "A Visit from St. Nicholas" (which began, " 'Twas the night before Christmas").

Nissenbaum provides an engaging analysis of the imagery in this poem, the poem's efficacy in achieving the goals of the Knickerbockers, and the subsequent transformations of Santa Claus iconography in the nineteenth century. He concludes that what changed as a result of this new paradigm "was not that the rowdier ways of celebrating Christmas had disappeared, or even that they had diminished, but that a new kind of holiday celebration was now being proclaimed as the 'real' Christmas. The rest of it—public drunkenness and threats or acts of violence, 'rough music'—had been redefined as *crime*" (99, Nissenbaum's italics).

Nissenbaum further points out that, in addition to facilitating this successful experiment in social control, the iconography of Santa Claus both as handcraftsman and as mythical mediator for the exchange of gifts also served to ease the guilt about indulgence and the ambivalence toward mass-produced goods felt by middle-class parents in the early nineteenth century. This made the "invented tradition" of Santa Claus of enormous value to manufacturers. As American manufacturing and its concomitant advertising became more powerful and sophisticated throughout the nineteenth century, Christmas—with Santa at its cultural epicenter—was appropriated by industrial interests not for controlling street rowdies but as a means to entice Americans into an annual orgy of buying.

"It was the figure of Santa Claus," Nissenbaum observes, "that permitted...[many Americans] to enter the world of commercial gift giving so quickly and completely. As early as the mid-1820s, Santa Claus was beginning to be employed to sell Christmas goods" (169). This, of course, gave rise to new concerns reflected in literature, all-too familiar today, marked by much hand-wringing about the immorality of greed and the dangers of spoiling children. "In about 1830," Nissenbaum argues, "the literature of

Christmas in America began to change. Before that date it dealt chiefly with questions of social disorder. Afterward a new concern emerged, an anxiety about private selfishness and greedy consumerism, especially as those affected children. . . . Consumerism was coming to supplant chaos as the new problem of the holiday season" (176–77).

In his superb book, Nissenbaum makes many additional points about the history of Christmas in America, but, as already mentioned, the aim here is not so much to summarize *The Battle for Christmas* as to acquaint the reader with those of Nissenbaum's contributions that have proved most engaging for the contributors to this volume.

It is worth noting that there was a preexistent scholarship of the American Christmas, though very little of it was particularly illuminating. In the year before Nissenbaum's book appeared, for instance, Penne L. Restad published *Christmas in America: A History,*[2] which, while extensively researched and rich with interesting minutiae, is largely devoid of any compelling analysis. In the same year, Princeton historian Leigh Eric Schmidt released *Consumer Rites: The Buying and Selling of American Holidays,*[3] which included a lengthy treatment of Christmas. Schmidt offers a superficial analysis that demurs from criticizing Christmas behavior on the grounds that *gift giving* is a universal part of human nature.[4] With such a pseudo-anthropological gloss to his perspective, Schmidt runs the risk of facilely equating modern American consumer excess with underclass traditions of the European past or other premodern cultures' traditions of gift exchange. It should be obvious, however, that Americans storming the malls to purchase the new toy craze their children demand as the result of a television advertising blitz constitutes markedly different cultural content than does gift exchange in, for instance, a potlatch society. And it is a markedly different cultural content that cries out for richer analysis.

The publication of *The Battle for Christmas* in 1996 dramatically overhauled and enhanced the study of this vast and highly significant cultural construct we call the Christmas season. Never before had the study of Christmas received such full and insightful treatment by a first-rate scholar. Where most scholars of Christmas continued to prospect in the same old played-out shafts, Nissenbaum mined a new vein that promises to yield rich ore.

Curiously, although widely hailed (and a Pulitzer Prize finalist), *The Battle for Christmas* has not yet generated the caliber of Christmas scholarship that it deserves. This volume intends to correct that. With Nissenbaum's socioeconomic analysis as a benchmark, the authors of these essays broaden, extend, and further apply Nissenbaum's germinal work in explorative—and often provocative—ways. The intention is not to pay homage to Nissenbaum, but to actively build upon his catalyzing work. It is hoped that this volume of essays will generate further scholarship and serve as a valuable point for discussion among its audience. It is further hoped that this volume will contribute to a new appropriation of Christmas by Americans away from the commercial paradigm that now dominates toward a model that will foster more humane and humanizing values—values that for the most part now lie latent in the imagery that has been created as received tradition.

Notes

1. Stephen Nissenbaum, *The Battle for Christmas: A Cultural History of America's Most Cherished Holiday* (New York: Alfred A. Knopf, 1996).

2. Penne L. Restad, *Christmas in America: A History* (New York: Oxford University Press, 1995). Even more analytically anemic is Karal Ann Marling's celebratory cultural history *Merry Christmas: Celebrating America's Greatest Holiday* (Cambridge, Mass.: Harvard University Press, 2000).

3. Leigh Eric Schmidt, *Consumer Rites: The Buying and Selling of American Holidays* (Princeton, N.J.: Princeton University Press, 1995).

4. See Schmidt, *Consumer Rites*, 8–10.

Part 1

The Formative History of American Christmas

Chapter One

The Armistice over Christmas
Consuming in the Twentieth Century

James Tracy

In *The Battle for Christmas*, a germinal book about the history of Christmas in America, Stephen Nissenbaum incisively demonstrates that the nineteenth-century iconography of Christmas (particularly the creation of Santa Claus) emerged first as a successful attempt at social control and later as a concomitant to the romantic cult of domesticity and the social construction of childhood. Nissenbaum's analysis, however, ends with the nineteenth century because, he states, "by the end of the nineteenth century, if not earlier, the Christmas celebration practiced by most Americans was one that would be quite familiar to their modern descendants. Between then and now the modifications have been more of degree than of kind, more quantitative than qualitative. The important changes—the *revealing* changes—had all taken place."[1]

One certainly cannot fault Nissenbaum, who has exhaustively mined the sources of three centuries from the Puritans to the Victorians, for placing a chronological limit on his narrative. Also, there is much truth in his assertion that the accoutrements and icons of fin-de-siècle America (Santa Claus, the Christmas tree, parental gift giving to children) would be readily recognizable to Christmas observers today. Yet it is worth considering whether Nissenbaum is too quick to assume that the changes in the twentieth century have been neither "important" nor "revealing."

Certainly, as he recognizes, there have been quantitative changes to the Christmas observance in the past century. Yet quantitative changes of sufficient scale often result in qualitative changes in the meaning and experience of cultural phenomena. What a century ago was a season of relatively minor indulgence encouraged by enterprising manufacturers is now so gargantuan a retail orgy that it is fervently monitored by Wall Street as a fundamental index and determinant of the nation's economic soundness. It is no exaggeration to predict that the American economy would lapse into recession if no one bought Christmas presents this year, while it would be difficult to make the same claim for any period that Nissenbaum analyzes.

It is true that Americans today continue to resonate with the Christmas imagery of a century ago. Indeed, the late-nineteenth-century Christmas imagery has become romanticized in popular culture as the dominant paradigm of Christmas celebration just as surely as Christmas cards printed with Currier and Ives images still sell at the mall. But, considered the other way around, would a nineteenth-century Christmas reveler magically transported to the present by the Ghost of Christmas Yet to Come recognize today's Christmas? In all likelihood, even a short exposure to the near-constant advertising assault on the senses, or the mall experience with its depersonalized assembly-line sales techniques and the shopping rage expressed by so many people determined to celebrate the joyous season in the style to which they feel obligated, would lead our imaginary Victorian to get down on her knees and plead with the Spirit to assure her that this is not the inexorable shape of the Christmas of her heirs.

It is noteworthy that many historians describe the culture of the nineteenth century as one marked by economic scarcity while the twentieth century might be fruitfully perceived as an era stamped with a culture of plenty. Considering the former, it was not until the very end of the nineteenth century that the productive capacity of the United States created excessive surplus. In other words, while Americans have often been blessed with "plenty" when compared to their European peasant counterparts,[2] nonetheless, throughout most of the nation's history, the productive forces of society have, by modern standards, barely kept pace with the most basic needs of the domestic market. Jeffersonian yeoman farmers might proudly display small pewter collections on their handcrafted cabinets, but the vast bulk of their market consumption was for staples—staples that production methods of the time could only just meet, with a very minor surplus to boot.

A society with underlying economic limitations tends, of necessity, to assume cultural norms and expectations consonant with scarcity. From pundits such as Ben Franklin to the moral crusades of the Gilded Age, middle-class Americans historically placed high premiums on such values as frugality, temperance, delayed gratification, and self-control. These were essential characteristics in a society that, during its best times, did not ensure opulence and that periodically went bust (witness the regular depressions of the nineteenth century). Even a successful planter and former president like Thomas Jefferson found himself—on his deathbed—attempting to raffle off his dear Monticello to pay creditors.

Self-control also reached into the most personal dimensions of life. One of the most remarkable demographic changes of the nineteenth century was a decline in white middle-class birthrates by about 50 percent between 1815 and 1900. This was necessary to ensure class replication, as middle-class children required more investment (in education, for instance) than farm children (who contributed to the family labor pool at young ages). It appears that the middle class accomplished this decline largely by way of abstinence.

After about 1830, as Christmas became one of the few times in the calendar year for regular family indulgence, Nissenbaum finds a new "anxiety about private selfishness and greedy consumerism" in contemporary literature.[3] Such anxiety about the ethics of indulgence seems quaint (or at least subordinated and muted) today, perhaps because the first emergence of Christmas as a time of consumerism occurred among a nineteenth-century middle class still wedded throughout the rest of the calendar year to the Yankee values of frugality and self-restraint.

In the early nineteenth century, northern financiers began to emulate the British industrial revolution with the creation of factory towns such as Lowell, Massachusetts. These developments were important harbingers of the future, and the industrial base of the North by the time of the Civil War would be an essential component to regional politics—as well as to Northern victory. Yet it was mostly in the thirty-five years from the end of the Civil War to the turn of the century that the industrial revolution first took complete hold of American life. In fact, it is arguable that America industrialized more rapidly during that period than has any other nation in a comparable period.

This, of course, resulted in tremendous upheaval. The farmers' Populist revolt of the 1890s may have been the largest protest movement in American history. Meanwhile, the union struggles of the late nineteenth and early twentieth centuries were bitter and not infrequently violent. A brief litany of some of the most prominent labor confrontations suggests the scale of industrial conflict during this period: the Great Railroad Strike of 1877, Haymarket Square in 1886, Homestead in 1892, Lawrence in 1912. Indeed, the period from 1877 to 1914 was marked by probably the most explicit class antagonism in American history.

In this context, Nissenbaum's finding that "during the nineteenth century … age replaced class as the axis along which the Christmas gift exchange took place"[4] is astounding. Indeed, while he further states that as "middle-class Americans were becoming concerned that the holiday season was an infectious breeding ground for juvenile materialism and greed," he posits that "the battle for Christmas was beginning to change from a physical struggle that pitted the classes against one another into a moral one that divided the generations."[5] This is especially remarkable insofar as he finds no significant resurgence of class as disruptive to Christmas observance even late in the century—by which time, as already noted, America was embroiled in class conflict on a scale unprecedented in the nation's history.

Given that the evidence supports Nissenbaum's contention, what could explain this apparent anomaly? In fact, an exploration of this very disjuncture potentially leads to valuable insight into the nature of America's industrial conflicts and the cultural significance of modern consumer capitalism. Historians (this one included), however, too often seek monocausal explanations of complex societal phenomena. In all likelihood, there were many contributing factors mitigating against the reappropriation of class as the central "axis" along which "the battle for Christmas" was waged at the turn of the century.

One factor was the extraordinary diversity of the American labor force during this period. The process of industrialization requires enormous demographic and labor transformation (as well as exploitation), which has resulted in varying degrees of conflict in every nation that has undergone such development. The United States, however, is the only nation in history to industrialize principally on the backs of immigrant laborers. While the Massachusetts mills were originally dependent on farm girls to meet their labor needs, by the period of the greatest industrial growth in the late nineteenth and early twentieth centuries, the consequent need for a large and cheap labor pool was met by successive waves of immigrants (Irish in the 1850s; southern and eastern Europeans later).

The ethnic diversity of American labor had many implications that stamped American class conflict and identity as *sui generis*. Ethnic and linguistic diversity discouraged cohesion among American immigrants. Indeed, the radical Industrial Workers of the World had difficulty organizing the Chicago stockyards in no small measure because their pamphlets had to be translated into a bewildering array of languages and dialects. Also, the immigrants were not recognized by middle-class Americans as having an entitlement to American culture (including political culture), and the immigrants themselves often felt that they had little leverage over the cultural symbols of their new home (symbols that might have become axes of confrontation in the hands of native workers).

Seen in this light, the labor confrontations previously discussed might be subject to some historical diminishment. In other words, it is important to ask the contextual question of whether the labor conflicts of the United States (which so often pitted immigrants against the native-born middle class and elites) were as violent or profound as those in other, particularly European countries undergoing similar industrial transformations while using predominantly native-born labor. The answer must certainly be no; there is no confrontation in the annals of American labor history to match the revolutions of 1848 or the Paris Commune or "The Making of the English Working Class."[6] Immigrants—even exploited immigrants—do not have that degree of unity or of leverage over the social, political, and cultural systems of their adoptive country.

The fact that the American working class was mostly composed of recent immigrants at the turn of the century mitigated against class conflict on a European scale in other ways as well. America's immigrants have been relatively conservative and pro-capitalist. Most of the self-selected members of Europe's working class (not indigent class) who chose to make the journey across the Atlantic in the nineteenth century were doing so because they sought a capitalist land of opportunity. They certainly engaged in labor struggles out of sheer necessity, but as a group they gravitated much more to those unions—such as the American Federation of Labor—that sought to wrest a larger slice of capitalist pie for labor while keeping the pie itself intact than to those groups that, for instance, espoused Marxist revolution.

Recognizing the typical turn-of-the-century worker in America as an immigrant who was rather conservative relative to her or his counterpart who remained in Europe may shed some light on the lack of conflict about Christmas Nissenbaum finds during this period. The immigrants from southern and eastern Europe encountered the Christmas celebration of Gilded Age middle-class Americans as a cultural construct with which they had little familiarity and over which they felt little leverage. Nissenbaum's wassailers of the colonial period, by contrast, felt a sense of ownership around class-based British Christmas traditions within which they and their social superiors were equally immersed. Viewed from this angle, it would have been remarkable if recently arrived sweatshop workers around 1900 had, in fact, made the American Christmas a new ground for class battle.

Quite the contrary, it is possible that Christmas served as a means of cultural assimilation for Europeans eager to Americanize. The modern American Christmas has such plasticity that it can be grafted easily onto many cultures (including, for example, non-Christians in Asia who now give gifts under evergreen trees). The secular Christmas of Santa Claus and family domesticity, coupled with aspects of traditional if domesticated peasant mid-winter carnivals, has been a celebration that was easily appropriated by disparate immigrant groups seeking cultural enfranchisement. Christmas has functioned for holidays much as baseball has functioned for sports—as a readily accessible means of cultural assimilation within the immigrant experience.

Recognizing American immigrants as fundamentally pro-capitalist offers perhaps even richer ore to mine in the exploration of Christmas during the last hundred years. Thorstein Veblen, perhaps the most insightful and certainly the most eccentric social critic of the American experience since de Tocqueville, explained much of American working-class behavior from precisely this assumption with the 1899 publication of *The Theory of the Leisure Class*. What has often been missed by readers of this iconoclastic work is that Veblen's concept of "conspicuous consumption" is best understood as a vehicle for social stability within an America whose workers are conservative. Veblen argues essentially that workers in America did not rebel against the elites conspicuously consuming in Newport—rather, they envied those elites and, to the extent that laborers did rebel, they did so in order to improve their means (and their children's potential) to emulate elite consumption patterns. Americans, Veblen would argue were he alive today, don't hate the super-wealthy; rather they sit at home watching shows such as *Lifestyles of the Rich and Famous* feeling envious and inadequate because they can't have all the leisure time and non-utilitarian status items that celebrities so prize and flaunt. Americans also emulate the rich by working long hours and maximizing credit lines in order to accumulate the trappings of conspicuous consumption associated with success—a sports utility vehicle, for instance, or a luxury car, neither of which makes sitting in traffic a markedly higher-quality experience than doing the same in a cheap compact.

The timing of Veblen's work is not surprising since, by 1900, the United States had far outstripped Great Britain to become the largest economy in the world—a status it held for the entire twentieth century. This meant a significant change in the relation of productive capacity to markets. Not only could American industry easily meet domestic staple needs by 1900, but it was indeed itself threatened by the fact that it could far out-produce those needs. A new discourse began to emerge in the late nineteenth and early twentieth century—a discourse about the need for new markets.

This concern deeply informed the publication of and response to Captain Alfred T. Mahan's book *The Influence of Sea Power upon History* in 1890. This book riveted the attention of imperialists such as Theodore Roosevelt who, among other reasons, sought to make the United States an imperial power commensurate with its economic prowess in order to ensure the continued healthy growth of the American economy.

Yet there was also a vast source for new markets that required going no farther than America's shores: the untapped potential of American workers' rising wages. While the success of mid-nineteenth-century retailers in marketing the new American Christmas is, as Nissenbaum shows, impressive, it is nonetheless of a distinctly primitive variety compared to the sophistication of marketing methods in the twentieth century. It is no coincidence that Madison Avenue's advertising agencies emerged in their modern form around the turn of the century, churning out sexual innuendoes and subtle feelings of inadequacy about shirt collars that weren't white enough just as the need for new markets necessitated the marketing of artificial needs.

Alan Trachtenberg argues that during this phase of what he calls "the incorporation of America," "the department store found its function...in dispensing images along with goods, and in this task the store counted increasingly on another great institution of the great city, the advertising industry.... The shift, just underway in these decades of vastly enhanced capacity in the consumer-goods industries, required that culture... stress consumption, to train people in new needs and new kinds of behavior."[7] Modern advertising, Trachtenberg adds, developed "a mode in which information as such now fused with a message about the product, together with a message about the potential consumer, that he or she *required* the product in order to satisfy a need incited and articulated by the advertisement itself."[8]

While the culture Americans had previously built within an economy hovering near sufficiency was marked by an emphasis upon frugality, self-control, and delayed gratification, the culture of consumer capitalism in an age of industrial overproduction is typified by excess, indulgence, and immediate gratification. This advertising ethos has been furthered and strengthened by the advent of ever-more powerful vehicles for the dissemination of the faith—radio and television.

With the emergence of consumer capitalism came entirely new industries—such as the leisure and entertainment industries—geared toward the masses. From Coney Island[9] to the Nickelodeon to Las Vegas with its massive entertainment venues, Americans with new change in their pockets and new sources of spending such as credit lines have sought to conspicuously consume leisure-time titillations as fervently as tangible goods. The eight-hour workday proved to be good for business.

Consumer capitalism has arguably been the most powerful cultural force of the twentieth century. Indeed, it has become a truly global phenomenon, led principally by American exports, significantly including cultural exports such as American music, movies, and television. Even attempts at countering the consumption ethos can work to further it. Free music in Haight-Ashbury in 1964 became big business by 1967. "The one real 'winner' of the sixties," according to David Steigerwald, "was the consumer culture. This proved nimble enough to absorb profound challenges to values and taste, even to the point of marketing many of the challenges."[10] Steigerwald further argues that "the U.S. establishment could ultimately accept cultural revolution because sex and rock-and-roll were so eminently marketable."[11] Indeed, it seems possible to build on Steigerwald's analysis to argue that the counterculture of the 1960s, far from being revolutionary, was, in fact, a consummate expression of the dominant culture—that immediate gratification without responsibility, sexual indulgence, primacy of leisure over work, and the commodification of experience (a drug available for every emotion) were more expressive of consumer capitalism than a revolt against it.

Working longer hours with record numbers of bankruptcies, spending more time shopping and commuting and less time with their own children than ever before while their junk overflows into storage facilities, Americans, of course, pay a heavy price for this secular faith in legitimating oneself by dying with the most toys. The earth, too, pays a terrible price in wasted resources, pollution, and appalling heaps of trash. (New York City's dump now rates as the largest human-made object.) Yet it would be an oversimplification to assume that Americans have been entirely duped into this.

As vigorously as industry has encouraged this new ethic of consumption capitalism, Americans have just as readily embraced it. After all, it fit into previous patterns of conservative pro-capitalist values and the social function of conspicuous consumption. Contrary to what some critics have maintained, in other words, the advertising industry only nudged (and sometimes elbowed) Americans along a path that they were predisposed to follow. After all, advertising culture is opportunistic, not prone to create *ex nihilo;* it latches onto and manipulates people's fears and desires but it does not create people's need to be popular or instill feelings of sexual inadequacy. Nor did it create Americans' materialism and desire to conspicuously consume; it simply amplified what Veblen had already identified as an American social phenomenon.

Similarly, advertising has not been very successful in commercializing holidays that previously lacked a strong consumption ethos. Thanksgiving, for instance, remains a relatively calm shopping affair. Christmas, on the other hand, as Nissenbaum so ably describes, entered the twentieth century with the perfect set of imagery, associations, and patterns already in place to make it the dream holiday for advertisers and sellers of American consumer goods.

More recent developments have only furthered its appeal in American culture. Multicultural movements of the late twentieth century have left only ethnically and religiously sanitized holidays such as Christmas largely uncontested. Court decisions removing crèches from public property have left the secular images so intertwined with consumption that, by default, they have become the only universally acceptable portrayals of Christmas.

Also, the disappearance of ambivalence about industrially produced goods or guilt about self-indulgence during the twentieth century has led to Christmas advertising that needs fewer cultural mollifiers. The Santa Claus story, which served in the nineteenth century as a palliative for those ambivalent about mass production by hearkening back to a time of handicraft,[12] is no longer needed in an age that is fully accommodated to industrialism and consumerism. Now the appeal can be directly targeted toward the relationship between the consumer and the mythic qualities ascribed by advertisers to the product, without the need for a mediating icon. Consequently, even venerable Santa Claus appears less frequently in Christmas advertising and television shows. Not only has Christ been taken out of Christmas; Claus is on his way out, too.

Nissenbaum's historical treatment of Christmas in America from the Puritans to the end of the 1800s is enormously valuable, but his assertion that there have been no "revealing changes"[13] in Christmas during the twentieth century is mistaken. This essay has been an attempt to suggest that rich areas for inquiry remain for social historians in exploring the development of Christmas as the religious expression of consumption capitalism in the twentieth century. As such, the history of Christmas holds significance for the labor, cultural, ethnic, and social histories of twentieth-century America.

Bibliographic Note

This essay constitutes an attempt to synthesize a broad range of historical interpretation. As such, it weaves together many historiographies, to which many more fine historians have contributed than can be credited here. The following bibliographic essay, then, represents only a selected sample of those books that have been most germinal in the formation of this overview. This, of course, does not mean that the works cited below or their authors espouse what I argue or the connections that I have made to other work.

Obviously, this essay owes a great deal to Stephen Nissenbaum, *The Battle for Christmas: A Cultural History of America's Most Cherished Holiday* (New York: Vintage Books, 1996).

With regard to the transition from a scarcity capitalism to a consumption capitalism, as well as the concomitant emergence of a leisure culture, a great deal has been written. I have been particularly impressed by the implicit, or explicit, use of these ideas in Kathy Peiss, *Cheap Amusements: Working Women and Leisure in Turn-of-the-Century New York* (Philadelphia: Temple University Press, 1985) and David Steigerwald, *The Sixties and the End of Modern America* (New York: St. Martin's Press, 1995). Also of interest with regard to American economic transformation as well as resultant cultural shifts are Jackson Lears, *No Place of Grace: Antimodernism and the Transformation of American Culture, 1880–1920* (New York: Pantheon Books, 1981); Alfred D. Chandler Jr., *The Visible Hand: The Managerial Revolution in American Business* (Cambridge, Mass.: Belknap Press, 1977); David Potter, *People of Plenty: Economic Abundance and the American Character* (Chicago: University of Chicago Press, 1954); Alan Trachtenberg, *The Incorporation of America: Culture and Society in the Gilded Age* (New York: Hill and Wang, 1982); Roy Rosenzweig, *Eight Hours for What We Will: Workers and Leisure in an Industrial City, 1870–1920* (New York: Cambridge University Press, 1983); William E. Leuchtenberg, *The Perils of Prosperity, 1914–1932* (Chicago: University of Chicago Press, 1993); David Riesman, in collaboration with Nathan Glazer, *The Lonely Crowd: A Study of the Changing American Character* (New Haven: Yale University Press, 1950); Kenneth T. Jackson, *Crabgrass Frontier: The Suburbanization of the United States* (New York: Oxford University Press, 1985); Estelle Freedman and John D'Emilio, *Intimate Matters: A History of Sexuality in America* (New York: Harper and Row, 1988); Carl N. Degler, *At Odds: Women and the Family in America from the Revolution to the Present* (New York: Oxford University Press, 1980).

On Populism, see John Hicks, *The Populist Revolt: A History of the Farmers' Alliance and the People's Party* (Lincoln: University of Nebraska Press, 1959); Richard Hofstadter, *The Age of Reform: From Bryan to FDR* (New York: Knopf, 1955); Lawrence Goodwyn, *The Populist Moment: A Short History of the Agrarian Revolt in America* (New York: Oxford University Press, 1978).

On Progressivism, see Gabriel Kolko, *The Triumph of Conservatism: A Reinterpretation of American History, 1900–1916* (New York: Free Press, 1973); Robert H. Wiebe, *The Search for Order, 1877–1920* (New York: Hill and Wang, 1967).

On labor conflict, an enormous amount has, of course, been written. Among the best on the subject are David Montgomery, *The Fall of the House of Labor: The Workplace, the State, and American Labor Activism, 1865–1925* (Cambridge: Cambridge University Press, 1987); David Montgomery, *Workers' Control in America: Studies in the History of Work, Technology, and Labor Struggles* (Cambridge: Cambridge University Press, 1979); Leon Fink, *Workingmen's Democracy: The Knights of Labor and American Politics* (Urbana: University of Illinois Press, 1983); Melvyn Dubovsky, *We Shall Be All: A History of the Industrial Workers of the World* (Chicago: Quadrangle Books, 1969); Herbert G. Gutman, *Work, Culture, and Society in Industrializing America: Essays in American Working-Class and Social History* (New York: Knopf, 1975); E. P. Thompson, *The Making of the English Working Class* (New York: Pantheon Books, 1963).

On immigration and internal migration, see Stephan Thernstrom, *Poverty and Progress: Social Mobility in the Nineteenth-Century City* (Cambridge: Harvard University Press, 1964); Nicholas Lemann, *The Promised Land: The Great Black Migration and How It Changed America* (New York: Knopf, 1991); Ronald T. Takaki, *Strangers from a Different Shore: A History of Asian Americans* (Boston: Little, Brown, 1989).

On nativism, see John Higham, *Strangers in the Land: Patterns of American*

Nativism, 1860–1925 (New York: Atheneum, 1963); and James Tracy, "The Rise and Fall of the Know-Nothings in Quincy," *Historical Journal of Massachusetts* 16 (January 1988): 1–19.

Works that have influenced my thinking on cultural transformation include Paul F. Boller Jr., *American Thought in Transition: The Impact of Evolutionary Naturalism, 1865–1900* (Chicago: Rand McNally and Company, 1969); Warren I. Susman, *Culture as History: The Transformation of American Society in the Twentieth Century* (New York: Pantheon Books, 1984); and Thorstein Veblen, *The Theory of the Leisure Class.*

Notes

1. Stephen Nissenbaum, *The Battle for Christmas: A Cultural History of America's Most Cherished Holiday* (New York: Alfred A. Knopf, 1996), xii.

2. I do not purport to explore the Angel Island immigration here, in part to contain the scope of the essay and in part because the Ellis Island immigration arguably had greater impact on the Eurocentric culture, based on the East Coast, that dominated turn-of-the-century America. Incidentally, the great migration of African-Americans to urban centers took place mostly after World War I.

3. Nissenbaum, *The Battle for Christmas,* 176.

4. Ibid., 109.

5. Ibid., 177.

6. A reference to E. P. Thompson, *The Making of the English Working Class* (New York: Pantheon Books, 1963).

7. Alan Trachtenberg, *The Incorporation of America: Culture and Society in the Gilded Age* (New York: Hill and Wang, 1982); in this portion of his analysis, Trachtenberg also utilizes David Potter, *People of Plenty: Economic Abundance and the American Character* (Chicago: University of Chicago Press, 1954).

8. Trachtenberg, *The Incorporation of America,* 137; emphasis in original.

9. See Kathy Peiss, *Cheap Amusements: Working Women and Leisure in Turn-of-the-Century New York* (Philadelphia: Temple University Press, 1985).

10. David Steigerwald, *The Sixties and the End of Modern America* (New York: St. Martin's Press, 1995), iv.

11. Ibid., 186.

12. See Nissenbaum, *The Battle for Christmas,* 175.

13. Ibid., xii.

Chapter Two

Christmas in the Sixties

Elizabeth Pleck

In December 1967 Mr. and Mrs. James Thatcher of Peekskill, New York, were mailing out their Christmas cards. On the outside of the card was an excerpt from a Carl Sandburg couplet which read, "There is only one child in the world / and the child's name is All Children." On the inside of the card was a photograph of a Vietnamese peasant holding a baby whose skin had been seared by napalm. Underneath the photograph was the inscription, "Christmas 1967."[1] Christmas in the 1960s was a special time of year to feel alienated. Rather than being simply a convenient expression for collective anguish in a deeply troubled, conflict-ridden decade, the term "alienation" was frequently invoked in relation to America's single most important holiday. In its December 1966 issue, *Esquire* wished its readers "a very, very alienated Christmas, a disenchanted New Year; some degree if you insist, of peace on earth; and whatever you may find to your advantage in good will toward men."[2] The founder of Kwanzaa also used the word to characterize the Black response to Christmas. He wrote of his dislike of Christmas with its "European cultural accretions of Santa Claus, reindeer, mistletoe, frenetic shopping, [and] alienated gift giving."[3]

Articles in popular magazines reveal a general increase in alienation toward Christmas during the "long 1960s," a period of social and political turbulence that began in the middle of the 1950s with the Montgomery, Alabama, bus boycott of 1955 and the appearance on the scene of Beat culture a few years later. The amount of complaining about Christmas in the late 1950s and early 1960s was greater than ever before. Folklorist Sue Samuelson paged through issues of *Seventeen, House Beautiful, Parent's Magazine,* and forty-one other magazines from the 1920s to 1982. She found a dramatic increase in what she called "festival malaise" in such magazines beginning in the 1950s, although the complaints became more vociferous in the next decade.

The pace of complaining slowed somewhat thereafter, as American society became more conservative and the sixties protesters turned into parents, homeowners, and investors. As a result, doing away with ritual was much less favored.[4] Instead, creating new ritual in both public and private life became the favored way of recognizing the Christmas season. The public and legal "solutions" to the problems Christmas posed have become lasting features on the December calendar: Kwanzaa celebrations, giant menorahs in the public square, holiday crisis hotlines, and divorce agreements specifying where the children will spend the holidays. Because the 1960s was an antireligious decade—the rate of churchgoing was plummeting—the solutions proposed were more secular than religious. In fact, some of the efforts of the 1960s were focused on undoing the religiosity of the 1950s—by taking Christ out of Christmas, rather than putting him back in.

What did the word alienation mean in the 1960s? It usually referred to lack of commitment to and cultural estrangement from shared values, normlessness, and (among Blacks and Jews) a sense of feeling excluded from the dominant holiday. Holden Caulfield in *The Catcher in the Rye* (1951) and James Dean in *Rebel without a Cause* (1954) personified alienated youth. There were also much older philosophical origins for the concept. Marxists spoke about the alienation of one's labor under capitalism, since the worker did not own the means of production, but merely sold his or her labor to the capitalist. In the late 1950s Marx's early writings, which discussed alienation, were first published in English.[5] By the early 1960s the existentialism of Jean-Paul Sartre and Albert Camus also appeared to view alienation (along with engagement in political struggle) as a proper philosophical response to the meaninglessness of existence. In *Growing Up Absurd* (1960), Paul Goodman, best classified as an anarchist, argued that American schools imposed needless conformity on American youth. Norman O. Brown in *Love's Body* (1966) held that the source of alienated consciousness was "a compulsion to work," induced by the profit-driven capitalist economy.

There is an obvious explanation why alienation from Christmas was so common in the 1960s: alienation from a variety of institutions was common then. The general climate of alienation arose from social movements influencing each other: a very large youth movement and youth culture; the civil rights movement; protest against the Vietnam War; and the women's movement. Disaffected youths of the 1960s, suspicious of authority, formed a counterculture, united by alienation from various public institutions, which they referred to as "the establishment" or "the system." (The counterculture's interest in New Age religion eventually led to celebrating the winter solstice in the 1970s, both as an alternative and as a supplement to Christmas.) The civil rights movement was the oldest of the protest movements, which produced ripples throughout the society, increasing social consciousness about political rights, raising concerns about group identity, and fostering awareness of neglected social problems. Government manipulation of information and lies about how the Vietnam War was faring contributed to a long slide in popular trust in the government and the military. The Vietnam War generated the largest domestic antiwar protest movement since the Civil War. It also helped escalate a youth rebellion into a wider challenge of all institutions—from the military to the church—marked by young activists shouting at the older generation and telling them they could not be trusted. Some of the key events in the development of an anti-Christmas Christmas occurred in the late 1960s, during the escalation of the Vietnam War—there was even extensive bombing of North Vietnam during the Christmas season—and the resulting increase in antiwar protest. The women's movement, which owed its origins to these other movements, adopted the slogan that "the personal is political." The slogan was intended to focus attention on everyday practices, social etiquette, and arrangements that showed the pervasive nature of gender inequality.

The times were ripe, then, for alienation from Christmas. What were the complaints? Certainly there were the perennial ones. Many Americans, for example, thought the holiday should be a religious rather than a secular one. Another perennial complaint was that Christmas was too commercialized, that the jingle of cash registers was drowning out the sacred hymns of the season.[6] This form of alienation from Christmas had deep roots. In the fourth century, St. Gregory Nanzianzen first voiced the fear that "in making merry" the populace was destroying the true meaning of Christmas. As historian Stephen Nissenbaum has shown, the worry that Christmas was becoming too commercial was voiced as early as the 1820s.[7] But in the 1960s, these older complaints against Christmas joined new ones.[8]

The new complaints concerned family life and private behavior as well as cultural and religious domination of public space. These newer complaints were mutually related and mutually reinforcing. Christmas was attacked for being White and for proving that the United States was not a religiously pluralist nation but a Christian one. Feminists decried women's burden as chief arrangers of the holiday; psychiatrists diagnosed a new form of seasonal mental illness, the holiday blues. In taking aim at Christmas and eventually creating a new style of public and private celebration, a number of dissatisfied Americans were engaged in providing material and symbolic definition of "cultural pluralism," which mixed politics, culture, and religion. Christmas was both cause and effect of this pluralism, as Americans came to redefine their religious, racial, ethnic, and gender identities in private and public life.

The range of protest movements in the 1960s provided diverse sources for the anguish Christmas was suddenly causing. Four of the sources will be examined here: Black nationalism, Jewish group consciousness, the role of psychiatric expert opinion in naming and diagnosing social problems, and feminism. These grievances, which arose because of the social climate of the late 1960s, were made known in magazine articles, lawsuits, and new rituals performed in private and public. In the 1970s and 1980s the list of disaffected groups spread until eventually almost every American was said to suffer from "holiday blues."

These four separate trajectories for alienation from Christmas developed at the same time but intersected only occasionally. There is no single thread linking the four, except that they all occurred in a decade of social unrest. The closest thing to a unifying force was the civil rights movement, which spurred a general search for group identity that was by no means limited to racial minorities. Certainly, both African Americans and Jews were registering their feelings of exclusion from the season of merriment. But only Black nationalists invented an entirely new ritual for the Christmas season. Then, too, the social climate of the decade was one of national governmental reform and major social legislation. During the 1960s, when poverty, child abuse, negligence toward consumers, and environmental hazards were rediscovered, Americans were becoming increasingly aware that individual problems were social in nature.

The particular form of alienation Kwanzaa expressed was the feeling of estrangement from the "White Christmas," the sense that Christmas was a holiday mainly for Whites. The year the first Kwanzaa was held was also the year the term "Black power" was first used. Kwanzaa was the cultural expression of Black power—a term with radical or moderate shadings, depending on the speaker—which generally referred to efforts to gain power (cultural, political, economic) through racial solidarity and increased pride in African heritage. Black power was urban (found mainly in northern and western cities), accepted violence as a tool of social change, and rejected racial integration as the major goal of Black collective action. One particular form of Black power, Black cultural nationalism, gave highest priority to cultural change through rediscovery of a lost African heritage and the public display of racial pride through hairstyle, clothing, naming, and the invention of new rituals.

Kwanzaa is extremely unusual as a Christmas ritual—indeed, as a national ritual—because it had a single inventor, Maulana Karenga (born Ronald Everett), and a distinct date of origin, the Christmas season, 1966. Karenga chose the Swahili word *kwanza,* meaning first fruits, as the name for the seven-day holiday he proposed. Because of the impact of Julius Nyerere's Tanzanian socialism on militant Blacks in the 1960s, Swahili became the lingua franca of Black nationalists in the United States. Swahili, while spoken by a large number of Africans, was also a non-tribal language, and therefore presumably more suitable as a pan-African language. Swahili also had the advantage of being relatively easy for English speakers to pronounce.

The origins of Kwanzaa lie in the Black nationalist responses to the Watts riot of 1965. While chanting, "Burn, baby, burn," Black residents of the Watts neighborhood of Los Angeles overturned cars, looted shops, and destroyed property. The Watts riot was the single largest urban rebellion of the 1960s, born out of frustration with police brutality and with continued economic inequality amidst the surface prosperity and civil rights legislative advances of the decade. The riot lasted five days in August 1965; it left thirty-four known dead and about nine hundred injured. Less than a month later Karenga, a graduate student in African studies at UCLA, founded a Black nationalist organization in Los Angeles called US (as opposed to them). The main task of US under Karenga's leadership was to create a cultural revolution that would revitalize African American life and eventually result in the formation of an independent Black political party—or a violent revolution. US was a vanguard movement led by a Black intellectual. At its height, the organization probably numbered no more than five or six hundred people.[9]

Karenga saw Kwanzaa as a Black alternative to Christmas. All of the decisions about Kwanzaa were entirely Karenga's, including the one to make it a seven-day festival beginning the day after Christmas and ending with a feast on New Year's Eve. He chose the post-Christmas season as a time for his new festival because many American Blacks had time off from work and could shop for modest Kwanzaa presents at post-Christmas sales. A little more than a year after US was established, the first Kwanzaa was celebrated in the apartment of an US member in Los Angeles. About fifty people gathered for the *karamu,* the feast held on New Year's Eve, the last night of Kwanzaa. US members brought food for a potluck dinner, which they ate seated on the floor. The participants at the first Kwanzaa performed African dances and listened to African folktales. (Much later Karenga added more scripting for the celebration.) The apartment was lit with candles in the Black nationalist colors of black, green, and red, and was decorated with baskets of fruit.

While Kwanzaa was designed to resemble an African harvest festival— and thus might be classified as a secular holiday—in the late 1960s Karenga was decidedly hostile to Christianity, which he then called "spookism." He made his views known in speeches between 1965 and 1967, excerpts of which can be found in *The Quotable Karenga* (1967). *The Quotable Karenga* was patterned after the "Little Red Book," *Quotations from Chairman Mao,* which was popular in leftist circles. *The Quotable Karenga* says, "Christianity is a white religion. It has a white God, and any Negro who believes in it is a sick 'Negro.' How can you pray to a white man? If you believe in him, no wonder you catch so much hell." Karenga also described Jesus as a "psychotic. He said if you didn't believe what he did you would burn forever." In the sixties Karenga did not think that African Americans needed to celebrate any religion, Christian, Muslim, Egyptian, or pagan. He believed that Black unity could best be achieved by having women adopt the role of nurturer of children and obedient servant of men, who were supposed to head the family. Nationalist gender beliefs were in fact a kind of secular religion, providing a rationale for male leadership of the nationalist movement. Thus, Karenga would argue that "[e]ach Black man is God of his own house."[10]

In the late 1960s Kwanzaa spread from Los Angeles to other Black nationalist centers. Initially, Kwanzaa was celebrated in the major northern and western cities and a few southern cities where cultural Black nationalism flourished—at a branch of US in San Diego, and in San Francisco, Brooklyn, New Orleans, Newark, Chicago, Durham, and Atlanta. Kwanzaa was mainly taken up by Black cultural nationalists who agreed with Karenga about the necessity for a revolution in cultural values. In those years, Kwanzaa was a statement of belonging practiced within the Black nationalist community, rarely noticed by the larger culture or celebrated in the public schools. Karenga's personality, role, and ideas, while crucial to the origins of Kwanzaa, also tended to keep Kwanzaa confined to this limited circle. The larger civil rights movement did not take note of Karenga's invention. Martin Luther King Jr., for example, never celebrated it. King's organization, the Southern Christian Leadership Conference (SCLC), instead arranged for a Soul Saint to visit Black schools, county jails, and homes for the elderly at Christmastime. Moreover, after King's assassination in 1968, the Reverend Jesse Jackson, also of SCLC, was demanding that department stores hire more Black Santas.[11]

Kwanzaa was initially a holiday of and for Black nationalist radicals, who were engaged in frequent armed confrontations with the police and shootouts with other Black nationalist groups between 1969 and 1971. US was also heavily infiltrated by FBI informers, who may have instigated some of this internecine warfare. In this period Karenga became more paranoid, even lashing out at his own followers. Eventually he was sent to prison for four years for assaulting two women—members of US—who he believed were trying to poison him. Kwanzaa did not become mainstream until the early 1980s when and because it lost its association with radicalism—and its close ties with Karenga. The holiday was redefined as a more familial event, especially appealing to the Black middle class and to the main holiday makers, Black women, who were seeking a child-oriented, highly sentimental Christmastime holiday as well as one of racial self-definition. As a family celebration, Kwanzaa embraced family history, photography, feasting, and homecoming. In 1983 the first articles about Kwanzaa appeared in *Ebony* and *Jet*.[12] By the mid-1980s, Kwanzaa was celebrated in many Black homes and was beginning to be noticed in public schools. Then, too, Kwanzaa was no longer seen as hostile to Christianity and came to be celebrated at Black churches.

As Kwanzaa became more successful, it became redefined as a supplement to Christmas rather than as an alternative to it. Kwanzaa could be touted as "the New Soul Christmas" or as the less commercial Christmas, therefore a holiday less sullied by the marketplace. It had other redeeming features as well. It could heal some of the wounds of racial bitterness the White Christmas inflicted. Black writers in women's magazines felt emboldened to announce that Kwanzaa was a Christmas holiday from which one need not feel alienated.[13]

Apparently Blacks paying the most attention to the new claims for the merits of Kwanzaa were middle class. There are no surveys to ascertain the social class of Kwanzaa celebrants, but newspaper and magazine articles describe events attended by beauticians and nurses, lawyers and administrators. In a post–civil rights era the Black middle class, while enjoying more success than ever before, did not feel its economic foothold was secure. Aware of the problems of the Black underclass and the epidemic of crack cocaine, worried that their children did not remember King, Hamer, or Malcolm X, the Black middle class looked to ritual to help their children acquire a proper racial identity. Kwanzaa allowed such families to feel comfortable with their economic success by reassuring them that they remained true to their racial identity. The racial aspect of Kwanzaa was combined with the festival's redefinition as a family occasion. Kwanzaa was decorative, festive, seemed to require dressing up, and involved giving of gifts.[14] The holiday also gained adherents from being commercialized—as a gift-giving holiday for children, but a less commercial one than Christmas.

Like Black nationalists, American Jews also had an alternative ritual to Christmas. Similar to American Blacks, many American Jews felt themselves to be outsiders at Christmas, for reasons of religion rather than race. However, making the relatively minor festival of Hanukkah into a major holiday was different than the development of Kwanzaa. There was no single creator of the American Hanukkah nor was the holiday associated with a specific Jewish organization or with Zionism. Unlike Kwanzaa, the growth in the popularity of Hanukkah was not an effort to recapture a lost Jewish heritage, but instead an attempt to make a Jewish festival competitive with the dazzle and allure of a major Christian holiday. The Jewish rediscovery of Hanukkah was not a protest or critique of Christian culture so much as a form of flattery, a recognition that Jewish children needed a seasonal holiday which could compete with the tinsel and trinkets of Christmas. The process of transforming Hanukkah was a gradual one that began as early as the 1870s and grew apace with consumer culture and marketing of Jewish products for Hanukkah after World War I. By the 1960s, the Jewish shopper was able to purchase Hanukkah records, greeting cards, gift wrap, and colored paper decorations for the living room.[15]

The Jewish response to Christmas has always been varied, ranging from acceptance and accommodation to protest and imitation.[16] But in the 1960s most Jews drew the line of acceptance at the front door. The majority of American Jews in the 1960s did not put up a Christmas tree. A survey of Jews in Kansas City in 1962 showed that only about 12 percent had a "Hanukkah bush," a bit of green most probably referred to by its more familiar name.[17] The feeling against having a tree was quite strong among many Jews. One Jewish homemaker told an interviewer, "The Jew who has a tree in an all-Jewish home is as much a hypocrite as if he'd have a cross on his wall. The Hanukkah bush is degrading to the Jew, as far as I am concerned. I feel it is a crutch for those who are ashamed or can't stand up for their ways."[18]

While her stance represented majority Jewish opinion in the 1960s, the term "the December dilemma," which seems to have appeared for the first time in a Jewish magazine in 1971, indicated that the decision about whether to put up a tree was becoming a perplexing one.[19] Even the homemaker in the 1960s distinguished between a tree in an all-Jewish home and a tree in a half-Jewish one.[20] The rate of Jewish intermarriage was climbing markedly, although an accurate count was not undertaken until the 1990s, when the figure was variously put at one-third or one-half of all Jewish marriages.[21] In the 1970s the intermarried began to admit their anguish. For example, an intermarried mother confessed in *Redbook* in 1971 that she and her husband celebrated both Hanukkah and Christmas because the couple "wanted to show him [their son] that people could participate in more than one religious observance."[22]

Initially, Jewish protest against Christmas consisted of Jewish parents complaining about Christmas celebration in public schools with many Jewish students. The first protest of this kind was a Christmastime boycott of New York City public schools by Jewish parents in 1906.[23] When Jewish children were a distinct minority of the school population, their parents usually kept quiet. Jews began taking a more assertive stance in the 1950s, bringing suits against school boards for erecting a crèche on school property. The courts invariably upheld the right to display Christian symbols on school property. But Jewish parents were not the only ones who were dismayed by Christian religious indoctrination in the public schools. By 1979, the issue of Christmas pageants in public schools got as far as the Eighth Circuit Court of Appeals in *Florey v. Sioux Falls District.*[24] What bothered a non-Jewish father of a kindergartner in Sioux Falls enough to sue was a Christmas quiz. Two classes of children, including the child of Roger Florey, had to rehearse, memorize, and perform answers to a "Beginners Christmas Quiz" at a Christmas assembly. The teacher asked a series of questions, to which the children responded. For example, "Teacher: of whom did heav'nly angels sing / And news about His birthday bring? Class: Jesus." The Eighth Circuit Court ruled that memorizing and performing the Christmas quiz was a religious activity and as such was not permissible in the public schools. The courts were trying to draw a clear line between the religious and the secular. In classrooms and in school districts, however, Christmas remained a matter of negotiation, a highly variable display of symbols, activities, singing, pageantry, and offering of sweets.

The 1950s was not merely a conformist decade, but a religious one, in which organized religion became part of Cold Warriors' antidote to Godless Communism. The Biblical epics of the decade from *The Robe* to *Ben Hur* were wide-screen advertisements for Christianity and the American empire, combining popular culture and spectacle with the story of the crucifixion. Starting in the 1960s, many lawsuits were attempts to undo the Christianization of public space, which had taken a major leap forward in the 1950s. Christian displays in department store windows and public squares grew rapidly beginning in 1949, when a group of Milwaukee mothers campaigned to put up posters and billboards bearing the slogan, "Put Christ back into Christmas." Organizations of Protestant ministers, Catholic lay associations, and community groups picked up the slogan. Merchants sometimes sponsored a display of the Holy Family in a store window or helped set up a crèche or Nativity scene near the entrance to their establishment. In one of the many historical ironies, they often did so precisely because they believed such efforts might promote Christmas shopping. Even more ironically, some of the merchants who contributed to putting up Nativity scenes were Jews.[25]

By the mid-1950s Jewish organizations were on the alert about "a wave of . . . efforts to put up religious monuments in public places."[26] The Jewish American Congress, which undertook a survey in 1958, found such displays becoming more common. Crèches or Nativity scenes could be found on public property, school grounds, or private land. However, in the 1950s, the majority of Jews in the United States wanted to avoid making a fuss. Most Jewish organizations disapproved of the display of any religious symbols. Nonetheless, in the late 1950s an occasional rabbi and his congregation sometimes accepted the dual display at city hall—a lighted menorah placed next to a Christmas tree.[27]

In the 1960s American Jewish organizations went on the offensive. The American Jewish Committee, established in 1906, was an American organization founded by wealthy central European Jewish immigrants to defend Jewish rights and build Jewish community relationships.[28] The AJC complained about a Christmas stamp issued by the U.S. Postal Service in 1968. The stamp was a reproduction of Van Eyck's *The Annunciation,* in which the archangel Gabriel, fitted with wings, announces to the Virgin Mary, standing in the doorway of a church, that she is pregnant with the son of God. The AJC preferred to enter into coalitions with non-Jews in bringing lawsuits, in part to prove that Christmas displays offended a variety of groups, not just Jews. The AJC found willing allies among atheists such as Madeleine Murray O'Hair and her organization, the Society of Separationists, the American Civil Liberties Union, and other religious groups. The AJC and the ACLU shared a civil liberties-individual rights approach to the question of displays of religious symbols.[29] The ACLU of Cleveland, for example, insisted that the singing of Christmas carols was a possible violation of the First Amendment. (The First Amendment establishment clause prohibits the government from favoring or opposing any particular religion.)

The first important Supreme Court test of the seasonal Christianization of public space was *Allen v. Hickel* (1970). The American Jewish Congress joined forces with the ACLU to sue the National Park Service. They wanted to end the annual Christmas Pageant of Peace on the Washington, D.C., Ellipse, with its life-size Nativity scene. The display consisted of lighted Christmas trees, a floodlit Nativity scene surrounded by a burning Yule log, and eight live reindeer borrowed from the National Zoo. As for the plaintiffs in *Allen v. Hickel*, the ALCU and the American Jewish Congress rounded up an Episcopalian minister, a Catholic priest, a rabbi, the president of the American Ethical Union, and an officer of the National Humanist Association. The priest testified that the religious meaning of the Nativity scene was debased by the symbols of the secular world. The court upheld the view that the display was legal and that the crèche was merely one symbol nested among several others.

In 1984 the United States Supreme Court revisited the same ground in *Lynch v. Donnelly,* mainly because lower courts had begun to rule that such public displays were unconstitutional.[30] *Lynch* involved a Christmas display in a park near the downtown stores of Pawtucket, Rhode Island. Pawtucket had no live animals, but topped Washington, D.C., in the number of Christmas symbols, which—as enumerated in the Court's decision—included "a Santa Claus house, reindeer pulling Santa's sleigh, candy-striped poles, a Christmas tree, carolers, cut out figures representing such characters as a clown, an elephant, and a teddy bear, hundreds of colored lights, a large banner that reads 'SEASON'S GREETINGS' and the crèche at issue here."[31] In a five to four decision, the Court majority held that Christmas—even a Christmas display that included a Nativity scene—was a presentation of the symbols of a secular national holiday, not a Christian religious one. Naomi Cohen argues that the *Lynch* decision had a profound effect in that it led many towns to erect a menorah alongside the public display of the crèche, despite the fact that the National Jewish Community Relations Advisory Council opposed *any* public religious displays.[32] Thus, *Lynch v. Donnelly* was significant not only in redefining public space but in redefining pluralism as both (or multiple) rather than none at all. There were several obvious reasons for the militancy of the American Jewish Congress in the 1960s and its continued court challenges up through *Lynch v. Donnelly.* The civil rights activism of American Blacks—and of American Jews within the Black struggle—spilled over into Jewish activism. It was easy to carry over the idea of the defense of constitutional voting rights into the defense of the constitutional right to separation of church and state. Heightened consciousness of the Holocaust increased the feeling that rights had to be defended or they might be taken away. Finally, the threat posed to the existence of the State of Israel, followed by Israel's quick triumph in the Six Day War in June 1967, altered American Jewish consciousness. According to Lawrence Grossman, the impact of the war was to awaken "a new fascination with the Holocaust as the paradigm of modern Jewish vulnerability, and [imbue] many American Jews with unprecedented pride in being Jewish as well as willingness to assert their Jewishness publicly."[33]

Except for many Blacks and Jews, was not Christmas for the White Christian majority still the season to be jolly? With Blacks and Jews the source of the alienation was social; they perceived themselves as belonging to groups which felt themselves to be outsiders at the dominant culture's beloved holiday. By contrast, sufferers from the holiday blues syndrome were individuals, tacitly Christian, who felt personally estranged from celebrating Christmas. Psychiatrists—the "experts" of the postwar world—reported that the Christmastime emotions their patients experienced were melancholy, depression, and loneliness. They published monthly advice columns in *Seventeen* and other magazines, warning about the problems Christmas might bring. To some extent, the psychological problem of overexpectation followed by disappointment had been a theme in writing about Christmas since the nineteenth century, but the naming of the phenomenon, the "Christmas syndrome" or the "Dickens syndrome," was new.[34]

The journalist Edwin Diamond's article in the *New York Times Magazine* in December 1967, "Singing Those Christmas Holiday Blues," coined the phrase that became the standard one. Psychiatrists had been diagnosing the blues while calling it a syndrome or giving it no name at all since the 1940s. However, their research had largely been confined to psychiatric journals.[35] Diamond turned the medical condition of a syndrome into a more popular, less serious-sounding malaise. Because of the theme of the decade—alienation, cultural critique, and fashioning of alternative (to) ritual—such esoterica now became mainstream.[36] Diamond claimed that there were more traffic accidents, murders, robberies, and bad checks passed at Christmastime than at any other time of the year. Diamond had interviewed psychiatrists, mainly in New York City, and also summarized a study done by psychiatrists in Salt Lake City in the 1950s. The psychiatrists reported that their patients suffered an emotional reaction to the pressures of Christmas. They claimed that they received more referrals at Christmastime and that their patients had more symptoms then, too. One psychiatrist told him, "with some patients I've come to expect my phone to ring on Christmas afternoon."[37]

To Diamond "the holiday blues" consisted of family quarrels, overeating, excessive drinking, loneliness, and despair. He noted (and subsequent stories bore him out) that suicide was infrequent before and during the holidays, but spiked just after New Year's Day. He moved easily from the problems of insiders to the difficulties of those who felt they were outsiders at Christmas. He touched on the difficulties Christmas posed for Jewish children, drawn to the festivity and joy of the Christmas holiday, who were being told by parents, grandparents, and rabbis that Christmas was not their holiday. He added that a Black psychiatrist thought that Black children needed Santas of their own race to reinforce the idea that God was not necessarily White.

Diamond's article also reflected the dawning initial recognition that divorce was wreaking havoc with Christmas arrangements. He mentioned the unhappiness of divorced or separated parents at Christmas who did not have their children with them or who had to compete for the child's affections with the celebration organized by the other parent. He also discussed sexual relations of married couples during the holiday season. Diamond suggested that with children on vacation from school and a mother exhausted from shopping, baking, and entertaining, sexual activity plummeted at Christmastime. Christmas might even cause tension in otherwise placid marriages, he suggested. Men were at home and had time on their hands, especially since women did most of the work of shopping and decorating the house for Christmas. Quarrels broke out precisely because a husband and wife were forced to spend many hours together.

Subsequently added to Diamond's list of Christmas woes were alcohol abuse, family violence, and acknowledgment of the difficulties of interfaith families. By the mid-1980s, magazine and newspaper articles expressed sympathy toward gays in deciding whether to go home for the holidays.[38] Gay hotlines, which provided health information as the plague of AIDS became visible, also began to provide counseling at Christmastime. Holiday blues had become such an accepted feature of the Christmas season that it was fast becoming a cliché. In 1981 Samuelson interviewed an editor at *Ladies' Home Journal* who could not decide whether to publish an article on this subject because it had "become something people do. You see it on television, you see it everywhere, and everyone knows that the suicide rate goes up. Well, we always look for something fresh, [but] you can't ignore it."[39]

While Diamond mentioned the impact of divorce, he did not allude to the problems of blended families created by divorced parents remarrying. The first issue of *Ladies' Home Journal* to do so appeared in 1981, the year the divorce rate reached an all-time high. The goal, according to the writer of the article, was for two sets of children to unite in a new family. The children of divorce might bring about this unity by purchasing Christmas presents together or working side by side to make and fill a parental Christmas stocking. Blended families were facing a bewildering array of difficulties, whatever holiday it was. Their dilemma—of achieving unity in the face of difficulty, unhappiness, and divorce—became a metaphor for the problems confronting the majority of American families at Christmas. Whereas for Diamond Christmas might cause problems in an otherwise happy family, by the 1980s the idea of "family dysfunction" was so widespread that it was assumed that the normal family suffered from multiple disorders. Therefore, the role of Christmas was simply to "aggravate a family's existing problems."[40]

What solutions were proposed for the problem of holiday blues? Diamond quoted the experts he interviewed who wanted to abolish the "wild office party." The psychiatrists he spoke to mainly prescribed therapy—the talking cure—along with reassurance to their patients that this syndrome was a common one. Newspaper columnists suggested alternatives—volunteer work or joining religious or secular organizations. People who did not want to visit their relatives were urged to go on vacation at Christmastime. Shoppers were told to buy gifts for themselves. The lonely were advised to throw a party, rather than waiting to be invited to one.[41] In the early 1970s churches and mental health clinics were beginning to establish workshops to help people cope with "Christmas blues." By the end of the decade, mental health experts and social workers were tackling the unequal gender division of labor at Christmas. They told family members to divide responsibilities, so that no "one family member was overburdened."[42] For Diamond and others, the holiday blues was a gender-neutral problem. Writers in women's magazines—because of their point of view, their gender, and their audience—tended to see holiday blues as a distinctively female problem.[43] Loneliness was missing from the homemaker's list of complaints, probably because such a woman was surrounded by family and friends.

Instead, she was thought to suffer from physical exhaustion and mental depression. The founder of the National Organization for Women, Betty Friedan, had once been a writer for women's magazines. In *The Feminine Mystique* (1963), she lambasted such magazines for their stereotypical views of women. The feminist climate of the late 1960s contributed to a subtle change in the content of some articles in these magazines. Some women columnists even began to convey a feminist message about Christmas.

To be sure, there is no women's liberation literature from the late 1960s that identifies Christmas as a special source of stress for women. Nor were the writers of Christmastime articles in women's magazines self-identified feminists. But the enormous popularity of Friedan's book gave permission for housewives to air their grievances—and for women writers to contribute to a culture of complaint. Articles in women's magazines described the exhaustion caused by preparing Christmas for a family. Since the readers of such magazines were assumed to be full-time homemakers, the articles were addressed to giving women permission not to sacrifice themselves unduly for the sake of others rather than to the conflicting demands of work and family. Female labor at holidays, such articles argued, was a specific form of the more general problem of housework—unpaid labor, wrongly defined as a labor of love, which deprived women of the necessary leisure. This unpaid labor was an unequal burden and was at odds with the concept of equality. It was assumed that women no longer could or should devote themselves to the preparation of the perfect Christmas. Homemakers were drained of energy, it was argued, because they were working part time—or perhaps engaged in volunteer activity. This analysis of inequality of leisure time was quite different from the grievances of Blacks and Jews toward Christmas. Blacks and Jews complained of feeling like outsiders. The complaint of the middle-class homemaker was that she was so much of an insider that all the work fell on her.

Long before the women's movement began, women writers had been publishing articles about the seasonal burdens of mothers. The initial listing of complaints—tired holiday shoppers and exhausted bakers of cookies—appeared as early as the first decade of the twentieth century.[44] Women writers had invariably dispensed the advice that their readers needed to become organized and cut back on their tasks. Was there anything new about the lead article in a 1966 *Reader's Digest* that described a housewife overwhelmed by her Christmas chores who broke down in tears while standing next to her dishwasher?[45] In her article "The Christmas Syndrome, or, Must We Hang Mother from the Tree?" (1967), Harriet Van Horne furnished the laundry list of women's complaints against Christmas. Horne was a forty-seven-year-old writer whose column became syndicated that year. She wrote, "It's all too much. Too much revelry, too much fatigue. Diminished antibodies. Tension and insomnia. Germs in the air. Result: Christmas cold and flu." What was new was that she urged women to buy goods rather than make them, and to purchase services rather than doing all the work themselves.

The impact of married women's employment was to shift the emphasis from greater organization and simplification to greater use of paid services and goods as a substitute for women's time and labor.

Women's magazines in the 1960s, it is now often claimed, aired only the grievances of the White middle class. But with the world shaking in revolt in 1968, *Ladies' Home Journal* published the holiday reminiscences of a Black woman and civil rights activist. In her article "Black Christmas," Myrlie Evers, the widow of the slain Mississippi civil rights leader, recalled with considerable bitterness the racial etiquette of Mississippi in her childhood. Her grandmother had been a maid for a White family. At Christmas she and her grandmother entered the employer's house through the back door. Her grandmother stood in the hallway while young Myrlie played the piano for the White family and was rewarded for her performance with a Christmas gift. She told the readers of *Ladies' Home Journal,* "I couldn't have put it into words then, but I know now what bothered me. It was seeking of approval and acceptance from white people who, however friendly, polite, and generous, could never really give it. How could they? They felt we were inferior. My real objection was that by seeking their approval and acceptance, we were acting as though we agreed."[46]

Although attacking Christmas was one of the most ancient of all Christmas traditions, the form of the attack and the "new traditions" created in the 1960s reflected the politicization of culture and tradition created by the social unrest of that turbulent decade. The social movements of the 1960s lent legitimacy to the airing of grievances against Christmas. Not just seasonal griping, such grievances could be understood as part of the larger critique of hollow and meaningless tradition and of institutions deemed to be unworthy.

The history of Christmas in the 1960s is thus partly a case study in how culture and identity were refashioned in the span of about a decade—as the reigning idea of nation changed from unity amidst homogeneity to unity through the celebration of differences. Group identities were to be recognized and validated. Public facilities were expected to host many coequal celebrations, rather than having none at all. As Kwanzaa and Hanukkah were added to the Christmas calendar, American society moved closer toward defining itself as pluralist. Hanukkah and Kwanzaa could be accepted readily as important holiday festivals because of new attitudes about group difference and because both holidays were easily marketable. The major fault lines had to do with who was to be included in the Christmas season, who set the terms for inclusion, and how to inject meaning into what many perceived as a meaningless ritual.

The issue of what kind of public celebration of Christmas should occur in public schools and town squares was an extremely sensitive one. In trying to limit the expression of Christianity in schools and public space, American Jews ran the risk of being denounced as troublemakers. Court decisions helped to define the extent of permissible Christianity in public. They generally urged the public schools not to step over the line between handing out candy canes and engaging in religious indoctrination. Meanwhile, the United States Supreme Court informed Rotary clubs and downtown merchants that they could define Christmas as a national, not a religious holiday. What steps would be needed to assuage minority sensibilities? The solution that Jewish groups eventually accepted was the dual public celebration, a giant menorah alongside a Nativity scene. In so doing, they stepped back from their firm stance against separation of church and state to a position that accepted state recognition of religion, so long as Jews were included.

What was perhaps most surprising is that in the 1960s homemakers, as the major creators of domestic tradition, would join in the general questioning of authority so characteristic of the decade. Women's magazines, known for their optimistic articles celebrating family life and their recipes for Christmas cookies, went so far as to declare Christmas "hollow and meaningless." Actually, it was Harriet Van Horne who announced to her middle-class female readers that Christmas had "become an obligatory, mandatory back-breaking ritual."[47] As a general principle, when ritual becomes meaningless, it becomes ripe for attack. How various were the complaints against Christmas in the 1960s, including van Horne's? Christmas, it was charged, was too White, too Christian, too commercial, too depressing, too labor-intensive. In subsequent decades, ripples of discontent spread to new groups and became part of a new and accepted way of celebrating, experiencing, and anguishing over Christmas. The Christmas capable of reinventing itself was not so alienating after all.

Notes

1. "Merry Christmas?" *Newsweek* 70 (December 25, 1967): 65.
2. "Black Christmas: Holiday Season in US Magazines," *Time* 88 (December 23, 1966): 44.
3. Maulana Karenga, *Kwanzaa: Origins, Concepts, Practice* (Inglewood, Calif.: Kawaida Publications, 1977), 15.
4. Susan Camille Samuelson, "The Festive Malaise and Festival Participation: A Case Study of Christmas Celebrations in America," Ph.D. diss., University of Pennsylvania, 1983, 184–87.
5. Morris Dickstein, *Gates of Eden: American Culture in the Sixties* (New York: Basic Books, 1977), 70.
6. For this form of criticism in the 1960s, see Philip Roth, *Portnoy's Complaint* (New York: Random House, 1967), 144.
7. Stephen Nissenbaum, *The Battle for Christmas* (New York: Alfred A. Knopf, 1996), 189–94.
8. For the history of these kinds of criticisms of Christmas, see Leigh Eric Schmidt, *Consumer Rites* (Princeton, N.J.: Princeton University Press, 1995), 106–91 and Nissenbaum, *The Battle for Christmas*.
9. Scot Brown, "The US Organization: African-American Cultural Nationalism in the Era of Black Power, 1965 to the 1970s," Ph.D. diss., Cornell University, 1999.

10. Imamu [Clyde] Halisi, ed., *Kitabu: Beginning Concepts in Kawaida* (Los Angeles: US, 1971), 7.

11. *New York Times,* December 7, 1969, 78; *New York Times,* December 25, 1970, 58.

12. Frank White III, "The New Soul Christmas," *Ebony* 39 (December 1983)· 29–32.

13. Desda Moss, "A Special Celebration," *Ladies' Home Journal* 111 (December 1994): 95.

14. Gerald Early, "Dreaming of a Black Christmas: Kwanzaa Bestows the Gifts of Therapy," *Harper's* 294 (January 1995): 55–61.

15. Jenna Weissman Joselit traces the growing Jewish affection for Hanukkah in "'Merry Chanuka': The Changing Holiday Practices of American Jews, 1880–1950," in *The Uses of Tradition: Jewish Continuity in the Modern Era,* ed. Jack Wertheimer (New York: Jewish Theological Seminary of America, 1992), 302–25. For more on this subject, see Kenneth N. White, "American Jewish Responses to Christmas" (ordination thesis, Hebrew Union College–Jewish Institute of Religion, 1982), 19.

16. Additional discussion of the Jewish response to Christmas can be found in Jonathan D. Sarna, "The Problem of Christmas and the 'National Faith,'" in *Religion and the Life of the Nation,* ed. Rowland A. Sherrill (Urbana: University of Illinois Press, 1990), 172–74; Elizabeth H. Pleck, *Celebrating the Family: Ethnicity, Consumer Culture, and Family Rituals* (Cambridge, Mass.: Harvard University Press, 2000), chapter 3.

17. Joseph P. Schultz, "The Consensus of 'Civil Judaism': The Religious Life of Kansas City Jewry," in Joseph P. Schultz, *Mid-America's Promise: A Profile of Kansas City Jewry* (Kansas City: Jewish Community Foundation of Greater Kansas City, 1982), 365.

18. Walter M. Gerson, "Jews at Christmas Time: Role-Strain and Strain-Reducing Mechanisms," in *Social Problems in a Changing World: A Comparative Reader,* ed. Walter M. Gerson (New York: Thomas Crowell, 1969), 70.

19. Esther Jacobson Tucker, "The December Dilemma," *Reconstructionist* 37, no. 9 (December 17, 1971): 19.

20. A 1990 survey found that most Jews did not have a tree. However, two-thirds of intermarried households had one, presumably because the Christian member of the couple wanted to maintain a childhood tradition. Since the rate of Jewish intermarriage in 1990 was high and was headed higher, the number of Jews who had trees was bound to increase. Sidney Goldstein, "Profile of American Jewry: Insight from the 1990 National Jewish Population Survey," *American Jewish Year Book 1992* (New York: Jewish Publication Society, 1992), 77–173.

21. Jack Wertheimer, Charles S. Liebman, and Steven M. Cohen, "How to Save American Jews," *Commentary* 101 (January 1996): 47–51; J. J. Goldberg, "Interfaith Marriage: The Real Story," *New York Times,* August 3, 1997, 13(A).

22. Evelyn R. Preston, "Mom, Are We Jewish or Christmas?" *Redbook* 48, no. 2 (December 1976): 85–90. For the opposite point of view, that children of a mixed marriage need to have "a sense of belonging to one group," see Dr. Alice Ginnott, "Can a Jewish Child Celebrate Christmas?" *Ladies' Home Journal* 95, no. 12 (December 1978): 94–97.

23. Leonard Bloom, "A Successful Jewish Boycott of the New York City Public Schools—Christmas 1906," *American Jewish History* 70 (December 1980): 180–88.

24. *Florey v. Sioux Falls School District,* 464 F Supp. 911, 192 (1979).

25. Naomi Cohen, *Jews in Christian America: The Pursuit of Religious Equality* (New York: Oxford University Press, 1992), 235.

26. Ibid., 233.

27. Ibid., 234.

28. For an earlier history of the American Jewish Committee, see Naomi W. Cohen, *Not Free to Desist: The American Jewish Committee, 1906–1966* (Philadelphia: Jewish Publication Society of America, 1972).

29. Stephen M. Feldman, *Please Don't Wish Me a Merry Christmas: A Critical History of the Separation of Church and State* (New York: New York University Press, 1997), 235.

30. *Lynch v. Donnelly,* 465 U.S. 668, 104 S. Ct. 1335 (1984).

31. Ibid.

32. Cohen, *Jews in Christian America,* 244.

33. Lawrence Grossman, "Transformation through Crisis: The American Jewish Committee and the Six-Day War," *American Jewish History* 86, no. 1 (1998): 27–54.

34. Harriet Van Horne, "The Christmas Syndrome, or, Must We Hang Mother from the Tree?" *Redbook* 130 (December 1967): 38.

35. Richard Sterba, "On Christmas," *Psychoanalytic Quarterly* 13 (1944): 79–83; L. Broyce Boyer, "Christmas 'Neurosis,' " *Journal of American Psychoanalytic Association* 3 (1955): 467–88; James Cattell, "The Holiday Syndrome," *Psychoanalytic Review* 42 (1955): 39–43; Jule Eisenbud, "Negative Reactions to Christmas," *Psychoanalytic Quarterly* 10 (1941): 639–45.

36. For the term "Christmas syndrome," see Fritz Leiber, "Christmas Syndrome," *Science Digest* 54, no. 6 (December 1963): 16–21; Edwin Diamond, "Singing Those Christmas Holiday Blues," *New York Times Magazine,* December 16, 1967, 32–33.

37. Diamond, "Singing Those Christmas Holiday Blues," 32.

38. Kath Weston, *Families We Choose: Lesbians, Gays, Kinship* (New York: Columbia University Press, 1991), 29–33.

39. Samuelson, "Festive Malaise," 92.

40. Carole Owens, "How to Avoid Holiday Hassles," *Ladies' Home Journal* 98 (December 1981): 52.

41. Amitai Etzioni, "Speaking Out," *Psychology Today* 10, no. 7 (December 1976): 23; *New York Times,* December 16, 1973, 1(X).

42. "Keeping the Christmas Blues at Bay," *U.S. News and World Report* 87, no. 25 (December 17, 1979): 68.

43. Samuelson, "Festive Malaise," 203.

44. For an example of this earlier form of complaint, see Margaret Deland, "Save Christmas!" *Harper's Bazaar* 46 (December 1912): 593.

45. *Time* 88, no. 26 (December 23, 1966): 44. Another subsequent statement of the blues was Gary R. Collins, " ' 'Tis the Season to Be Jolly'—or Melancholy," *Christianity Today* 18, no. 5 (December 7, 1973): 5–6.

46. Mrs. Medgar Evers, "Black Christmas," *Ladies' Home Journal* 85, no. 12 (December 1968): 23, 84.

47. Van Horne, "Christmas Syndrome."

Part 2

The Culture of
American Christmas

Chapter Three

Christmas on Celluloid

Hollywood Helps Construct
the American Christmas

Max A. Myers

Moviegoers going to see *Destination Tokyo* in 1944 might have gone merely to view the romantic comedy lead, Cary Grant, play a submarine commander in an action movie. Viewers would not have been disappointed, but they would have seen more than a new war film about an American submarine operating in Japanese waters. Once the submarine got out of San Francisco Bay and entered the war zone, the crew celebrated Christmas at sea. The celebration itself was makeshift and had a tone of comedy, but the interesting point is that it mimicked the sort of Christmas celebrated in many other films of the period. The Christmas celebration had precisely the effect that it was supposed to have. As the crew members ate Christmas dinner in the mess, sang carols, and exchanged gifts, they became bonded with one another. From an odd assortment of disparate individuals, they were shaped into an organic whole. They also, through their brief recollections and statements of hopeful expectation, became bonded with the "folks back home," and with America's consumer-oriented Christmas to which they looked forward in the postwar future.

The viewer would not have found this attitude strange, for the mythic convention was being established at that period that Christmas could represent everything that the armed forces were fighting to save now, and what they hoped for in the future. This notion was then being constructed by all branches of the mass media: advertising, radio, magazines, and newspapers. But nowhere was it more potent than in the films of the 1940s. A number of films made in that decade had "Christmas" as their theme, some with a religious aspect, some without. All, however, had the effect of making Christmas, and specifically the American consumer Christmas, an integral part of the normal social world of Americans.

The construction of the American Christmas as iconic of home and prosperous consumption in the American mythic consciousness can be discerned through a close examination of three popular films of the era: *Holiday Inn*, *Miracle on Thirty-Fourth Street*, and *It's a Wonderful Life*.

Hollywood's classic depiction of Christmas constructed a cultural complex that reached its peak in the forties in its most popular, characteristic, and enduring films dealing with the holiday, although they usually referred to earlier films, stories, and poems. The depiction is "classic" because it formed the canonical version of Christmas for American life and culture that persists up to the present day through the recycling of the films on television and videocassettes. Many of the elements of the cultural complex, of course, existed before the forties. A major aspect of the Christmas complex is that it carries a nostalgia for old times that is historically bogus. In fact, "Christmas" as an American tradition was an invention of the very films that celebrated it. Some of its component elements can be traced back to the second quarter of the nineteenth century as Nissenbaum has shown in *The Battle for Christmas*. Even in the British Isles, the home of the Dickensian Christmas so important to Hollywood, there were large segments of the population that did not observe Christmas at all until after the Second World War, for explicit religious and cultural reasons, and scorned those who did—in Scotland, for example. In America, where the Puritans had forbidden its celebration in some New England colonies by law, observance was quite spotty, and by later standards extremely Spartan and plain, well into the Depression era. In the eastern urban centers, large stores had spent considerable sums of money on lavish window displays and other forms of advertising to promote a family Christmas where gifts were exchanged and homes were elaborately decorated. Despite all this, however, the mass market had not been transformed into consumers of a standardized vision of Christmas. For this transformation, a new medium was necessary.

Movies played an important role in American culture in the early twentieth century, especially in the construction of normal social reality. Historically, other societies had traditional ways of socializing new members through the repetition of myth and ritual, through the teaching of the folkways of the culture in a thousand daily activities, and through the inculcation from birth of a native language with all of the values that are implicit in its usages. In these ways and others, new members are brought into a society and come to share its distinctive ways of behavior and its practical notion of what is normal. This inculcation, of course, usually takes place from infancy through puberty in traditional societies. American society, however, had to take a radically different tack. Because of the huge migration of people from very different cultures, the traditional ways of enculturation were not sufficient. Some means had to be found to bring these new immigrants into the social world of American culture. By a lucky coincidence, the movies began to assume this role, just at the time they were most needed.

The movies were a medium extremely well-suited for this task of transmitting American culture on to the new immigrants—particularly the silent movies whose apex occurred just at the beginning of the century when the immigration from eastern and southern Europe was at its peak. Since silent movies by their very nature had to rely on images of movement and gesture rather than verbal language, they were readily understood by people who were not native speakers of English. Indeed, because of the montage of film, they could convey nuances of meaning even to those who could have been incapable of understanding the finer shades of the English language. Moreover, the viewer of a film is placed in the world of the narrative in such a way that she or he begins to grasp the "instrumental complex" of the culture in a nonverbal way. Almost unconsciously, the viewer begins to inhabit the world depicted on the screen. What is normal in American culture—styles of clothing, ways of transacting business, and ways of interacting with others in public—begins to seem normal to the viewer as well. Among the main topics of interest in the new medium were work, leisure, and time, particularly time and its importance for social life. As part of this emphasis on time, the movies also depicted holidays and communicated appropriate behavior on holidays. Christmas quickly became the most important holiday on screen, perhaps because of its visual appeal. Many immigrant groups had no distinctive traditions concerning the celebration of Christmas. Some, such as Jewish groups, had no traditions related to Christmas at all. All new immigrants had to become self-conscious about their native traditions and learn the Christmas traditions of their new culture.

The earliest movies adopted the familiar icons of Christmas from print media, particularly Thomas Nast's drawing of Santa Claus. One of the first silent films depicted the Nativity of Christ, and Santa Claus made some brief appearances in other very early movies. Walt Disney and other producers made cartoons of the poem "A Visit from St. Nicholas," but the story line was too thin and simple for anything longer than a "short," even with writers' embellishments. On the other hand, as the major winter holiday, Christmas could play a part in full-length films rehearsing the seasonal narrative.

It has long been the practice in Western culture to unfold a narrative in harmony with the change of seasons: springtime as a time of new beginnings and romance, summer as a time of growth and normalcy, autumn as a time of maturation and decline, and winter as a time of old age and death. The seasons have become symbolic of particular attitudes, emotions, and events in the lives of individuals and groups—summer symbolizes flourishing and enjoyment while winter can symbolize isolation, silent suffering, and despair. Christmas, therefore, can represent attitudes and events associated with winter. A particularly blatant example is the film *Meet Me in St. Louis*, made just after World War II, in which Judy Garland sings her best-known Christmas song, "Have Yourself a Merry Little Christmas." The major crisis, the father's decision to leave St. Louis and move the family to New York City for professional advancement, is announced Halloween night, after a long exposition of the characters and their world in the summer. The plot comes to a climax on Christmas Eve, when the father decides to give in to his family's desires and to stay in St. Louis on the holiday meant to celebrate

home and family. In this mythic reference, the film plays on the symbolism
of death and renewal at year's end.

What might have accounted for the public reception of the Christmas
complex and its mythic images in the mass media? There is always a general
receptivity to programming in any period, but were there specific factors we
can point to that might help explain the reception of the American Christmas
complex? The 1940s were a time of great stress, uncertainty, and danger.
Economically, in 1939, the nation was still in the grip of the Great Depression. Despite all the innovative New Deal programs, the nation was still
facing high unemployment, labor unrest, and the threat of political disintegration. Politically, the people were losing faith in the nation's basic ideology
and the nation was teetering on the edge of war, which had just broken out
in Europe. The population was torn between support for one of the groups
that advocated violence—the Nazis, the Communists, or the traditional allies, the British and French, on the one hand—and isolationism and total
pacifism, on the other. In high culture, an elite modernism swept the arts,
poetry, and music, which remained almost wholly incomprehensible to the
mass audience of radio and the movies. The mood of the period may be
evoked by considering the near mass hysteria provoked by Orson Welles's
radio broadcast of "The War of the Worlds." This phenomenon points to
a population gullible, easily influenced by mass communication, and on the
edge of panic. This suggests that in 1939 the popular culture in America
was without any effective means to withstand potent images in the media
by rational thought. Moreover, the intellectual elite was viewed with some
suspicion because of its perceived assault on traditional values and beliefs,
especially religious beliefs. Given this mood, the commercial interest in promoting a traditional holiday as a means of increasing economic consumption
dovetailed nicely with the felt national need to affirm images and behavior
seen as traditional and reassuring. If these images could be given potency
in the new media, there was little to stand in the way of their acceptance,
and if the intellectual and cultural elites were critical of them, so much the
worse for the standing of those elites.

With respect to the film industry itself at this time, another important historic factor must be mentioned: the imposition of the Production Code on
all Hollywood movies, beginning in the late thirties. In fact, the moment of
the effective enforcement, though not the creation of the Production Code,
can be pinpointed to late 1934 when studio executives and the original official judge of movie morals, Will Hays, gave the arbiter of the code, Joseph
Breen, public power of review. The reasons for giving Breen this power
were as complex as were its effects, of course, but some are relevant to our
discussion. First, the Production Code represents a delicate balance of the
cultural and economic power of three forces: the studio executives, who
were almost all Jewish; the rising urban Roman Catholic hierarchy, which
had demonstrated power over theaters in large cities through the Legion of
Decency; and the older Protestant elites who distrusted both groups and the

power of film itself over the masses. The immediate effect of the imposition of the code was to stop dead any traces of the cultural radicalism that made some movies of the twenties and early thirties so vital and interesting. Conservatives and right-wing cultural critics identified the radicalism as Jewish. This terrified the studio executives, who were all too aware of the rising tide of anti-Semitism in Europe, especially in Germany, Italy, and France, and its incipient upsurge in certain quarters of the United States. Under the Production Code, the studios replaced radicalism with a return to American nationalist themes and "safe" cultural values, such as the home and traditional holidays. This trend was tailor-made for the idealization of Christmas, which, as we have seen, was being reinforced by other factors as well. In any case, neither Roman Catholics nor Protestants were going to object to movies that involved the sentimentalization or glorification of Christmas, and that was good both for business and for the image of the movie industry. It may also be mentioned that, as a by-product, the whole process of submitting movies to a moral censor instilled the habit of judging movies by the standards of "American values," a habit which proved useful both to the government and to conservatives during World War II and the Cold War.

It was in this context that a series of movies with a Christmas component were made that proved to be popular and helped to create a successful cinematic theme. The three films that I have chosen to consider in detail are *Holiday Inn, Miracle on Thirty-Fourth Street,* and *It's a Wonderful Life.* All three were released in the forties and all three deal with some aspect important for the construction of the American Christmas complex. I have also chosen them because of their continuing influence, as measured by their re-release, remakes, and repeated showings on television during the Christmas season.

Holiday Inn, starring Bing Crosby and Fred Astaire, was released in 1940. This film is important for our theme because its real message was the importance of celebrating holidays, and because it introduced the classic version of the song "White Christmas," which became a kind of anthem for the specifically modern American Christmas. More than any other song, "White Christmas" came to symbolize the religiously rather nondescript Hollywood Christmas complex and inspired a whole genre of similar popular Christmas songs. It is rather fitting that "White Christmas" was composed by a Russian Jewish immigrant, Irving Berlin, because the version of Christmas that it celebrates has little to do with anything specifically Christian but takes its place among the other popular songs that Berlin wrote celebrating American life within the context of consumer capitalism. In a similar way, the fact that it is sung by a "crooner" who was publicly identified as a Roman Catholic is also fitting, because it signals the end of the sole Protestant ownership of American religious symbols. It is also a recognition of the existence of significant Roman Catholic ethnic groups in the urban centers of the nation and their more relaxed attitude toward holidays and celebrations involving alcohol. In the opening scene of *Holiday Inn*, the Crosby character berates modern society for the relentless pursuit of money through continuous industry and professes the belief that more celebration of holidays must be good for the nation's spiritual and mental health. This attitude apparently resonated deeply with the audience. It is hard not to hear in it a kind of Catholic plea for a change from the Protestant ideal of constant hard work and frugality to a cultural calendar with many sanctioned days of celebration. One of the keynotes of classic American culture from the Puritans onward had been the ideal of hard work and saving, with a strong prejudice against consumption—the Protestant Ethic. Until the second quarter of the twentieth century, most American holidays were civic occasions. Unlike much of the Old World, particularly the Mediterranean cultures, Americans did not celebrate with elaborate displays of consumption, ostentatious idleness, or relaxed sexual behavior. During the nineteenth century Christmas had not been universally celebrated in America and its observance in many places was relatively simple. After the large influx of immigrants from predominately Roman Catholic cultures in the late nineteenth and early twentieth centuries, this rigid Protestant culture was in increasing conflict with the proclivity of many of these recent immigrants toward the observance of many holidays by not working and by conspicuous spending for exchange and display. After all, many of the immigrants had come from cultures that observed a whole series of holidays, many of them totally unknown to American culture. Many times they celebrated by taking several days off from work and, at least in the eyes of many Protestant leaders, by public drunkenness and rowdiness, if not bawdy behavior. It also did not escape the notice of either side that the recent immigrants were very often workers employed by Protestant capitalists, who stood to lose days of production by these celebrations, just as the workers stood to gain some respite from hard and unremitting toil.

The segment of *Holiday Inn* that was vastly important for establishing the very atmosphere in which the Christmas complex could live and breathe, along with its implicit assumption that holidays themselves are valuable, was the scene in which the Crosby character sings the song "White Christmas." Given its subject, it is ironic that the song is introduced by Crosby singing to a woman in a room lit only by a fireplace and a Christmas tree while they are alone in a country farm house on a wintry Christmas Eve; that is, it functions as a song of seduction. It is not too much of a stretch to suggest that it is really the audience that is being seduced into accepting the whole complex of attitudes and actions associated with the modern American Christmas. If one cultural item could be said to be the trigger for an entry into the desired holiday mood at that time and for at least the next decade, it was surely the song "White Christmas" as sung by Bing Crosby. As has been noted many times, during World War II Crosby's version of "White Christmas" was heard by armed forces service personnel throughout the various theaters of war as well as at home. The image of soldiers or sailors in battle gear on foreign soil or at sea dreamily listening to this song on the radio came to define Christmas from 1941 to 1945. It also provided a link between those family and friends at home and their relations overseas, a kind of communion through the media of mass culture.

In the introduction to the song, the narrator/singer places himself or herself in Beverly Hills on Christmas Eve, writing Christmas cards to friends while gazing at palm trees. This situation calls forth memories of past Christmases in, one assumes, the northern United States, where there is snow and children sing Christmas carols. It also calls forth a yearning for that lost time. It ends with a wish that the correspondent's Christmases be "white" and "merry and bright." The accompanying music is rather slow and lugubrious to the point of melancholy, unlike many popular Christmas songs, which tend to be fast and upbeat, like "Jingle Bells." In fact, the music and its lyrics leave the impression of a strong contrast between the singer's and the correspondent's present life and the remembered joy of the past. In the song, "white" seems to symbolize lost happiness, beauty, and innocence: youth as seen from the vantage point of one who is older and can no longer participate in those things associated with the holiday that gives happiness to children. This attitude of sorrowful wisdom may be appropriate to the theme of winter as symbolic of aging and death, but it would seem to have little to do with a holiday celebrating birth.

Within what we have been calling the Christmas complex, I think it is possible to see "White Christmas" as an adult counterpart to Santa Claus. Santa Claus, as the personification of the child's wish for gifts, provides children with emotional access to Christmas, but it could hardly function that way for adults. "White Christmas"—as the expression of an adult's nostalgic longing for a happier and more innocent, purer time—provided the adult listener with an emotional connection to Christmas that was at once acceptable to the adult persona and provided a motivation to ensure that others, whether one's own children or not, had the sort of experience that they, in their turn, could recollect when they became mature. This motivation, of course, could be easily channeled into purchasing goods for children in order to ensure that they had a happy experience of Christmas. However, like all such attempts, the result of this one must be uncertain because we can never actually engineer another's happiness through buying or giving goods and because children and others, if they do find happiness, must experience it in their own way and according to their own timetable and inner psychic economy, not according to a date on a calendar. This very uncertainty, however, only serves to fuel more and more spending, since in a consumer-oriented culture the way to ensure happiness is to buy more goods and more expensive goods. Given this basic dynamic, it is no wonder that Christmas is such a frustrating and depressing season for so many people.

If *Holiday Inn* was the prewar vehicle of the anthem of the Hollywood Christmas for the war years, *Miracle on Thirty-Fourth Street* is the prime example of the postwar adaptation of the Hollywood Christmas to a changed situation. Two contradictory strains in mass culture emerged after the war and the end of the Great Depression: the progressive tendency, which tried to continue many of the liberating movements in art, the economy, culture, and ideology that the thirties had spawned; and the conservative trend that attempted to return to some version of an earlier, simpler, and more "virtuous" America. Politically, the progressives tended to be Democrats who wanted to continue Roosevelt's legacy in the direction of social welfare legislation, a more democratic society with civil rights for all, feminism, and freedom of intellectual inquiry. On the other hand, the conservatives tended to be Republicans who wanted to reduce government, regulate labor unions, return to traditional values and modes of thought, and reinstate more traditional roles for Blacks, other minorities, and women. Even though the film industry contained both types until the Red scare and the House Un-American Activities Committee hearings, Hollywood's status in corporate America practically foreordained that it would for the most part fall in line with the conservative agenda. *Miracle on Thirty-Fourth Street* is almost a paradigm of that agenda, with special reference to Christmas and women.

In the beginning sequence of *Miracle on Thirty-Fourth Street,* we are thrust unquestioningly into the world of the commercial American Christmas with all its assumptions of proper images and values intact. The film opens with preparations for Macy's Thanksgiving Day parade, and focuses on a woman executive at Macy's who must get an actor to play Santa Claus on short notice. For our purposes, the symbolism is particularly apt, since Macy's was one of those large retail stores that were most responsible for the creation of the American Christmas and for the elevation of Santa Claus into position as its primary icon. Furthermore, their Thanksgiving Day parade, which is always referred to as *Macy's* Thanksgiving Day parade, was, unlike traditional parades, at once an "instant tradition" and basically an advertising scheme. As the plot unfolds, an older man is hired as a temporary Santa Claus at Macy's, but this man creates the film's dramatic conflict by calling himself Kris Kringle and causing everyone to believe that he actually thinks that he is the "real" Santa Claus. The ostensible point of the movie is that even such a deluded old man, if he has good will, really can be Santa Claus. Further, the modern world can and should be manipulated into admitting that such a Santa Claus exists, since Santa Claus is, in reality, a diffuse spirit of giving and good will. The movie's Kris shows this truth in the course of the plot by bringing happiness to all involved, in spite of themselves.

That is the ostensible plot of *Miracle on Thirty-Fourth Street.* The real plot, whether intentional or not, is quite different and turns out to be rather reactionary in its implications. American business corporations, symbolized here by Macy's, are shown to be only superficially uncaring, exploitative, and wholly driven by the profit motive. Their operations ultimately are good and, left to themselves or with only gentle nudging by concerned individuals with imagination and decent motives, will produce valuable products at reasonable prices while caring for the welfare of their employees and for the larger community. The only truly evil officer of Macy's is a psychologist, unmasked by Kris as a fraud and a petty tyrant, who preys on vulnerable people and schemes to commit the good Kris to an institution. Although the script does state, in small print as it were, that the psychologist is not a real psychoanalyst, the fear and resentment of common sense against talk about the unconscious, complexes, and drives are not hard to place in the coded language of Hollywood at that time. Furthermore, the evil psychologist is portrayed as a bureaucrat who uses bureaucratic machinations to commit Kris. In contrast we have the basically good individual owner of the store, Mr. Macy, who, like his counterpart and rival Mr. Gimbel, is easily swayed by Kris's humanity, especially when he grasps that Kris's good will really serves to give Macy's a better public image. The owner's favor, of course, only further exacerbates the irrational hatred of the evil psychologist for the good Kris. This brings into play two of Hollywood's stock notions of collective morality. First, that the public is spontaneously drawn to the good because it is good, and ultimately recognizes the embodiment of good. This creates resentment in individuals who work through rationally created structures such as bureaucracies—they use the power of those structures to destroy the embodiment of the good. Second, that the leaders of large and powerful organizations are inherently good and will respond to the good when it is presented to them personally in an individual encounter. The underlying message here is that the basic problems of society are caused by the manipulation of the rules of institutional structures by clever and evil people who manage to hold positions of power—these evil persons put the bearers of real good in a bad light and isolate the good leaders from a true understanding of the situation. Both of these features, which are the background assumptions of innumerable Hollywood films, are clearly at work in this movie.

In *Miracle on Thirty-Fourth Street,* however, the person most in need of redemption, for her own good as well as that of her daughter, turns out to be an independent woman: the Macy's executive who hires Kris and who is raising her daughter by herself, having divorced her husband before the film begins. She is presented as cold and loveless, a hard-bitten realist herself, presumably because of her treatment in her former unhappy marriage, who intends to give her daughter "a modern upbringing." This child raising strategy includes, it is announced, teaching her daughter not to believe in fairy tales, such as Santa Claus and a handsome prince who will rescue the fair damsel from loneliness. The redemptive figure for this woman is a bachelor lawyer who lives in the apartment next door. The lawyer befriends Kris, on the one hand, and the daughter, on the other. Throughout the movie he carries on a battle on two fronts: to save Kris from being committed to an institution by the evil psychologist, and to save the female executive and her daughter by wedding the woman and leading her to give up her foolish modern notions. The dynamic here is that a male, by allying himself with a child and with the spirit of Christmas, is able to overcome an independent woman, reduce her to wife and mother, and thereby bring true happiness to all.

The conclusion of the film shows the new family, on Christmas Day, entering their new suburban home, supposedly a gift from Kris, to create the sort of life that would be idealized in the fifties as the natural and normal pattern for all Americans. This was especially appropriate as an ending for a film such as this, made right after the end of World War II, for it fit the trend of postwar middle-class flight from the urban centers into the suburbs and tied the spirit of Christmas to suburban life. This connection was immensely important for the postwar period and helped to justify and sanctify the new home and highway construction of that era as well as the normalization and conformity of suburban middle-class life in America.

As important as the new idealization of the suburbs was, however, one other main feature of the film was equally or even more significant: an expression of the tension concerning feminist values and the need to overcome them by a modern form of patriarchy. One of the unintended consequences of World War II was the discovery by thousands of women of their self-sufficiency and independence through their participation in war work. The need to hire women workers for factory and other traditionally male jobs, both to replace the men who went to war and to handle the increased production caused by the need for war materiel, gave women a confidence in their own ability and a taste of freedom outside the traditional female occupations and roles. It also, of course, gave them the chance to develop new skills and control over their own income outside the power of fathers or husbands. However, after the war was over and men began to return to civilian life, there was a need to convince women to go back to traditional female roles and to let men resume their former jobs and some of their former authority over women. Thus, the same Hollywood that had glorified Rosie the Riveter began to cast women in a more romantic, "feminine light." In *Miracle on Thirty-Fourth Street,* this light is rather glaring and the message almost blunt, although wrapped in the garb of Christmas.

The most famous Christmas movie of the forties, certainly the most frequently broadcast on television and for many viewers the *sine qua non* of their season, is *It's a Wonderful Life.* Indeed, it was broadcast so frequently that it has recently been limited to one or two showings a season in order to prevent overexposure. In light of its recent popularity, it is interesting to note that when it was initially released, although it did reasonably well at the box office, it was not an outstanding success. *It's a Wonderful Life* became a much more popular film in Reagan's America of the eighties than it ever was in Truman's era, despite the fact that it captures so much of the small town postwar ambiance of America at the time. There are telling reasons why this should be so—and they have little to do with the critics' complaint, at the time of its release, that *It's a Wonderful Life* was too gloomy and dark—a comment that seems a bit odd now, when it is often described as the quintessential "feel good" movie.

It's a Wonderful Life qualifies as a Christmas film because its action takes place during a few hours of the Christmas Eve of 1945, as the fictional town of Bedford Falls, in upstate New York, awaits the arrival of a local war hero soon after he had been fêted in Washington. This anticipation is spoiled for George Bailey, however, the war hero's older brother, who runs the family business, a small savings and loan company. George has fallen into deep despair over some missing funds and prepares to commit suicide in order to collect the only money he has access to, his life insurance policy, by jumping off a bridge into the icy river running through his hometown. The rest of the film until the last few minutes is a flashback of George's entire life leading up to this crisis. The particular conceit of the film is that most of his life story is told by a senior angel to a fledgling angel named Clarence, who must win his wings by saving George Bailey, the character played by James Stewart, from himself. Clarence does this first by appearing to drown in the river just at the moment George prepares to jump, causing the super-responsible George to jump in to save him. After George rescues him, Clarence shows him a vision of how much worse the town would have been without him if he had not lived his life the way he did. After this insight, George reaffirms the meaningfulness of his life and "real time" resumes. During the last few minutes of the film, which take place under the Baileys' Christmas tree, the whole town chips in to make up the missing money. George realizes that he does, in fact, have a wonderful life because of the affection of all the friends that he made by his good deeds. In the course of the film, evil is portrayed by a crippled old banker named Potter who is prevented from having total control over Bedford Falls only by the interventions of the self-sacrificing Baileys, George and his father before him. It is Potter who precipitates George's Christmas Eve crisis by keeping the missing funds which have accidentally fallen into his hands and then complaining to the authorities.

At first sight, it is hard to account for the recent extreme popularity of *It's a Wonderful Life* as a fixture of Christmas television viewing, since the connection with Christmas appears to be rather tangential. The real drama seems to be what today we would call a midlife crisis about vocation or possibly even identity. George is a character familiar in American film and fiction, the talented small town native who never escapes to realize his or her potential, but remains out of responsibility to family, which may or may not be a rationalization for a fear of failure. The plot becomes more poignant by being played out on Christmas Eve, with the contrast drawn between the supposed merriment of the season and the subjective despair of the main character. But this contrast is one of the few links between the story of George and Christmas. In fact, one gets the feeling that the turn-of-the-century scene on the Christmas card drawings that provided the background for the opening credits were somewhat out of place and may have been added as an afterthought. The fact that Clarence is an angel may relate the plot to Christmas themes, but Clarence has no specific reference to Christmas, and the angelology of the movie is, in any case, rather odd. In the opening scenes the angels are presented as stars that flicker when they speak and who hear the prayers intended for God and answer them on their own—proficiency in doing so elevates ordinary saints to angelic status. The cloying notion expressed in the last scene that whenever a bell rings an angel gets its wings not only has nothing to do with Christmas, but also is apparently unknown outside the world of this film.

In contrast to the other films discussed in this essay, *It's a Wonderful Life* has increased in popularity since its initial release and even today it remains connected with Christmas in America in ways that other films do not. Given the conservative capitalist ideology of many Americans since the Reagan-Bush era, it may seem natural that a film extolling a hardworking, responsible, independent, and patriotic business- and family man who lives in the same small town all his life would be popular with many who might see in it an idealized vision of their own father. It was even made in the era when Reagan's own film career, such as it was, was at its height, and it requires no great leap of the imagination to picture Ronald Reagan himself in the role of George Bailey. The only feature of the film that might give some of Reagan's supporters pause is the fact the organized religion plays almost no part in the plot. The Baileys not only never go to church, they never mention religion, and, in fact, they seem to be the perfect secular, civic-minded family. Prayer, though, is mentioned three times—once at the beginning of the film when the prayers of his neighbors for George are seen ascending up to the angels; again later in the film when his wife urges the children to pray for George after he storms out of the house; and finally, immediately after that scene, at Nick's Bar where George has retreated and where he prays for help after admitting to God that he is not a "praying man." Although this might trouble some of Reagan's supporters on the Christian Right, it may not have bothered Reagan himself, since he seemed to be remarkably lax when it came to actual worship as opposed to rhetorically invoking religion.

However, there is a much larger paradox here. *It's a Wonderful Life* makes a hero of the sort of anti–New Deal businessman who, at least in popular mythology, helped the honest worker through the Great Depression by sound capitalist lending, as George does in the middle part of the film. In Republican rhetoric, this person did not resort to large organizations, or to social engineering, or to the government, but relied on himself alone and encouraged the working class to do the same, although most workers were misled by politicians to rely on the government or some other external organization. Republicans relied on this kind of imagery to appeal to the working class from the time of Herbert Hoover on through the forties to the fifties when Dwight Eisenhower offered a different rhetoric of professional competence and international diplomacy more suited to the Cold War. It was precisely in the administration of Ronald Reagan that this earlier vision of the world became popular among the majority of Americans. During Reagan's era, however, a business and a style like that of George Bailey's savings and loan were as obsolete as a Model T Ford. Reagan, after all, presided over a period in which banks and lending institutions were deregulated and encouraged to merge into gigantic operations through takeovers, hostile and friendly, leveraged buyouts, and all the other "new" financial techniques that appeared in the eighties. They also engaged in an imaginative array of practices ranging from the legal but unethical to the felonious. This in turn led to widespread collapse, especially of savings and loan companies, governmental receivership, and indictments of former financial officers at the cost of billions of dollars for all of society.

The real George Baileys, if they had survived into the eighties, would have controlled assets that would have made Potter's bank look like a mom-and-pop store, and would themselves have likely been indicted for fraud. There should be no surprise in this, however, because this is the classic function of ideology. It is supposed to distract us from reflecting critically on the real situation by instilling illusions about that situation in members of society, while the historical factors that the illusions both represent and conceal continue their work along quite other lines. The image of life that is presented as inevitable and righteous both justifies the real institution that can claim similarity with that image and blinds us to its actual function in non-movie life. This is what holidays can do also, unless thought is given to their liberating potential through critical and prophetic proclamation. Such a context, of course, is precisely what movies like *It's a Wonderful Life* and the holidays themselves do not ordinarily get. Their context is commercials and sales, and this brings us to our final points about *It's a Wonderful Life*.

Ostensibly, *It's a Wonderful Life* is a celebration of the family and community over time and the way their interactions support one another. The Bailey family members, including a Black female servant, each have their places in the order of things. In this hierarchy, as presented at the beginning of the film, the father is the leader and the eldest son is groomed to take his place, while the mother remains a somewhat shadowy figure even though she remains alive throughout the entire film, unlike the father. When the father dies, George, as the eldest son, takes his place in the family business, a fact symbolized by the dead father's picture overlooking both home and office. George assumes this role despite the fact that his talents and interests tempt him elsewhere and into a different profession, architecture. The narrative of the film presents this, rather bluntly, as the correct understanding of responsibility, an understanding of community built on the eldest son replicating the role of the father. Even the father's enemy, Potter, automatically becomes the eldest son's enemy.

The other members of the family, including George's wife, Mary, who in this sense replicates the role of George's mother, are peripheral to this structure: they are of service to the structure, but remain in the background. In the case of the wife, this subservient and dependent position is underlined by the fact that, during George's nightmare vision of the disorder that would have ensued if he had never been born, and hence never had taken his father's place, Mary is seen as an "old maid," an unmarried, pathetic spinster who wears glasses, works in a library, and is hysterically frightened of men. This vision is rather curious in one respect. In the story, George has to struggle for his wife's hand in marriage with his rich childhood friend who has gone to New York City to make his fortune and has succeeded. In fact, Mary's mother makes it clear that she would have preferred that Mary wed the rich suitor rather than George. Are we to assume that George was responsible for Mary's attractiveness to other men as well as for their own children? Even in the world of the narrative, it would seem that if George had never lived, Mary would have been married to some other man who was George's social or economic better. It should be noted as well that in Capra's visual vocabulary, glasses and books are not deemed suitable for real women.

Thus, the deep code of the film is that correct order, created order as opposed to chaos, is found in the recapitulation of the father's role by the eldest son, and the son's own interests and aims, insofar as they are independent of his father's inheritance, are evil and disordered. This comes out clearly in the crisis scene. Because the "good son," the one who repeats the father's behavior, is rendered inoperative by the missing money and its consequences, the "bad son" can emerge as the "real" George Bailey. It is the bad son who strikes Uncle Billy for losing the money, yells at the children, and destroys the order of the home that the good son has worked so hard to shore up. It is the "angry stranger" who is allowed to come out of hiding in this chaos, especially when he drinks too much at Martini's Bar and literally tries to kill George Bailey by jumping into the river. All of the appurtenances of the responsible life of the good son are suddenly rendered hateful, from the banister ornament that is not firmly fixed to the stuck door of the old car that is still being driven long after it should have been replaced. Especially galling on this Christmas Eve is the Christmas wreath George was to have brought home in preparation for the return of his younger brother, the war hero who actually did all of the sorts of things that the good son was prevented from doing because he was trapped in the role that his father had handed down to him. If Christmas is the holiday of the American system of consumer capitalism as we have been arguing here, then one of its functions must be to legitimate the social structures that make that system work. Chief among those structures is the family structure, which is reaffirmed in this film and which defines the responsibility that has George trapped and divided. If we are dealing with a "deep code" here, then perhaps *It's a Wonderful Life* is more integral to the theme of Christmas than would appear at first glance. Christmas here represents the reestablishment of hierarchical order out of chaos and the consequent affirmation of the socioeconomic system as the best guarantor of personal happiness and fulfillment.

Some comment must be made about the last scene of the film, the Christmas Eve scene in the Bailey home into which everyone from the town, except Potter, crowds in to contribute money for George's redemption. It has always seemed to me that it concludes with a false note, particularly the last lines between George and his youngest daughter, Zu Zu, about bells tinkling when angels win their wings. It is awkward not only because its sentimentality and cuteness go beyond the sentimentality of the rest of the film, but also because it tries to mask the fact that the plot does not have a real resolution. The immediate crisis of the plot may be solved, but the underlying conflicts that led to it are left unresolved. The good George Bailey did not die, drowned in the depths of the river to be reborn as an integrated person. Instead, the good George is simply reaffirmed and the bad George is once again repressed. The crisis in George's life was not caused by Potter's accidental discovery and appropriation of the missing money—that was only the precipitating event that led to its eruption. The real cause of the crisis was the network of preordained relationships into which George was thrown and which he was unable to confront and renegotiate. As long as George allows those relationships to control his life, he remains a fragmented self with part of his being at war with the part that accepts that control. This means that the "bad" George will always be latent, ready to break out of hiding when another precipitating event presents itself. In this view, George's redemption on Christmas Eve is not a redemption at all, in the original sense of setting free. Instead, it is a temporary equalization of forces between the internal dynamics of George's self and the structure of power in the external institutions of family and community. When that equilibrium is disrupted, as it will be at some point in the future, then the sort of crisis played out in this film will be repeated, until there is a disintegration on one side or the other. Given the usual situation, the self is normally the side that disintegrates first, in death, madness, or some other destructive solution such as alcohol.

It's a Wonderful Life may be more truthful on this point than it wants to be, or than its director intended it to be. The dynamics outlined above are precisely the way that holidays, and particularly Christmas, functioned in the psychic economy and ecology of American culture in the postwar period. They are still a recognizable syndrome in the lives of many people, as is apparent to anyone who works with people, especially during the Christmas season. There are a number of ways in which the "bad self" manifests itself at Christmastime, from suicide, as in the film, to sexual acting out, drunkenness, spousal or child abuse, to generating huge amounts of debt. What is called for, from a Christian point of view, is a genuine transformation from a divided and fragmented self to a healthy, integrated self. Of course, this is easier to talk about than to achieve, particularly since it involves the death of the old divided self, both good and bad, and the pain that accompanies that death. This is a task made more difficult by the fact that both the good and the bad selves are experts in surviving by convincing the person that the transformation is complete long before it actually is. As hard as truly changing the self is, however, that is not the real problem with this sort of radical transformation. The real problem is that it involves social and cultural change as well, since the family and community structures that contribute to the fragmentation of the self must be confronted and changed or left behind if authentic transformation is to take place.

The other point I wish to raise has to do with the notion of community presented in *It's a Wonderful Life*. In perhaps the most famous scene of the film, the Christmas Eve gathering we have just commented on, the whole community of Bedford Falls, or at least its representatives, gather around George in his hour of need and reciprocate his service to them over the years by helping him. The interesting point here is that both the need and the help are presented in the form of money. This is a true capitalist community built on a cash-nexus. In fact, George's accountant underlines this by setting up his cash register to receive and record the contributions of the town's folk in front of the Christmas tree in George's living room, almost as an altar on which the townspeople all leave their votive offerings. The subtext is plain: real need is lack of cash, real help is giving cash, and cash is the appropriate gift at Christmas. In the context of the film, it is literally the exchange of cash that brings people together out of their private worlds and makes them into a community. In this scene, aside from the association of Christmas with capital visually, we also see the expression of human relationships take the form of money. Insofar as this is the climax of the film, we are entitled to ask whether it is money after all instead of authentic human relationships that makes life wonderful, just as its absence earlier made life miserable.

The three films we have been considering all have played an important part in constructing the American Christmas and the American psyche during the postwar period. As we have seen, they all play a part in integrating the self into the culture and economy of American society in that era, even as they share as a background the icon and narrative of Santa Claus to which they have added their own contributions. They have—in common with the icon of Santa Claus—a view that what is of ultimate importance is independent of the Christian narrative and wholly in conformity with consumer capitalism. They all also function as ideology by providing symbolic answers to real problems. *Holiday Inn* attempts to persuade its audience that holidays and specifically Christmas have an important social function. *Miracle on Thirty-Fourth Street* attempts to persuade its audience that patriarchy and social conformism are more satisfying than liberation. *It's a Wonderful Life* attempts to persuade its audience that repression is a better way to deal with the conflicts and contradictions of modern capitalist society than transformation. Much about these films may be dated, but one can still fruitfully ask whether Christmas in contemporary America does not share their ideology even if the trappings are different. Many will also want to ask whether the values and solutions proffered by that ideology are compatible with their own religious or human values or whether, as I have argued, they should be challenged.

Chapter Four

Still Dreaming

War, Memory, and Nostalgia
in the American Christmas

Kathleen M. Sands

> Painful memories merge into motivated forgetting
> with special ease.
> — SIGMUND FREUD, *The Psychopathology*
> *of Everyday Life*

> I'm dreaming of a White Christmas
> Just like the ones we used to know.
> — IRVING BERLIN

There are pieces of popular culture that we are embarrassed to enjoy but
do, despite (or perhaps because of) their cheesiness. For me, the 1954 Hollywood musical *White Christmas* is one such tasty bit of cultural junk food.
Judging from its yearly replaying on network television and its soaring video
sales, I am far from alone. Here is my excuse: released in the year of my birth
to parents who both served in World War II (my mother as an Air Corps
nurse, my father as an Army MP), it condenses for me a myth of family
origins. I grew up on my parents' war stories that, like *White Christmas*,
were always of friendship and good times refracted through an earnest sentimentality. Listening to those stories was like sleeping between my parents,
drifting in the dreams that made me secure in the knowledge that the worst
battles had already been fought for me, and won. The fantasy was offered
up to all of America: this was how we used to be, how decent and wholesome, how cheerful and patriotic. Since the 1980s, with its new nostalgia for
the presumed era of "traditional" American families, the fantasy has been
doubled. Now the 1950s, which were themselves all about forgetting, have
been memorialized as supposed touchstones for the prelapsarian American
past. Like *White Christmas,* artifacts of the 1950s have thus become living, power-charged symbols. And Christmas, as a romance of the American
family, has become—in every sense of the word—still "whiter."

In my family, it would take decades for the rougher side of my parents' war stories to be told—the shock of dismembered or dead bodies, the remorse for killing "under orders." For the nation, it would take the Korean War, whose memory could be suppressed but not sentimentalized, and the Vietnam War, which would not submit to either strategy, to trouble the much-needed moral rest of the post–World War II era. Even so, neither the nostalgia of war nor that of Christmas has been defeated; it emerges again and again, as antidote and anesthetic. For nostalgia is not simply sanitized memory: it is an *alternative* to memory, a kind of "motivated forgetting."

Christmas in our country has always been that. At one level, the nostalgia concerns the story of Jesus, which if remembered would actually be a story of poverty, "illegitimacy," genocide, and political domination.[1] But the Jesus story, though a pre-condition of the American Christmas, is neither what we are chiefly remembering nor what we are laboring most vigorously to forget. If it were, then the lack of reference to the Nativity would count against the credibility of our Christmas products and productions. However, in the case of *White Christmas* and in countless others, it does not. Amazingly, the emotional efficacy of Christmas artifacts is reduced not a whit by the absence of Jesus, nor even by the absence of "religious" referents as such.

No, the aim of Christmas in the United States is not to recreate the founding event of Jesus' birth. Rather, the aim is to reenact a previous and presumably ideal celebration of Christmas itself—a Christmas "just like the ones we used to know." As Stephen Nissenbaum shows, Christmas today is an "invented tradition," designed specifically to appear "old-fashioned." Constructed mostly in the nineteenth century, by 1900 our Christmas had become most of what it is today—that is, a festival that weds consumerism and the family in a distinctively American way. Indeed, he argues, "Christmas itself had played a role in bringing about both the consumer revolution and the 'domestic revolution' that created the modern family."[2]

Christmas thus came to be not only a fantasy, but also a distinctly domestic fantasy. In idealizing the middle-class nuclear family, it also idealized a nation which, to put in it contemporary terms, often equates "family values" and "American" values. The effect of the family-centered Christmas, too, was domesticating, compared to earlier styles of Christmas celebration. The Christmases of early America, although far less extensive than those that were to come, had been rowdy public affairs, typically involving demands of the poor upon the beneficence of the rich. As Nissenbaum shows, upper-class folk in the nineteenth century very deliberately shifted the celebration from street to home, so that the recipients of gifts were no longer the poor of society but the children of the house. Even as it was vastly expanded, Christmas in this new, American version would be tamed and its potential for social critique severely blunted.

Nostalgia is historical misrecognition, which in turn enables misrecognition of how our present culture is established and enforced. Catherine Bell argues that cultural misrecognition is facilitated by processes of "ritualization." In Bell's sense, ritualization can happen through any cultural practice, not just when we are doing things explicitly marked "religious." It works by appearing to resolve tensions that the ritualization itself produces.[3] For example, a tension may be posited between an innocent time "then" and a fallen time "now." Ritualization purports to resolve that tension by re-shaping the "now" according to the supposed norms of the past. In fact, however, that vision of the "past" is being conjured up in the present and it may not be the best blueprint for the future. To discern whether it is, we would need to critically scrutinize the norms that are being proposed to us through the invocation of this "past." This is exactly where ritualization, in Bell's sense, intervenes, for ritualization is that sleight of hand by which such critical scrutiny is suppressed. Ritualization tosses a handkerchief over the sources of cultural authority, and when the handkerchief is removed—presto!—norms are re-infused with power. If the ritualization is persuasive and engaging, so are the norms.

Through ritualization, then, norms become hegemonic. In this context, "hegemony" means a style of dominance that relies on unreflective consent. Hegemonic norms pervade not only political and economic space, but also psychic and cultural space, until they become so internalized that they can "go without saying." Such norms do not appear coercive; in fact, they hardly appear as norms at all. Instead, they present themselves as "normal," spontaneous desires, dispositions, and behaviors—that just happen to be deeply conformist. To put it in financial terms, hegemonic norms are the ones we collectively "buy into." This makes them not less but more powerful than other kinds of rules. As historian Michel Foucault noted, coercion is a weak form of power, because it requires dominant elites to actively police their subordinates. The power of hegemonic norms, in contrast, is strong power—the kind of power that is gained when subordinates can be made to regulate themselves.[4]

If Bell is right, ritualization seems uniquely suited to the establishment of hegemonic norms. We should suspect, therefore, that where cultural practices are most heavily ritualized, that is where the internalized norms are most concentrated. Christmas is certainly one of those sites in United States culture where to call the festival into question is to invite accusations of misanthropy. Literally as well as metaphorically, there is no set of rituals Americans "buy into" more deeply, since the lion's share of consumer spending takes place in this season. But the American Christmas is not only a secular ritual; it is also what could be called *a ritual of secularization*. In religious rituals, what is draped from view are the worldly forces that shape religious rules and beliefs. With Christmas, however, nearly the inverse takes place: the religious referent is draped from view, so that the ambiance and authority of religion can be surreptitiously transferred to secular culture. And that may account for the unique cultural power of Christmas. For while many of us have learned to critically scrutinize religious ritual, far fewer of us have learned to critically scrutinize rituals that present themselves as secular.

After all, Christmas can command the center stage of American culture for eight or more weeks a year only because it is secular. Only as secular can Christmas attach such an incredible array of social norms and conventions—about family structure and cohesion ("I'll be home for Christmas"), the economy of sex roles ("Santa baby, slip a sable under the tree for me"), wealth and its display ("Silver and gold, everyone wishes for silver and gold"), childrearing ("you'd better not shout, you'd better not cry"), romance ("Merry Christmas, darling"), marriage and parenting ("I saw Mommy kissing Santa Claus"). And only as secular could Christmas become, as it did in *White Christmas* and has ever since, an emblem of America as prototypically White, Christian, middle-class, and heterosexual.

Most significantly, it is only as secular that this protracted ritual and the package of norms it rewraps and redelivers each year could become socially compulsory. To choose or reject religious beliefs, to display or not display religious symbols, to observe or not observe religious holidays— these are counted among our most basic political freedoms. But to refuse the Christmastime giving and receiving of gifts, the parties and songs, the decorations and shows—is to face penalties ranging from ridicule to social excommunication. Religion, we are entitled and even urged to discuss and reflect upon. But those who question Christmas are chastised for making too big a deal of customs that are, supposedly, nothing more than pleasant trifles. Economically speaking, however, Christmas *is* one of the biggest deals around. Yet, like other aspects of popular culture, it deflects critique by passing itself off as morally or philosophically trivial. Religion can never be openly trivialized in the United States, but secular practices can be. Ironically, then, it is under the cover of its secularism that Christmas and the consumer culture it irrigates become binding on all Americans.

The sleight of hand that confers this power on Christmas is more than the illusion that secular conventions have nothing to do with institutional religion. More fundamentally, it is the illusion that Christmas, unlike religion, is informal rather than formal, spontaneous rather than forced and repetitive, based on our hearts' desires rather than on social constraint or obedience. Not coincidentally, these are the very features that legitimate our political economy. Like Christmas, that economy presents itself as an outgrowth of voluntary choices, natural or spontaneous desires, individual initiative, and impartial, non-arbitrary processes. The ritual that extracts the bulk of consumer spending is thus also the means through which the consumer economy legitimates itself as free, rewarding, and accessible to all.

The problem with our secularized, consuming celebration of Christmas, then, is not just that it enshrines as American a story drawn from a single religious tradition, a tradition that is less and less representative of our pluralistic society—though that is indeed a serious problem. Nor is it that this secularized version of Christianity erases the diversity and conflict within

Christianity, including conflicts about the political economy—although that too is among its deleterious effects. The most serious problem that I am suggesting is that this intensively ritualized season mystifies social and economic relations that detract from all our lives, and we therefore urgently need to understand it. My purpose in this chapter is to reach beyond that mystification in order to remember more truly both our present Christmases and "the ones we used to know."

Warm Nostalgia and Cold War

It should not surprise us that *White Christmas,* a fabrication of nostalgia and misrecognition, was anything but original. The lack of originality extended even to the music of the musical, all of which was written by Irving Berlin, but not all for *White Christmas.* Most notably, the theme song "White Christmas" had already appeared in the 1942 musical *Holiday Inn* and had become the surprise hit of that earlier film. Its resonance in 1954, then, was because during the war the song already had been popular with servicemen. In fact, in the movie *White Christmas,* the song is first performed in a frontline Christmas show, as the battle-weary soldiers long for home and for Christmases like the ones they used to know. Through the song "White Christmas," Christmas is represented not only as a consoling memory for soldiers at war, but also as an emblem of American-ness itself, the home for which they were fighting.

The film belongs to the sub-genre called the "backstage musical," in which the main characters are theatrical performers and their performances are included within the story's plot line. In *White Christmas,* the main characters are Bob Wallace (Bing Crosby) and Phil Davis (Danny Kaye), former army buddies and now a song-and-dance team. The buddies met during the wartime Christmas show just mentioned, at which the character Wallace, supposedly a showman in "real" life, sang "White Christmas" for the troops. As the story gets underway, it is several years after the war, and Wallace and Davis have achieved fame and fortune with their act. But Davis, the younger, is eager to be rid of the chaperonage of his older friend. Devising a plot to marry his friend off, Davis not only succeeds in pairing Wallace with a suitable mate (played by Rosemary Clooney), but also (surprise!) in marrying himself off as well (to a character played by Vera Ellen).

The site of these pairings, however, is equally significant. It is a New England inn, which is faltering due to lack of its main attraction—snow—and which turns out to be owned by Wallace and Davis's former commander, the kindly and paternal General Waverly. Wallace and Davis decide to rescue the general financially by gathering their old division, plus wives, at the inn for a Christmas Eve show. So the story ends as it began, with Wallace singing "White Christmas" for his fellow soldiers and their general. Only now they are home in America, the home they were longing for in the opening scene. And now each and every soldier is matched with an appropriate female. Meanwhile, on stage, Wallace, Davis, and the girls, dressed in ridiculously silly Santa suits, finally resolve their tiffs and misunderstandings and constellate into their destined couples. Around them, dressed like miniature Santas, are dancing children who dreamily prefigure Christmases-to-come, the nuclear families of the postwar era.

But even this tightly repetitious plot was hardly original for Berlin. He already had written a war-centered musical called *This Is the Army,* which opened July 4, 1942, and was performed for millions of American GIs worldwide before it closed in 1945. The reach of TITA, as it was called, was extended even further by its film version, starring Ronald Reagan, released soon thereafter to become the most popular film ever released by Warner Brothers up to that time.[5] To make things still more complicated, within *This Is the Army* there are reminiscences about a *previous* Irving Berlin musical, *Yip Yip Yaphank,* made during World War I and, like TITA, also (supposedly) performed by "real" soldiers. In TITA, these World War I veteran-performers prepare their sons to perform their own musical (*This Is the Army*), mobilizing the new generation—both musically and militarily—for World War II. Thus the assimilation of war to theater, which we see in *White Christmas,* was anything but new. In the later film as in the earlier, the dense repetitions of plot and music were giddily deliberate.

Moreover, the settings, character, and plot line of *White Christmas* all doggedly reiterated those of yet another Berlin musical, *Holiday Inn* (1942). *Holiday Inn* was, in fact, the template for the film *White Christmas.* The settings in both are a matched pair: on the one side, there is the fast, shallow life of show business in the big city (quintessentially New York); on the other side, there is the domestic tranquility of country life in a New England inn (one in Connecticut, the other in Vermont). The lead characters, too, are a matched pair. One is comprised of dancers, the other of singers; the former are slick, sexy, and untrustworthy; the latter homey and guileless. In both films, these pairs have to be constituted in the course of the narrative, and the coupling of like with like is the central, predictable piece of plot work. In both movies, the event that completes this coupling is a Christmas show at (or, in the case of *Holiday Inn,* referring to) the New England inn, and this show is at once a private homecoming and a public performance, a wedding and a moneymaking bonanza.

Another pairing occurs between the films, in the parallel between Bing Crosby's character, Jim Hardy in *Holiday Inn,* and General Waverly of *White Christmas.* Lest we miss that these characters are both innkeepers in economic straits, both stranded in emasculating isolation with unmarriageable women, there is more: our first glimpse of the general in *White Christmas* has him carrying the same armload of firewood as had Crosby/ Hardy in *Holiday Inn.* Crosby thus becomes, in both films, the bearer of the old. In *Holiday Inn* he is the father figure; in *White Christmas,* the father's eldest and favored son.[6] Moreover, his engagement to marry is the resolution of both films. Marriage, the classical comic ending, usually represents a victory of the new over the old, a renewing and even subduing of old conventions by fresh new passions.[7] But there is no dancing on graves in these musicals, particularly not in *White Christmas,* where the rights of age are doubly underlined by the link between the fatherly Crosby and the elderly general. Instead, there is an assertion of marriage over sex, of stability and restraint over rambunctious mobility.[8] Inevitably, a secret place is still reserved for youth and sex, and for the loose women who become the complements to good wives. But if the young characters of *White Christmas* benefit from the plot, it is because the spotlight is *not* fixed on them but on the marriage of their elders, allowing the young to dance off into the dark.

The New England inn, the setting of each film, warrants some special attention. On one hand, an inn is a home where people eat, sleep, take baths, have sex, maybe even conceive children. It is a private, intimate place where people can let down the pretense of their worldly lives. On the other hand, the inn is a public establishment—not just somebody's home but *everybody's* home. At least everybody who counts. As the exemplary, normative, "American" home, these inns replicate the hierarchies and exclusions of their society. Non-White people are present either as servants, as in *Holiday Inn,* or not all at, as in *White Christmas.* Given that Christmas is the main event at these inns, non-Christians obviously would feel like aliens. And, judging from the high-class food, clothing, and decor, even people better off than Mary and Joseph could not afford a night at either place.

As a public-private consortium, the inn-household is an economy—*oikonomia* in the Greek sense. It is a site not only of consumption but also of production and exchange, generating romance and families as well as money, and establishing the patterns of social domination. The means through which these socioeconomic functions come together in the films are, explicitly, "productions"—song and dance shows upon whose success the life of the household hangs. As *domestic* productions, they make a show of domesticity itself as simultaneously a production and a performance. Although totally staged and commercial, the productions present themselves as an expression and indeed as the measure of authentic American life. They take place not in ordinary time, but in the ritual time of Christmas, when families try to squeeze themselves—if only momentarily—into the American ideal of family. (This odd equation of authentic home life with elaborately staged holidays perhaps explains the curious contradiction at the heart of *Holiday Inn:* Crosby/Hardy decides to leave show business because he wants holidays off. Yet, in his new setting at the Holiday Inn, holidays will be the *only* days he works!)

There is, however, at least one telling difference between *Holiday Inn* and *White Christmas.* Interestingly, it has to do with the role of Christmas, which is more specific and more exclusive in *White Christmas* than in the earlier film. *Holiday Inn* revolved around American holidays, and it was as such that Christmas and Easter are tossed in alongside the Fourth of

July and Lincoln's birthday. In *Holiday Inn,* then, Christmas appears under the heading "American." But in *White Christmas,* the relation is reversed: now "American-ness" appears under the heading of Christmas. Christmas, all by itself, could now represent the home and country for which the war was fought and to which soldiers return when it ends. On Christmas Eve, when Wallace and Davis, their girlfriends, their division, and all the wives sing "White Christmas," their gala performance represents the whole nation, postwar, reconsolidating itself as family. Christmas, quite without the support of any religious celebration, now could function as the anthem of both personal and national life.

This postwar family, like the Christmas celebration that showcased it, was also an "invented tradition," something new that is validated by being made to appear old. More than anything, what was new at the time of *White Christmas* was the temperature of war, which had shifted abruptly from hot to cold. For in 1954, the enemy was not Nazi fascism or Japanese imperialism but Soviet Communism. This new circumstance, the Cold War, gave a distinct shape and intensity to certain exigencies of postwar culture as such. These exigencies were, most obviously, economic—the shift from defense to consumption, from sustenance to abundance. But they were as much social and psychological—the shift from the patterns of war, with its mobility, excitement, and same-sex communities, to those of peacetime, with their stable, even staid, heterosexual couples and nuclear families. In the context of the Cold War, however, the consumer economy and the nuclear family that sustained it gained unprecedented significance as the American counterpoint to Communism. Christmas, so closely linked with this family and this economy, took on an even greater significance. For it now heralded, in effect, a new economy of "grace," abundance, interpersonal love, and individual freedom—an economy understood to contrast dramatically with the Communist economy of "works," sustenance, socialist citizenship, and state control.

The new significance given to Christmas and with it, conventional sexuality, was also due to the distinctive interpretation that postwar Americans gave to Communism, in contrast with other political enemies. Much more than Nazism, Communism was felt to be an internal threat rather than just an external one, not so much a political viewpoint as a kind of creeping degeneracy or corruption. This threat, ideologically, was cast as distinctly sexual. As Elaine Tyler May shows, Communism became ideologically assimilated into fears of a moral, specifically *sexual* chaos that could only be contained by vigorous promotion of the nuclear family.[9] The nuclear family and nuclear weapons thus became the linked arms of American defense in the Cold War. Perhaps the paradigmatic illustration is the famous "kitchen debate" between Richard Nixon and Nikita Khrushchev; Nixon, pointing to a display of elaborate household appliances, argued that the American system was superior because it was designed "to make things easier for our housewives."[10] The suburban home, staffed by a stay-at-home mother and possessing every device needed to be a comfortable, self-sufficient unit, thus became the microcosm of an American identity.

This was an "invented tradition" because the middle-class, suburban, nuclear family, with its particular arrangements of gender and labor, private and public life, was new in a number of ways. Indeed, its existence was substantially indebted to World War II because the GI Bill played a massive role in enabling it.[11] Nonetheless, this particular pattern of life was understood as the mainstay against Communism. Subversion therefore was attributed not only to those with left-of-center politics, but also to those with unconventional versions of gender and of sexuality. This explains the association of Communism with homosexuality and the fierce persecution of homosexuals in the military, in government, and in civilian life throughout the 1950s. As May writes, "Gay baiting rivaled red baiting in its ferocity, destroying careers, encouraging harassment, creating stigmas, and forcing those who 'confessed their guilt' to name others with whom they associated."[12]

The other main target of the anti-Communist hysteria, as we recall, were Jews. This returns our attention to the unique role of Christmas in postwar America, not just as the holiday in which family and consumer spending each reach their apex and are welded together, but also as the secular ritual through which American identity is established, both religiously and racially, as Christian. Or, to put it differently, as the ritual through which Christmas is established not only as American but as "White." Christian anti-Semitism, conterminous with Christian history itself, has always pivoted between being a religious and a racial-ethnic prejudice, as Rosemary Ruether and others have shown.[13] Even when Jews converted to Christianity, they remained suspect in Christian culture, on the conviction that in some deep, ineradicable—that is, "racial"—sense, they remained Jews. Like Communism, it seemed American-ness was something more than—and maybe something other than—a political choice. It was, most deeply, a racial-ethnic character, something in the blood.

Nazi ideology seized upon and developed that racial side of an anti-Semitism that has to be acknowledged as, from its inception, fundamentally Christian. In historical retrospect, Americans remember the evils of Hitler and Nazism, exemplified in the genocide against the Jews, as the chief justification for World War II. The power of this account, despite its inaccuracy, is that it underlines the moral heroism of our side. If indeed the American part in that war had been a repudiation of anti-Semitism, an affirmation of our nation as religiously free, it is inconceivable that *White Christmas* could have been made into the musical score for that memory. (Christmas, after all, would not have been a strong point of distinction between American troops and their German enemies!) If racist fascism were the imagined enemy of the war nostalgically recalled in *White Christmas,* could that film or its audience be comfortable with the representation of our nation as totally, blindingly, White?

The fact that neither the Whiteness nor the Christian-ness of the America represented in *White Christmas* were noticeable problems underlies the film's chief sleight of hand—the implicit, unselfconscious substitution of "Godless Communism" for Nazi fascism as the enemy. For the welding of Communism to the notion of Godlessness, in addition to erasing long and still-living traditions of religious socialism, also welded American-style capitalism to American-style religion. That is, to Christianity—*not* Christianity as a system of beliefs, but Christianity as an economy, a class, a set of sex-gender relations, a culture, and even a "race."

White Christmas, then, revolves around two sets of misrecognitions. One is political—the substitution of Cold War for hot war, of Communism for fascism as the counterpoint to American identity. The other is psychosocial—the transmutation of life-scarring trauma into romantic drama, of grief and remorse into sentimentality. The patterns of gender and sexuality, race and religion, that shaped *White Christmas* and Cold War America were by no means natural, traditional, or inevitable. Far from returning to "the way we were" prewar, they required vigorous and sustained denial of contrary realities that wartime America, not long before, had experienced firsthand. That denial, in *White Christmas* and in Christmases ever since, was enabled by nostalgia, a forgetfulness that poses as memory, but through which real memory threatens to erupt.

Gender and Sexuality: Coming "Home"

The most evident nostalgia and denial within *White Christmas* are related to sexuality and gender. In 1954 this was different for men and women and different pre- and postwar. Here too the contrast with *Holiday Inn* is instructive. In both films, the men must transition from an initial state in which they relate intimately to each other, to an end state in which they relate intimately only to women. In *Holiday Inn,* however, the men in their initial state do not relate only to each other but also to a woman (the sleazy, "dancing" Lila Dixon). Moreover, in *Holiday Inn,* the male bonds have not been compacted or complicated by the experience of military service. There was never any love lost between Jim Hardy (Bing Crosby's character) and Ted Hanover (Fred Astaire's character). On the contrary, they connected only through their competition, which was both professional (the contest between singing and dancing), and sexual (their battle over the wholesome, "singing" Linda Mason). In the end, their connection is resolved through termination, when each man is matched with his characterological "like," singer with singer and dancer with dancer. Thus, by mating with their female characterological likes, the men are parted from their male sexual likes.

In *White Christmas,* the singers and the dancers will also end up in heterosexual pairs, but the whole process is more difficult because Wallace and Davis are bound by the deepest of emotional ties: during the war, the younger has saved the older's life. Ostensibly, the plot's problematic is to separate these two, dislodging them from the sexual latency of buddyhood into the sexual maturity of marriage. In the end, however, what parts them is their romantic pairing with women who happen to be sisters. From here to eternity, we are led to imagine, they will be related through marriage. This is explicit when onstage, during the Christmas show, the engagement between Bob Wallace and Betty Haynes is finally sealed. With the foursome briefly hidden behind the Christmas tree, Davis turns to Wallace and says, "Welcome to the family." Wallace and Davis have thus become "legiti-mates," to borrow a term from Mary Daly. They are at once relieved of the embarrassing appearance of being married to each other, and joined together on a permanent basis. The same trick is enacted on grand scale when the entire division of soldiers, gathering *en masse* before the general with their wives, not only receive his blessing on their marriages but also ritualize their indissoluble bond with each other.

In *White Christmas,* the threat of homosexuality is recognized and denied much more vigorously than in its template—no doubt also an exigency of military experience and its Cold War aftermath. Despite the official policy that homosexuals were not to be admitted to the military, they were everywhere. Allan Bérubé estimates that of the eighteen million men interviewed for military service, only four to five thousand were turned away for homosexuality; for women the rate was even lower.[14] Ironically, the war contributed something to the gay rights movement that was to come into being within two decades: it was in the service that gays around the country first found each other, and it was at the points of military discharge, such as New York and San Francisco, that large postwar gay communities were to develop. This contradiction, between the de facto participation of gays in the military and their de jure exclusion, meant that the war effort depended significantly upon a sustained and collective act of denial.

This denial embraced more than the homoeroticism of self-identified homosexuals. Homoeroticism also was and is a standard, albeit denied, aspect of military life among those who see themselves as sexually "normal." As a sailor who served in the South Pacific reported, "A lot of friendships became intense and men were getting closer and closer. People ended up lovers. The ship was crawling with them. It was an accepted thing."[15] Bérubé argues those who saw themselves as heterosexual often felt more free to engage in what he calls "situational bisexuality" than did servicemen and women who knew they were gay and feared to be exposed as such.[16] Moreover, even when not actively homoerotic, military life was (and is) profoundly homo*social*. During the war, men and women had lived in sex-segregated communities where they had experienced the most intense adventure, attachment, camaraderie—and often loss—with members of their own sex. Postwar, it could not have been easy to relinquish those same-sex communities, friendships, and, not infrequently, erotic bonds, for the nuclear family. In that newly insular life-world, both sexuality and adult intimacy were supposed to be restricted to one and only one person—the marriage partner. As men's and women's lives were relegated back to separate spheres (hers to the world of home, his to the world of work), that intimate adult partner was less and less likely to actually share the experiences and interests of one's daily life.

By the time *White Christmas* was made, then, "normal" adults who had lived through the war would have been missing the same-sex bonds of wartime, yet also recalling those bonds with some anxiety. The anxiety was evoked partly by shifting, contradictory ideas about sexual preference that were destabilizing the whole concept of sexual normality. Through the rising influence of Freudian psychology, homoeroticism (or "sodomy") was being reinterpreted. It was now no longer understood simply as a criminal act (as it had been in World War I) or a sinful act (as it has been throughout much of Christian history), but rather as rooted in a pathological and probably unchangeable personality type. At the same time, however, there was a widespread view (held for example by William Menninger, chief consultant in neuropsychiatry for the Army from 1943 to 1946)[17] that even "normal" men would experience homosexual feelings and perhaps even engage in homosexual behaviors under the abnormal conditions of war. Then, shortly after the war, the famous Kinsey report (1948) had suggested an alarmingly high rate of homosexual interest (about 50 percent) and, at least occasionally, of homosexual behavior (about one-third) among the entire population of American men. As Eve Sedgwick has argued, these two views of homosexuality, which have dominated the twentieth century, are linked and yet contradictory: on one hand, there is the conviction that homosexuality is a fixed, pathological, and hence non-contagious condition. On the other hand, there is the conviction that, under particular circumstances, any "normal" man might experience and enact homosexual feelings—in which case, homosexuality is a universal and fearfully contagious tendency.[18]

So, although men and women who thought of themselves as sexually normal had a great interest in distinguishing themselves from "real" homosexuals, during the war this distinction would not have been easy to make, for several reasons. As already noted, real but closeted homosexuals were everywhere within the military, and the stability of military life depended on not taking much explicit notice of who they were. Since homosexuality was thought to be usually either latent (unknown to oneself) or hidden (from others), there was no certainty about who was or was not a true homosexual—an uncertainty that could easily be extended to oneself. Moreover, even explicit confessions of homosexuality by men were not taken at face value, because they were regarded as possible malingering (as a tactic to avoid combat).[19]

After the war, although it was no easier to prove or disprove who the "true" homosexuals were, the stakes in doing so had skyrocketed. Even as postwar Americans were contending with the loss of same-sex bonds, persecution of homosexuals had begun in every arena of life. In the ideology of the McCarthy era, homosexuality (like Communism and Jewishness) was a hidden degeneracy, a pathological condition rather than just a behavior, belief, or style of life. Anyone was susceptible to the accusation of being homosexual; while these charges were hard to refute, they wreaked havoc on jobs, political careers, and personal lives. There was, in fact, an increased sense of male vulnerability to homosexuality postwar, because of the loss of soldierly roles, the risk of unemployment, and the postwar confinement of men to passive, bureaucratic jobs. All this, it was feared, could endanger men's masculinity, hence their sexuality, making the nation as a whole more penetrable by Communism. Therefore Cold War homophobia had an intimidating effect not only on self-identified homosexuals, but on all Americans, particularly men.[20]

If it was necessary, both during the war and after, to aggressively deny homoeroticism, that is evidence of how dreadfully present this sexual "deviation" was felt to be. It is important to remember that denial pertains to what is real, for there is no need to deny what is not felt or feared to be real. The result was an astonishing degree of sexual doublethink—a constant, collective "protesting too much." One example during the war was the "homosexual buffoonery" that was commonplace in barracks, showers, and similar settings. According to Menninger, these raucous parodies of homosexuality were "carried to such extremes that no one participating in it ever considered in his own mind the disturbing possibility of any seriousness in it."[21] Yet if *parodies* of homosexuality were permitted and even required, that was only because *actual* homoeroticism required constant denial.

During the war, a major vehicle of denial was the drag show. In World War II, soldier-cast shows ("blueprint specials") were a regular part of military life, and drag was a standard part of these shows.[22] One show, for example, included eight full pages of dress patterns in its production notes, along with choreography for men in tutus. The official rationale was that shows were a vital part of military life, and that female roles, in the absence of women, had to be played by men. But that rationale was surely disingenuous, because servicewomen did become available for female roles early on, and the response of servicemen was resentment rather than relief. Moreover, drag shows actually created a need for gay soldiers. In order to cast and staff the shows, the military was always on the lookout for the appropriate "types" in its ranks, such as soldiers adept at costume design, makeup, or drag. Unsurprisingly, this drew a large number of gay soldiers into military shows. Drag numbers were thus a volatile mix of repression and acting-out, simultaneously providing the flamboyant display and the aggressive denial of homosexuality. For gay soldiers, this meant that drag was a way of hiding in the open—signaling gayness to other gay men via the codes of camp, while asserting to the rest of the military that their effeminacy was only a put-on, requiring laughter but (ideally) forbidding ridicule. But it was a dangerous game, because the gay soldier who pressed too hard at the boundaries of denial was risking his honorable discharge, his postwar employment, and his personal safety within the military.

Phil Davis, the character played by Danny Kaye, seems to dance on this razor's edge. Kaye himself, rumored to have been gay or bisexual,[23] spent fifty years in a marriage that may have been largely a cover-up. His character is equally ambiguous in his sexuality. This is especially evident when Judy suggests to Davis that they pretend to be engaged, as a way of enticing Wallace and her sister into romance. Unaroused by Judy's hand as its slithers up his inner thigh, the rattled Davis skitters away from her, protesting that his feeling for her is not unlike the affection he feels for his cocker spaniel. His reaction lends itself equally well to two interpretations: it can be either a manly resistance to sexual commitment, or a sissy's fear of heterosexual impotence. Under cover of the former interpretation, viewers are freed to implicitly recognize the latter. The same dynamic is at work in Kaye's number "Choreography" which, while ridiculing effete modern dance and the rising beat generation, also parodies the effeminacy of (presumably) homosexual choreographers. Yet (and this is so regardless of the truth about his sexual preference), Kaye's *gender* presentation, and therefore that of all his characters, was undeniably, exuberantly effeminate. In "Choreography," then, he is *pretending to be what he really is*. He is pretending to be pretending.

Gay men, in other words, were making use of the same mechanisms of denial used by "straight" men in the army. But while gay men often were consciously delivering double messages, straight men saw themselves as delivering an unambiguous message about their own normality. As remarkable as it seems from the perspective of our more sexually skeptical era, most servicemen doing drag evidently felt no sense of exposure as they publicly enacted these transgressions of gender and sexuality. Quite the contrary. An especially vivid illustration is the number "Mandy," as it appeared in TITA.[24] ("Mandy" was also to appear in *White Christmas,* but of that performance, more below.) In TITA, "Mandy" was still a drag act and, to make the performance still more revealing, it was also performed in blackface, which was worn by both the "women" and the men. What the performance presented, then, was White GIs, pretending to be Black, pretending to be women, and pretending to be "queer." Which is to say, White GIs showing that they are *not* women, *not* Black, and *not* queer.

In *White Christmas,* Crosby and Kaye perform a drag act together that is a combination of these historical strands. Standing in for the Haynes sisters, who are fleeing an angry landlord, they perform the girls' number, called "Sisters." Thus, by parodying the "real" sisters, the partners Wallace and Davis demonstrate that they *not* "sisters," a euphemism for male homosexuals; their swishy gestures evoke not real women, but effeminate men. In the context of the film as a whole, and in the context of the public's familiarity with Kaye and Crosby, viewers would surely have noticed that Kaye's drag is much more "natural" than is Crosby's. While Kaye is pretending to pretend, Crosby is (supposedly) *really* pretending. In the doublethink of military drag, very familiar by 1954, the audience could register Kaye's effeminacy as something to be enjoyed but not scrutinized, and Crosby's stiff performance as evidence of his secure masculinity. Yet, even as it carefully defused the threat of homosexuality, this drag performance was allowing postwar men to regress to the wartime pleasure of drag shows and the male bonding they secured.

In addition to shifting their affectional or sexual bonds, postwar males also had to find ways to preserve their masculine gender identities in the milder, mixed-sex context of the home. This was not only a social but also a political exigency. Postwar policy legislators and policy makers were understandably concerned that demobilized soldiers, unless quickly domesticated, would grow dangerously restive and even subversive (as had the "Bonus Army" of World War I veterans, which lay siege to Washington, D.C., in July 1932),[25] and this was a large impetus behind passage of the GI Bill.

The impact of the war is again evident in differences between *White Christmas* and *Holiday Inn.* In the earlier film, men's transition into domesticity was not complicated by the intervening experience of war. For example, in *Holiday Inn,* Crosby/Hardy is not embarrassed to don an apron over his tuxedo and stir the soup. And when man-to-man conflict threatens to erupt with Astaire/Hanover, he retreats demurely with the excuse, "I have to turn the roast." In *White Christmas,* however, the gender role dissonance is much more severe, because the men have been enacting manhood at its most hyperbolic—as warriors. In the case of the general, this is underlined by his isolation with an aged spinster and his pubescent granddaughter, an impotence at once sexual and financial. Crosby sings the dilemma of the general's temporary genderlessness with a sympathetic lyric, "What can you do with a general when he stops being a general?" The general's division can sympathize because they too, in the postwar years, have lost something of their masculine edge. In his mock inspection of his former troops, who have stuffed themselves back into uniform for the occasion, the general barks, "You're soft, you're sloppy, you're unruly, you're undisciplined" but then, changing to a tender tone, concludes cornily, "and I never saw anything look so wonderful in my whole life." Acceptance by women would not suffice; instead, men had to see the postwar deflation of their masculinity as a collective situation. On that basis, with a sigh, they could loosen their belts.

From another angle, the domestication of masculinity was also the remasculinization of the domestic sphere. But to shut down the anomalous wartime economy and jump-start it with men at the wheel was no mean feat. At a practical level, it required the return of men to wage work, yet there was widespread fear of unemployment and, as after World War I, of another Depression. This was resolved largely through the GI Bill, which busied millions of veterans with college studies and, when they had finished, provided opportunities for improved employment. In *White Christmas,* the challenge of remasculinizing the home is thematized by the general's sad situation at the inn, in which both production and reproduction are at a standstill. What will save him, of course, is a "production"—a show—but a show that in turn depends on heterosexual pairing with procreative intent. Were it not for the romantic reconciliation of Crosby and Clooney (who plan to have nine or so children), the Christmas show could not have been successfully performed. And were it not for the return of the soldiers and their wives, it could not have made money. Thus the film dramatizes the resumption of moneymaking and baby making under male leadership. The fact that this, like Christmas, is a gala *performance* seems to intensify its persuasiveness as an ideal, even as it belies its shakiness as reality.

The female characters, in contrast to the men, *are* "sisters." Sister stories, as subplots of Hollywood musicals, were not unusual, but again this sister act was newly inflected with, or threatened by, the recent memory of the war years. These were years in which women had unprecedented opportunities to work with, live with, and, if they chose, form sexual bonds with other women. For women, like for men, wartime life was sex-segregated. This was true not only for those who went into the military, but also for those who stayed at home and entered the work force. The war years fostered the migration of many women into urban areas, where lesbian communities were to form in the 1940s and 1950s. In the cities, women were able to work and live with other women, outside the supervision of parents, spouses, or boyfriends. Within the women's military, as noted, lesbianism was effectively accepted—by officials, for reasons of expediency, and by military women themselves with an attitude of evident nonchalance.[26]

Intimate emotional and erotic attachments among women had every opportunity to blossom in the war years. As lesbian activist Lisa Ben wrote in 1947, "Never before have circumstances and conditions been so suitable for those of lesbian tendencies."[27] Unlike in nineteenth-century middle-class life, these attachments could no longer be ambiguously labeled "romantic friendship"; psychology's invention of the "invert" or the "homosexual" as a personality type forced all women to consider the meaning of same-sex attachments in a more frankly sexual light. For all these reasons, lesbians, like gay men, found that the war years vastly expanded both their sexual opportunities and their consciousness as a group. And few straight women could have come out of the war, especially not out of the military, without having known, tolerated, and perhaps loved women who, by the next decade, would be persecuted as sexual deviates.

For women, just as for men, the postwar years would put an end to any nonchalance about homosexuality. In the 1950s women's sexuality, intensified and channeled exclusively toward their husbands, would become the glue that held the nuclear family, hence the nation, together against the threat of Communism. So the sister act of *White Christmas,* like the Wallace-Davis parody of it, had to do a double service for the postwar audience. On the one hand, it had to provide a nostalgic memory of sisterly intimacy in the war years; on the other hand, it had to show that sisterly love was a distant second to the romantic love women were soon to find in marriage. Indeed, the theme of the song "Sisters"—the one and only number Betty and Judy Haynes perform together—is the immediate preparedness of the sisters to separate from each other in the event of a marriage proposal. Its comic re-

frain, repeated half a dozen times in the film, begins by espousing sisterly
loyalty—"Lord help the mister who comes between me and my sister"—but
ends with the punch line "and Lord help the sister who comes between me
and my man." Its message is, in effect, that "Sisterhood is Powerful: NOT."

In addition to the characters' biological sisterhood, the age difference between them also defuses the intensity of their relationship. Betty Haynes,
played by Rosemary Clooney, is visibly older and far less sexy than her
younger sister Judy (played by Vera Ellen). Their relationship is that of
mother hen to baby chick, and, since neither of them is a chick anymore, it
is about time for someone to "fly the coop." The sisters therefore show no
regret about the end of their shared career and companionship. For example,
when Clooney/Betty sheds tears on the night of Judy's engagement, the tears
are not because she is losing her lifelong intimacy with her sister, but because her day-old romance with Wallace has been briefly derailed. Betty in
particular seems to represent the ideal middle-class wife of the postwar era.
That she is a "natural" for marriage and motherhood is indicated through
her distaste for show biz life, where "everybody's got an angle." Despite
her fame and glamour, Betty cannot wait to give it up for the presumably
more authentic married life with the staid Wallace. Her solo number ("Love,
You Didn't Do Right by Me") has her dressed in black, mourning the ever-
so-temporary loss of her one and only man, who at that very moment is
adoringly observing her from the audience.

Watching Betty and Judy, postwar female viewers could nostalgically recall their own war years, comfortably repackaged as a prelude to marriage.
In truth, most women did not wish to stop working when the war was over;
in fact, many did not stop. Contrary to the prevailing image of the 1950s,
the number of working women actually rose after the war. What did change
was that women were generally removed from the "men's" jobs some had
held during the war, their wages fell, and the labor market became even more
sex-segregated. Although 75 percent of the women who had been employed
in war industries were still employed in 1946, 90 percent were earning less
than they had during the war. Women's average weekly pay after the war
decreased by 26 percent (in contrast to the national postwar decrease of 4
percent), and Black women earned less than half of what White women took
home. Even female veterans were ineligible for many of the benefits given to
servicemen under the GI Bill.[28] Women rearing children, therefore, although
they were not unlikely to work for wages, were made deeply dependent on
the economic support of men.

In *The Feminine Mystique*, Betty Friedan would argue that the 1950s reduced middle-class women quite completely to marriage and motherhood.[29]
Recent scholarly assessments suggest a more complex picture; for example,
that women's magazines, in addition to their fictional stories of domesticity,
also included non-fictional accounts of admirable career women, many of
which were told without any reference to the woman's marital status.[30] But
women's reassignment to domestic labor, their increasingly sex-segregated

jobs, the professionalization of homemaking and childrearing as women's work—all this was certainly as much a matter of social compulsion as personal choice. In particular, what seems to have been compulsory, at least for respectable women, was *ideological* loyalty to domesticity. Regardless of whether this ideology matched their work or family realities, their personal histories, or their deepest feelings, middle-class women in the 1950s did as a rule espouse the belief that their most important job, and their deepest fulfillment, lay in being wives and mothers. Even those who openly supported women's employment no longer did so on grounds that work outside the home was vital to a woman's personal development, an argument that had been made in the 1930s. Now, the only acceptable rationale was that women's work could benefit her family or her country. Women might explain that they were working to buy a specific item or raise the family's level of consumer spending. Or an expediency argument was made: women's employment helped to strengthen the economy and maintain in women a level of expertise in the event that it became necessary to mobilize for war against Communism. (The latter rationale, strange but not uncommon, used the same Cold War anxieties that confined women to the home to make, at least for a certain number of women, the opposite case.)[31] In short, tensions and contradictions within the ideology of domesticity were already afoot in the 1950s, but it was not until the 1960s that those contradictions would be identified as such, enabling or even forcing women to make a choice.

Even within *White Christmas,* points of tension in the ideology of domesticity peek through. For one thing, their marriages will not end this sisterhood, just as the marriages will not really separate Wallace and Davis. Also, the women in *White Christmas* are permitted some lighthearted recollections of the greater heterosexual freedom that was available during the war. In the boy-girl number, "Gee, I Wish I Was Back in the Army," the postwar girls pine for "a million handsome guys / with longing in their eyes / and all you had to do was pick the age, the weight, the size." These are not precisely the measurements taken by women seeking marital chastity, the film winks, even while it places a partition between the youthful days of sexual freedom and the present reality of mature, married life.

In the character of the younger sister, Judy (Vera Ellen), the tension between sexual freedom and marriage, sexiness and wifeliness, appears much more strongly. Judy suggests the kind of uncontained, promiscuous female sexuality that was a major repository for Cold War anxieties.[32] Bearing a striking resemblance to the images of female bodies men in the air force had used to decorate their fighter planes, she is the epitome of the female "bombshell"—an expression we owe to the war years. Her solo ("Mandy)" is, in sharpest contrast to her sister's number, the most highly sexualized number in the film. The lyrics betray an anxiety to marry her off ("Mandy, there's a minister handy"). Yet the visuals seem curiously at odds with the lyrics. Vera Ellen's "bridal gown," though virginally white, is designed to expose every millimeter of her gorgeous legs, and the train, its one concession to bridal modesty, is soon cast off entirely. In addition to her main partner, an anonymous man, she dances with a whole gang of other anonymous men, suggesting—depending on what one wants to see—that she belongs to all of them or that they all belong to her. Even as she "ties the knot," this "bride" seems to remain a "woman on the loose."

The character Judy also enacts what the number "Mandy" conveys. Unlike her elder sister, she has plenty of angles. She initially pursues the men only for purposes of career advancement and, when she moves in on Davis, seems more interested in sex than in marriage. Like Davis, her characterological "like," she seems to prefer glamour and money over love and marriage; like him, her initial aim is to marry off her elder chaperon, not herself. Just as "Mandy," despite her song, remains a woman on the loose, so Judy, even at the film's end, has never avowed love for Davis/Kaye. So although Davis welcomes Wallace "to the family," Judy herself has done nothing to make Davis her "family"; her marital interests, instead, are entirely fixated on her sister's status.

Judy is thus the bearer of the tensions within the postwar sexual ethos. These tensions are partly those of the double standard itself, which encourages men to both require and resist the chastity of women—or, to put it the other way around, to require and prohibit women's sexual availability. Contradictory even for men, the double standard is also a double bind for women. One gesture toward resolution is to intensify the sexual expectations from wives, so that the marital relationship itself will be more rewarding, and this indeed was a marked change in the postwar understanding of marriage. Yet for both men and women, this new effort to infuse marriage with the sexual intensity of life "on the loose" would also have stirred vivid recollections of the war years, in which sexual life really was far looser than could be openly replicated in the postwar years. Even more profoundly, the sexualization of wifehood introduced new levels of sexual expectation—and of frustration—that within a decade would lead to open attacks upon the double standard and upon traditional sexual ethics in general.

All these shifts—from multiple relationships to monogamy, from homosociality and often homoeroticism to strict heterosexuality, from adventure and mobility to security and stability—operated as they still do, in the style of hegemonic rather than coercive power. *White Christmas* works hard to make these dramatic and compulsory changes appear like a homecoming, a return from the artificiality of the theater and the danger of war to the safety and sincerity of family. Christmas is a key means by which these changes are affirmed as free and natural, as hearts' desires, even as they are grafted onto the consumer economy.

The "Whiteness" of Christmas

Through Christmas, both literally and symbolically, the postwar economy was made dependent on the gift. As a cultural practice, gift giving absolutely demands the pretense that gifts are unexpected and even unwarranted. ("You _shouldn't_ have!")[33] So it comes as no surprise in _White Christmas_ that what refuels the general's failing _oikonomia_ is a massive, unexpected gift. It is love that makes this new economy go 'round, the musical seems to say, not compulsion or intimidation, competition or scarcity, exploitation or profit. Romance, generosity, friendship, luck, surplus, affection, and happy destiny—Christmas makes the economy a miracle of "grace," rather than a rat race of "works."

But Christmas, as already noted, was itself the most ambiguous of gifts, particularly in terms of Americans who were not Christians. Here we must pause to recall the strangest of ironies: that it was a Jew, Irving Berlin, who gave us both "White Christmas" and "America the Beautiful." Berlin's own first memories, according to biographers, were of a pogrom in his native Siberia. From that trauma, he was to conclude the superiority of American democracy to Bolshevism, and to become, by the Vietnam era, a fierce Cold Warrior. However, he did not internalize the other message implicit in his early persecution: that its roots lay not only in political but in religious and racial antagonisms. To dwell on that other message, in the American context, would not have been very comfortable. Berlin's solution, like that of many other Jews, was a defensive assimilation to the American ideal. He saw this assimilation as cultural and political, not religious; in his mind, for example, "White Christmas" was a patriotic and not a religious song.[34] In a sense, Berlin himself contributed to the secularization of Christmas through the writing of that song. The question, however, is whether that secularization ever was or could be something other than the absorption of all Americans into an identity that was tacitly Christian—where "Christian," again, stands less for a set of beliefs than for a culture, an ideology, a political economy, and a race.

The history of Jews in the United States, even in Hollywood itself, answers that question resoundingly in the negative.[35] Before the United States had become involved in World War II, Hollywood produced a number of unabashedly propagandistic, war-preparedness films. Isolationist politicians interpreted these films as expressing the hatred of Jewish studio heads for Hitler (as if antagonism for Hitler would have been unwarranted). They went so far as to initiate a congressional investigation of these studios, in which accusations were made in explicitly anti-Semitic terms.[36] Once the war had begun, that investigation was quickly dropped; Hollywood was suddenly receiving money and even unsolicited artistic advice for producing pro-war films. But after the war, as the Cold War commenced, it would not be long before Jews—and in particular Hollywood Jews—would again find themselves, under McCarthyism, a suspect group.

Just as Nazism drew on the racial side of Christian anti-Semitism, so McCarthyism, in its theories of "degeneracy," drew on the racial-ethnic aspect of Cold War ideology, in which only Euro-American Christians were natural (or, as it was called at the beginning of the century, "native") Americans. In that context *White Christmas,* whatever Berlin's intent, was not only a show about Christmas (and thus of Christian-ness) but also *a show of Whiteness.* Again, these social norms operated differently postwar, in *White Christmas,* than they had at the war's beginning. In *Holiday Inn,* the innkeeper (Crosby/Hardy) had openly functioned as a White master in relation to his Black, mammy-like servant Mamie (played by Ethel Waters), and her two Kewpie-doll children. In one particularly offensive scene, Whites in blackface represent plantation "darkies" singing the praises of "father" Abraham Lincoln. Offstage, in the kitchen, Ethel Waters's character sings along in earnest agreement. In the social reality of 1942, it was inconceivable that Waters would sing on the same stage as her White colleagues; in the film, the White characters do not even know she is singing with them.

White Christmas, in contrast, replaces Mamie and her children with a White woman and child—the spinster Emma and the general's granddaughter, Susan. The tune "Abraham" is repeated but, interestingly, only as a dance number, *sans* lyrics; viewers only know that the song is about Lincoln and the "darkies" because they remember its previous performance in *Holiday Inn.* In *White Christmas,* absent Mamie and her children, every single character is White. Similarly, the number "Mandy," which in TITA had been a drag act in blackface, in *White Christmas* has been entirely Whited-out. The racism lingers, but much more subtly, for the song is still framed within a larger "minstrel" show. In *White Christmas,* then, Whiteness has become the only show in town. It no longer appears in contrast to Blackness or as the "master" race, as it did in *Holiday Inn.* To dissociate itself from the bellicose racism of Nazism, *White Christmas* now presents Whiteness not as a race, but as a kind of racelessness—a tacit norm of humanness and American-ness that, precisely because it is "normal," disappears.

But if Whiteness "disappears" in *White Christmas,* that is so only for Whites whose method of sustaining White supremacy is to not notice it. For Americans of color, however, it could hardly be ignored. As African Studies scholar Gerald Early writes, when he was growing up in the 1950s and 1960s many African Americans responded to Irving Berlin's "White Christmas" with "a kind of measured irony," as a song "not about weather but about culture." The benediction "and may all your Christmases be white" was heard as "the white man's hope for the future."[37] Ideological White supremacy makes the same connection. For example, the inaugural issue of a Neo-Nazi newspaper, which appeared in January 1989, announced "Good News America! There is a White Christmas in Your Future!"[38]

The shift to a more subtly ubiquitous form of racism in *White Christmas* also owes something to the experience of war. In the service, young White men from different regions and ethnicities were brought into a closer unity than they had ever known. But at the same time, all White servicemen were made to witness and support the racial segregation of the armed forces, so that those who had never seen or participated in official, systemic racism now did. I remember my father describing how he had to pull the bodies of drowned Black GIs out of the water in North Africa, a shock heightened for him by the deep purple hue of their corpses. They had been stevedores, forced to unload supplies from American vessels even though the shoreline was being strafed at the time, as if their lives were completely expendable. In some cases, African American servicemen refused to continue performing these jobs. In the Navy, a group called the Chicago 50 was convicted of mutiny for refusing to return to their job of loading ammunition onto ships, following an accidental explosion that had killed 320 of their fellow Black sailors.[39] The understandable anger of Black men did indeed make Whites fear to place guns in their hands (President Truman's postwar order in 1948 to integrate the troops was as fiercely resisted as are uncloseted gays in the military today). And not for nothing was there anxiety about the disturbance that military experience might create in America's racial hierarchy; African American veterans were indeed among those who, by the 1950s, were initiating the earliest stage of the civil rights movement.

Another American color buried in the drifts of *White Christmas* was that of Asian Americans, particularly Japanese Americans. The interment of Japanese Americans, which continued from April 1942 to December 1944, is even now a barely acknowledged injustice. Just as the "racial" side of Jewishness made Jews vulnerable to anti-Semitism even when they converted or assimilated to Christianity, so the race of Japanese Americans placed them under suspicion even when their political identity was plainly American. Postwar films did not help, for they continued to portray Japanese soldiers as ruthlessly indifferent to human lives, including their own. Whatever real horrors of war those memories, like the memories of Nazism, may have held, they covered over as much. For it was the United States, not Japan, that committed the unprecedented sin of nuclear annihilation. It was easier to demonize the Japanese as people indifferent to life, than to remember American indifference to *their* lives.

The Whiteness of Christmas, both as the color of Christianity and as the color of American-ness, was in the most profound sense a question of the color of God. The God of *White Christmas* is certainly White, as symbolized by the white-haired General Waverly, who resembles both Uncle Sam and the Euro-Christian God. Despite having won the war, the God/nation depicted in General Waverly is presented as oddly debilitated. He seems to have lost something in the war and, like Tinkerbell, needs the faith of others to restore his former glow. This debilitation is best understood if we grasp the general's Whiteness as not only a matter of color but also a matter of morality. For it is this second kind of "whiteness"—moral innocence—that is the subtext of General Waverly's dilemma, and that of his country. Instructively, the film reverses the dilemma. The general is presented as absolutely and infinitely benign; instead, the problematic of the film is how, returned to the home front, he can regain his wartime stature. This was a comforting reversal of real memories of generals of World War II, who had exercised the power of life-and-death over a whole generation of men. Even when decent and honorable, they could hardly have been remembered as either impotent or morally innocent.

The general's problem, in effect, is a political version of the theological problem known as "theodicy"—that is, the problem of reconciling the infinite goodness and the infinite power that are both imputed to God. Most efforts at solution end up denying the infinity of one quality or the other. *White Christmas* chooses to deny the power, and it does so in order to restore faith in the general's goodness. But whether used for the purposes of theology or for those of Hollywood, this tactic evades the most crucial questions. For example: Could any absolute power, such as the absolute destructiveness of the hydrogen bomb, be good? And, given the unfathomable tragedies of World War II alone, could goodness ever again be thought of as the force that runs the world? War cannot but place the goodness of power and the power of goodness in the most profound moral doubt. But this doubt was much more easily faced in regard to the fascist equation of might and right than in regard to the evils done and the losses endured by the United States and its allies. The general's infirmity, like that of his country, was moral, a wound bandaged at the time with forgetfulness but that in the long run, could only be healed in the open air.

Secularization: From Theater to Film

Christmas, I have argued, is a ritual of secularization in several senses; *White Christmas,* in its trite and schlocky way, exemplifies them all. It reinforces an entire ensemble of cultural norms bearing on race and sexuality, nation and family. It makes these norms appear perfectly free, in fact the expression of our hearts' desires, even while inscribing them as socially compulsory. Wishing a Christmas dream for every citizen, *White Christmas* thoroughly kneads into American identity a hegemonic Christianity that enshrines racial Whiteness and middle-class status as much and often more than religious practice. And it lends indispensable support to the consumer economy, a substantial portion of which it renders socially requisite. Ideologically, it mystifies the workings of the economy into grace and gift, freedom and desire, protecting the impersonal, constraining mechanisms of corporate capital from rational scrutiny.

The shift from theater to film, as well as their ongoing connection, sheds light on Christmas as a ritual of secularization, because *film is to secularity as theater is to religion.* In twentieth century America, religions, like theater, are ritual performances that we choose to attend or not attend, rules and doctrines that we consciously accept or reject. Religion, like theater, is something we can look *at;* while secularity, like film, is a normative filter we look *through.* Film, as much as religion, presents norms for us to imitate and by which we measure ourselves. But because these norms are presented as entertainment, they are not subject to reflection or choice. Again, this is why the norms that circulate this way are so powerful.

The musical *White Christmas* represents, in a double sense, a "stage" in these processes. First, it is an example of the "backstage musical," most popular in the period when the power of theater was being transferred to the much more naturalistic and popular medium of film. In the backstage musical we are shown the stars both onstage and offstage. In this way, their offstage appearances—that is, their *filmic* appearances—are established as authentic in contrast to the artificiality of their staged performance. The backstage musical, then, helped to establish film as a realistic window onto American life—that is, to establish film as a means through which we could be trained to follow rules, while experiencing ourselves as simply observing the way things are.

There is a ridiculously obvious example of this at the end of *Holiday Inn*. Hollywood, the plot tells us, has decided to cash in on the success of the "real" Holiday Inn by making a movie about it. However, the plot concludes, this movie (within the movie) could not possibly have been convincing, because *its* characters were just acting. The Christmas scene in the movie (within the movie) only becomes convincing when the "real" sweethearts, Jim Hardy and Linda Mason, sing "White Christmas" together and return to their "real" home, the Currier and Ives postcard that is the "real" Holiday Inn. Viewers are to imitate this filmic image of authenticity as the American ideal, even while telling themselves that this, in contrast to the phoniness of Hollywood, is the "real thing."

By *naturalizing* the filmic frame, the backstage musical also helped to naturalize the activities of courtship, marriage, and domesticity that the film represents for ritual mimesis. And by *staging* these activities, the backstage musical infuses them with the hyper-reality of theater—or, to put it differently, with the ideality for which ordinary life strives but which, as ordinary, it can never achieve. In *White Christmas*, therefore, the climactic moments of filmic satisfaction are those in which theater and "life" come together, either because the show floods into its audience, or because people find themselves on stage, enacting and resolving the very struggle they had been going through offstage. The best example is the final scene, when Wallace and Betty Haynes, having had a fight that disrupted their implicit engagement, are on the stage performing "White Christmas." But their performance is at first stilted because they are "acting" like sweethearts but are no longer "real" sweethearts. That is, until Wallace finds the "white knight" in his stocking, indicating that Betty has again accepted him as her fiancé, an authentic and therefore marriageable man rather than a guy with "an angle." It is then, when the stage couple becomes a "real" couple, that the Christmas performance becomes a real Christmas. And we can tell it is real because, offstage in heaven, God acknowledges its authenticity with the gift of snow.

By the time *White Christmas* was made, the transition from theater to film—and with it the waning of the backstage musical—was well underway. So in *White Christmas* the theater-film dichotomy, which transfers credibility to film, could assist in the formation of the religion-secularity dichotomy, which transfers the authority of religion to secular norms, practices, and beliefs. The normative authority once monopolized by religion thereby is given over to market forces; simultaneously, these market forces are made to appear not as market forces at all but rather as the free expression of personal desire and choice.

This brings us back to the theater where we began—the theater of war. It is war from which *White Christmas* flees and to which it nostalgically and compulsively returns. The film makes war, quite literally, into a theater; the only war scene we see is one in which a song-and-dance show is occurring on the frontline. Quite without the song and dance, we know that war is called a theater. To name it "theater" is to say that war is bound in time and space, that the roles we play here are not our real selves, that the actions we perform are not ones that we ourselves have chosen, that the life-and-death conflicts we have there are not the stuff of ordinary life. But to the extent that the economy and the *oikonomia* under which we live are compulsory and exploitative rather than gracious and free, then war and its shadow are the stuff of ordinary life. Historically, war unfortunately has been far more than a "stage" for us, and the theater to which it truly belongs is the tragic theater, as more recent filmic treatments of World War II have recognized.

The alternative to the theater of sentimentality, however, is not no theater at all, just as the alternative to nostalgia is not an unequivocal moral judgment upon our history. Nor is the alternative to a consumer-fetish Christmas an austere refusal of joy, friendship, romance, family, or sensual indulgence. A better American holiday would be larger, not smaller. It would be larger in the peoples and traditions it celebrates, in the homes and the nurturance it provides. And it would leave space at table even for the restless spirits of the unfinished past.

I grew up in a postwar neighborhood where the fathers, and sometimes the mothers, had plenty to forget. There, with the help of the GI Bill, houses and families sprang up quickly through the 1950s. A few doors from our house I had a friend, just about my age, whose name, oddly, was Anne Frank. She was the child of an American serviceman stationed in Nagasaki and a Japanese woman. In the years after the war, it was said, Anne's mother had gone insane and eventually killed herself. Anne was being raised by her paternal grandparents, who lived on our street, and it was to them that she owed her Germanic name. When we were around nine, she developed a cancer; the last time I saw her she had a massive tumor on her neck and was soon to die.

Anne Frank was my first up-close look at death, and my first confrontation with the death of a peer. It was a disturbing memory, not the kind one wants to dwell on. It took many years for me to wonder about the name and the fate that linked my friend with the other Anne Frank, and to wonder whether her cancer, or her mother's suicide, might have had something to do with the bombs that my country had dropped on hers. It was an alternative memory, painfully resurrected, like the ghosts of Hiroshima and Nagasaki, whom mourners urge down the river in candle boats each August. There is no telling the truth in the story of the life and death of my young friend, but we do know that true memories, healing memories, must be more than nostalgia. What is buried beneath those cool, sentimental drifts is nothing so simple as unmitigated evil, for neither we nor our enemies were ever that. But along with the courage and the love, there is remorse, confusion, and unspeakable loss. Such memories may trouble our sleep but, in so doing, portend a better dream.

Notes

1. See chapters 6 and 7.

2. Stephen Nissenbaum, *The Battle for Christmas* (New York: Alfred A. Knopf, 1996), xii.

3. Catherine Bell, *Ritual Theory, Ritual Practice* (New York: Oxford University Press, 1992).

4. Michel Foucault, *Discipline and Punish* (New York: Vintage Books, 1979), 27.

5. Allan Bérubé, *Coming Out under Fire: The History of Gay Men and Women in World War II* (New York: Free Press, 1990), 69–71.

6. This symbolic function was abetted by the fact that the actual Crosby was older than five of his six fellow leads (Danny Kaye, Rosemary Clooney, Vera Ellen, Marjorie Reynolds, and Virginia Dale) by a margin of ten to twenty-five years.

The exception was Fred Astaire (of *Holiday Inn*), born in 1899, who was actually five years older than Crosby, but was regularly cast as a youth and, as he aged, paired with women who were on average twenty-two years his junior. See Rick Altman, *The American Film Musical* (Bloomington: Indiana University Press, 1987), 245.

7. This emphasis on marriage and sexual stability is evident also in *This Is The Army,* where the plot line revolves around the eventual decision of Ronald Reagan's character to marry before going off to war. In a heroic effort to spare his girlfriend possible widowhood, he had resisted her persistent suggestions of marriage, but in the end he is convinced that marriage and family are in fact what the war is all about—that is, what he is supposed to be fighting for.

Encouraging marriage for servicemen was also official government policy. For example, a radio ad of 1942, sponsored by the Office of Facts and Figures and intended to mobilize young men to enlist, has a young man's voice saying to his girlfriend: "That's one of the things this war's about.... About love and gettin' hitched, and havin' a home and some kids, and breathin' fresh air out in the suburbs.... " Cited in Elaine Tyler May, *Homeward Bound: American Families in the Cold War Era* (New York: Basic Books, 1988), 60.

8. This preference for the old mitigates *White Christmas*'s participation in the comic backstage musical, and establishes some connection with what Rick Altman calls the "folk" Hollywood musical. See Altman, *The American Film Musical,* 274.

9. May, *Homeward Bound.*

10. Ibid., 16–18.

11. See Michael J. Bennett, *When Dreams Come True: The GI Bill and the Making of Modern America* (Washington, D.C.: Brussey's, 1996).

12. May, *Homeward Bound,* 94–95. The political attack against homosexuals first began in February 1950, the same month McCarthy issued his first accusa-

tions about communists in the State Department. In part, the supposed link between Communism and homosexuality was predicated on the notion that homosexuals were susceptible to blackmail. However, as D'Emilio and Freedman argue, "the growth of a gay subculture" (which occurred postwar) "also called into question the strength of another prop of Cold War society, the family." See John D'Emilio and Estelle Freedman, *Intimate Matters: A History of Sexuality in America* (New York: Harper and Row, 1988), 292–95, especially 294.

The sexually contained, heterosexual nuclear family, with breadwinner father and housewife mother, was felt to be the mainstay against Communism, which in turn was understood not simply as a political view but as a kind of moral and psychic degeneracy into which weak individuals could be easily seduced. Male homosexuals, who were seen as weak and self-indulgent, were thus felt to be points at which America was particularly penetrable by the communist. For a thoughtful and thorough analysis of this dynamic, see May, *Homeward Bound,* 92–102, especially 92–96.

13. Rosemary Radford Ruether, *Faith and Fratricide: The Theological Roots of Anti-Semitism* (New York: Seabury Press, 1974).

14. Bérubé, *Coming Out,* 33. There were a number of reasons for this de facto acceptance of gays and lesbians in the military during World War II. One, which applied both to men and to women, was the need for draft boards to meet their quotas for military personnel. Additionally, in World War II psychiatrists saw homosexuality as a pathology and a condition, not (as in World War I) a criminal action. Many psychiatrists, some for humanitarian reasons, were not motivated to expose homosexuals, given the persecution that classification as homosexual might cause in their later lives (for example, difficulties in gaining employment). Also, because of patriotism on one hand and fear of persecution on the other, gay men were likely to lie or dissimulate in their induction interviews in order to gain admittance to the military. See Bérubé, *Coming Out,* 8–33; also D'Emilio and Freedman, *Intimate Matters,* 292–95.

The situation for lesbians in the World War II military was even more favorable. For while the symptoms attributed to male homosexuality (primarily effeminacy) were understood to make gay men unsuitable for combat, just the opposite was true for women. Mannishness, independence, competence, physicality, and even the desire to bond with a group of women were all seen as high qualifications for women in the military. So, although the military went to pains to project an image of the femininity of its female personnel, there was, as one high level military woman put it, "a firm public impression" that the female military was full of lesbians. Based on accounts of women who were in the military at that time, as well as official documents indicating tremendous concern over this issue, that public impression was correct. See Lillian Faderman, *Odd Girls and Twilight Lovers: A History of Lesbian Life in Twentieth Century America* (New York: Penguin Books, 1991), 118–30.

15. Bérubé, *Coming Out,* 188–89.

16. Ibid., 41, 188–89, 191, 192, 260.

17. See Menninger's postwar report on homosexuality in the army, excerpted in Jonathan Ned Katz, *Gay/Lesbian Almanac: A New Documentary* (New York: Harper and Row, 1983), 634–39.

Menninger defined "homosexual interests" as "emotional attachments to members of our own sex" and regarded this as a normal phase of psychic development. In adult life, many people continue to find "sublimated homosexual gratification" in same-sex organizations. Therefore, when denied heterosexual opportunities and thrust into the same-sex context of military life, it was to be expected that homo-

sexual satisfaction would be among the "substitutes" for "normal sexual energies."
In the army, according to Menninger, one of the most common forms of homosexual
satisfaction was what he called "homosexual buffoonery"—parodies of homosexuality that were standard behaviors in any situation of male physical intimacy
within the army. (Drag shows, in this view, would presumably have been a more
public expression of this buffoonery, offering homosexual satisfaction but at the
same time insulating men from their fears of actual homosexuality.)

However, Menninger also observed that many men in the army, to their own
surprise, did experience conscious "physical interest in other men," and that many,
"including many married men, found 'women' to satisfy their need." (The scare
quotes around "women" evidently indicate homosexual relations with "passive"
partners, which would have felt less threatening to the self-concept of the "active"
partner.)

Presumably most of these behaviors would belong within the third of Menninger's
four-part typology of homosexuality: (1) latent homosexuality; (2) conscious and
self-accepting homosexuality; (3) occasional homosexuality (for example, under the
influence of intoxication); and (4) a group of homosexuals that, while small, was
a "social menace," openly displaying homosexual interests and actively attempting
to seduce other men. However, the notion of occasionality does not seem quite
consistent with the pervasiveness the various homosexual satisfactions Menninger
describes.

It should be noted also that a primary aim of this report was to argue that military response to homosexuals was often punitive and unfair. In issuing this protest,
Menninger again shifts from the view of homosexual feelings as common and in
some degree normal, to the view of homosexuality as the pathology of a minority.
In the view of psychiatrists, he contended, homosexuals have immature personalities "which make them and their lives and some of their personal relations grossly
pathological. Like any sick person," he added, "they deserve understanding instead
of condemnation."

18. Eve Kosofsky Sedgwick, *Epistemology of the Closet* (Berkeley: University of
California Press, 1990).

19. By 1945, this became an official army regulation, although without the knowledge of his office, according to Menninger. See Menninger in Katz, *Gay/Lesbian
Almanac*, 638.

20. As Barbara Ehrenreich wrote, "fear of homosexuality kept heterosexual men
in line as husbands and breadwinners.... The ultimate reason why a man would not
just 'walk out the door' was the taint of homosexuality which was likely to follow
him." Quoted in D'Emilio and Freedman, *Intimate Matters*, 295.

21. Menninger in Katz, *Gay/Lesbian Almanac*, 635–36.

22. For a full discussion of the remarkable role of drag among U.S. troops, see
Bérubé, *Coming Out*, 67–97.

23. In a biography of Laurence Olivier, Donald Spoto claimed to have proven a
ten-year affair between Olivier and Kaye. This assertion has been much contested,
for example in a more recent biography of Kaye by Martin Gottfried (*Nobody's
Fool: The Lives of Danny Kaye* [New York: Simon and Schuster, 1994]). However,
even Gottfried made note of Kaye's "covert sexuality," but preferred to interpret it
as "of a piece with his general emotional repression rather than being a signal of
any alternate sexual activity" (quoted by reviewer Desmond Ryan in the *New York
Times Book Review,* November 13, 1994, 47).

24. "Mandy" also exemplifies the patterns of repetition within Berlin's war musicals. It was originally written in the World War I era (1917). Within TITA (1942), which had been written to embolden the young soldiers of World War II with the example of their veteran fathers, "Mandy" therefore served to evoke World War I. When the number was repeated in *White Christmas* (1954), it would have brought back memories not only of the widely popular TITA, but also patriotic recollections of World War I.

25. See Roger Daniels, *The Bonus March: An Episode of the Great Depression,* Contributions in American History 14 (Westport, Conn.: Greenwood Publishing Co., 1971); also Walter Waters (as told to William White), *B.E.F.: The Whole Story of the Bonus Army* (New York: Arno Press and the New York Times, 1969).

Fear of similar restiveness among World War II vets was, by some accounts, a decisive factor in the approval of the GI Bill. See Bennett, *When Dreams Come True.*

26. Faderman, *Odd Girls and Twilight Lovers,* 125.

27. Ibid., 129.

28. May, *Homeward Bound,* 76.

29. Betty Friedan, *The Feminine Mystique* (New York: Laurel Books, 1963, 1974).

30. Joanne Meyerowitz, "Beyond 'The Feminine Mystique': A Reassessment of Postwar Mass Culture," in *Not June Cleaver: Women and Gender in Postwar American, 1945–1960,* ed. Joanne Meyerowitz (Philadelphia: Temple University Press, 1994).

31. See Susan Hartmann, "Women's Employment and the Domestic Ideal in the Early Cold War Years," in Meyerowitz, *Not June Cleaver.*

32. See May, *Homeward Bound,* 92–113.

33. See Pierre Bourdieu, *Outline of a Theory of Practice,* trans. Richard Nice (New York and London: Cambridge University Press, 1977).

34. Susannah McCorkle, "Always: A Singer's Journey through the Life of Irving Berlin," *American Heritage* 49, no. 7 (November 1998): 74.

35. See, for example, Naomi Morris, "Jews in Tinseltown: Was the American Dream Born in Eastern Europe?" *Maclean's* 111, no. 10 (March 9, 1998).

36. Beginning in 1939, a number of Hollywood films had been made to encourage U.S. entry into the war, some but not all stimulated by Jewish studio heads. In September 1941, a subcommittee of the Interstate Commerce Commission, led by Senator Gerald Nye, held hearings on "Motion Picture Screen and Radio Propaganda." Nye's accusation, that Jewish studio heads had created a conspiracy to push the U.S. into war, became moot within a few months, when Pearl Harbor was bombed. See Allan Woll, *The Hollywood Musical Goes to War* (London: David and Charles, 1981), 3–8.

37. Gerald Early, "Dreaming of a Black Christmas," *Harper's* 294, no. 1 (January 1997): 55 (7).

38. Elinor Langer, "The American Neo-Nazi Movement Today," *The Nation* 251, no. 3 (July 1990): 82.

39. President Clinton issued a pardon to Freddie Meeks, one of the last survivors of the Chicago 50, two days before Christmas in 1999. See John Aloysius Farrell, "Fifty Years Later, a Sailor Is Pardoned," *Boston Globe,* December 24, 1999, 1(A).

Chapter Five

The Holy Days and
the Wholly Dazed

Christmas and the "Spirit of Giving"

A. P. Simonds

It is Thanksgiving weekend. In the *New York Times Magazine*, Tiffany & Co. opens the holiday season with a two-page advertisement that brings us straight to the heart of the matter. On the left side is a tightly framed black and white photograph of a couple embracing. Her handsome face is meticulously well-cared for and we know, from just a small glimpse of the back of his head, shirt collar, and suit, that he is comparably attractive: a man of means and authority. She looks down with eyes closed, leaning lightly against his neck and shoulder. It is a moment of deep intimacy: a reaffirmation of the love of a lifetime. And the magic that infuses the moment takes material form in a small box lodged, ironically (or perhaps entirely appropriately), in between them.

I said this was a black and white photograph, but that is not quite true. For the box, tied in elegant white ribbon, is a pale, blue-tinged, green—only barely chromatic against the grayscale of everything else, but green enough to impart an ethereal aura that seizes attention and attests to the emotional or even spiritual importance of the box and, by extension, to its contents. We know, even before we look to the adjoining page, that it is a gift from him to her (a not insignificant inference; see note 33). We know that it is something of great value; no egg timer or paperweight could be a token of such a moment. Looking to the right, we see what she is soon to unwrap. In a sea of white space sits a bracelet and just three lines of text. The first identifies Tiffany's in thirty-point type. The last, in tiny eight-point letters, provides a phone number for information about store locations. In between, a description of the product:

> ABOVE ALL ELSE. Platinum mesh buckle and bracelet with diamonds, $14,000.

Though the meaning of these words is perhaps not quite so straightforward as at first they appear (a matter to which we will need to return), many questions will occur to the reader who takes the message at face value but pauses before turning the page. How does an object come to be associated with the deepest attachments of the heart, much less a measure of their authenticity? Why should we suppose that value in the sense of "price" has anything to do with value in the sense of emotional, moral, or spiritual "worth"? Perhaps most pointed of all, how did we arrive at a position in which it is thought appropriate and indeed entirely unremarkable to see the purchase of such a gift as a fitting way to celebrate the birth of one who counseled that "a man's life consisteth not in the abundance of the things which he possesseth"? (Luke 12:15 KJV).

Bearing Gifts

Questions and doubts such as the ones I have just raised are scarcely unfamiliar; they probably cross the minds of most adults, at least briefly, at some point during each Christmas season. Nor, according to Stephen Nissenbaum, are they particularly novel: the practice of complaining about commercialization, he indicates, is nearly as long-standing a feature of Christmas tradition as Santa Claus himself.[1] But important as it is for historians to remind us that there is nothing new under the sun, so too do they help us to see, as James Tracy points out, that quantitative changes at some point become qualitative, that differences of degree can turn, almost seamlessly, into differences of kind.[2] Beginning early in the nineteenth century, Nissenbaum shows, a public, unruly, class-centered, carnivalesque Christmas was domesticated: it moved from the streets to the hearth, from the expression of social unrest to the embodiment of familial order, from noblesse oblige to parental love, a holiday that was henceforward child-centered and, perhaps most important, "commercial at its very core."[3] There can be no faulting Nissenbaum's description of Christmas past; indeed, his book is perfectly splendid. But it is a very long leap from his perfectly reasonable claim that contemporaries would find the nineteenth-century Christmas "quite familiar" to his suggestion that Christmas present is essentially similar: that "the important changes—the revealing changes—had all taken place" by the turn of the twentieth century.[4] It is as if one were to say:

> by the middle of the nineteenth century, the organization of production in the most developed countries of the world had shed its feudal and mercantile forms, and the practices of capitalist producers took a form that would be quite familiar to their modern descendants. Between then and now, the modifications have been more a matter of degree than of kind, more quantitative than qualitative. The important changes—the *revealing* changes—had all taken place.

Well, yes. But...

To see what makes recent changes revealing, it is necessary to unpack our images of domesticity, of childhood, of commercial motivation, and especially, of gift giving.[5] As Richard Horsley points out, the contemporary American holiday season is properly considered a two-month festivity, inaugurated by Thanksgiving and concluding with the Super Bowl in late January. But Christmas is the season's focal point and gift giving is, for good or ill, securely lodged as the centerpiece of Christmas. Spiritual expression, reenacted tradition, family values, and of course commercial motivation all converge here. Yet it is not easy to parse the overlaying meanings and consequences of the practice. Certainly they are not all benevolent, even as they affect their ostensive primary beneficiaries, children. While the holiday "wish list," for example, can certainly be, as Horsley observes, "an important expression and validation of personal identity" within the family,[6] it can also turn gift giving into simple order-fulfillment, something that threatens to generate as rich a yield of disappointment and surrender of self as it does gratification and self-validation. The wish list of fifty years ago typically took the form of a handwritten "Dear Santa" letter asking for generic presents: a doll, a sled, a baseball glove. (A wish list cast in the form of a letter, even to a fictive gift giver, would probably also toss in a few niceties along the lines of "How are the reindeer?" or "Hope you and Mrs. Claus are keeping warm.") During the following decades, product focus became ever sharper, the Christmas list evolving not just toward greater specificity, but toward brand-name-sensitive specificity: "It's a Barbie doll I'm looking for, Santa." By the last Christmas of the century, the wish list has been directly embedded in the business logic of the toy retailer: in the form of the personal gift registries found on nearly all on-line merchandising sites, it is literally an order form enumerating product, model, and price next to a convenient one-click order button. Under this sort of Internet retailing model, "What will I get for Christmas?" is displaced by "How much will I get?" (the child has already specified the "what"), and space for the unscripted and unexpected present recedes toward the vanishing point: Uncle Elmo in the Philippines has the same access to Etoys.com as Mom and Dad.[7]

The point here is not to bemoan the putative loss of yesterday's innocence; there is doubtless something to be said for, as well as against, the new way of doing Christmas business. What is of interest is the reality of change and the importance of understanding both its sources and its likely consequences. If the unsophisticated "Dear Santa" letter is a thing of the past for all but the very youngest of children, this should be credited neither to the inexorable march of technology nor to some general loss of innocence or moral decay. It is the result of a series of deliberate marketing decisions that were made possible by technologies such as television and the Internet but which were motivated by identifiable economic and political interests that are independent of either. At mid-century, toy industry advertising was negligible—some one-tenth of one percent of annual sales volume, targeted chiefly at purchasing adults rather than consuming children.[8] Three decades later, sales were some twelve times higher; advertising expenditures, on the other hand, had risen by a factor of three hundred, or roughly 2.5 percent of sales. In 1998, the two toy powerhouses Mattel and Hasbro both spent more than 16 percent of United States sales on national advertising.[9] Does this mean that parents at the end of the century see vastly more toy ads than their own parents and grandparents? Probably not: the new advertising artillery was aimed at what was, in the late fifties, an entirely new target audience: children themselves. Children's television programming made possible the creation of brand-consciousness in the toy business, but it was extended and amplified in dozens of ways in the ensuing decades: product placement in films, cross-marketing that turns films and television programs into ads for not only toys but food, clothing, and other entertainment products including books, music, videos, live performances, and sporting events. As a result of these changes, the Y2K Christmas wish list takes not just a different form: it has a different content. When the seven-year-old girl unwraps her Millennium Barbie and says "It's just what I wanted!" says Peter Arnell, chief creative officer of AG Brand Consulting, what she means is, "This is the brand I wanted!" And he continues: "The system that allowed Barbie to live is the brand."[10]

If the contemporary Christmas is in these ways "post-domestic," it also retains many of the elements that Nissenbaum identifies as residues of the pre-domestic patron-client exchange. While our cultural self-understanding of Christmas gives priority to the bestowing of gifts on children (the image of Santa Claus epitomizes this), children's gifts account for but a small portion of Christmas spending and probably always have. Expensive gifts bestowed by men on women continue to have the biggest impact on the dollar volume of seasonal retailing. December sales of jewelry stores in the United States, for instance, approach 25 percent of annual sales—considerably higher than the "Christmas spike" in general.[11] Alluding to Christmas jewelry advertising in 1809, Nissenbaum writes: "Women, like children, were dependent members of the household. Only later were adult men included as appropriate recipients of Christmas presents."[12] It is not clear that we have rid ourselves of this anachronism, and it is but one of multiple functional and moral guises assumed by the Christmas present: the gift-as-bribe (the tip that keeps the newspaper from being tossed in a puddle), the gift-as-guilt-absolver (the poinsettia plant or box of chocolates for the office secretary), the gift-as-business-expense (for clients, Super Bowl tickets say ABOVE ALL ELSE even better than that bracelet), the gift-as-stimulus-to-indulge (the fact that the Christmas sales spike continues for a while after December 25 supports the suspicion that Christmas gift giving feeds acquisitive impulses as well as generous ones).

The afterlife of gift-exchange is also problematic, since the conversation that begins "What did you get?" is widely understood to be a surrogate for "How important are you?" or "How loved are you?"—whether it takes place in the school yard, by the water cooler, or at the country club. The seasonal distribution of suicide rates may be nearly as significant and revealing as that of retail sales. Before and during the holidays, the evidence indicates, they are well below normal; afterward, they shoot upward in what has been termed the "broken-promise effect."[13] Broken promises, failed hopes, false pretenses: from the perspective of Christmas's discontents, we may find ourselves tempted to conclude that an English-speaker's best guide to the underlying meaning of "gift" would be found by looking it up in a German-English dictionary.

Yet however widespread the discontent, however many people share the sense that Christmas is somehow not what it used to be, or at least not what it should be, it is stunningly difficult to see what we should do about it. There are at least two reasons for our dilemma. The first is that any effort we might make to swim against the currents of commerce seems doomed before drawing first breath. The frenzy of excitement mobilized in younger children each December is overwhelming, and while there are some opportunities for channeling expectations in a direction that diminishes the prominence of commercial transactions without cruelly disappointing expectations, they are severely circumscribed. The situation is not substantially different in the adult world. Where Christmas marketing manufactures expectations, counter-gestures (homemade gifts or gifts of service, charitable contributions "in the name of," down-scaling, etc.) are extremely difficult. Our culture provides the language by which we communicate, and if the word for "I care about you" or "You deserve to be celebrated" is "expensive gift," then we can find ourselves trapped in a corner from which escape seems impossible.[14] The other circumstance that makes practical diagnosis so difficult is the fact that Christmas represents such a complex mixture of positive, negative, and problematic elements. Gift giving (and there is, of course, much more to the celebration of the holidays than this) can be many different things, sometimes simultaneously: it is an act of grace, of empowerment and validation, of discovery, of simple pleasure, of control or manipulation, of imprisonment, of cruelty. Christmas is wonderful and it is dreadful. So what do we do?

In this chapter, I propose to do two things. The first is to try to elucidate the effect of commerce on Christmas by looking more carefully at the development of the language of commerce itself. By language of commerce I mean, essentially, advertising (though the principles and the logic embodied in advertising pervade increasingly wide spheres of public life). And while the history of advertising extends—in its enormity and its complexity—far beyond the reach of our immediate concerns, attention to two significant shifts of meaning in the past make it easier to see the way commercial messages work in the contemporary environment and, more particularly, shape the practice of Christmas. On the basis of that account, I propose to return to the larger question that underlies so much of this volume: just what is the relationship between the celebration of Christmas and consumer capitalism, and how might an understanding of that relationship help us to wage the ongoing "battle for Christmas" with greater self-awareness and effectiveness?

Blowing Smoke

The meaning of "advertise," we learn from the Oxford English Dictionary, was "at first simply an alternative form of *advert*," that is, to turn toward something rather than away (avert), against (controvert), aside (divert), back (revert), and so on. The object turned is attention, and, at least after the sixteenth century, this is understood to mean not one's own attention but the attention of others. This remains, of course, the core meaning of "advertise" to this day. But the way in which the practice has been framed and understood, both by advertisers and by their audiences, has shifted significantly.

Before the nineteenth century, an advertisement was understood to mean, essentially, a "public notice" or "announcement." Commercial motives were certainly not excluded by this understanding, but they did not define it. For a representative example of early printed advertising, we can look to one of the earliest regularly published papers: the twice-weekly *Domestick Intelligence Or News both from CITY and COUNTRY*, which appeared almost immediately upon the lapse of the British Licensing Act in 1679. The December 23 issue, consisting of two double-column pages, gives news of actions at Court, hangings at Tyburn, and general goings-on about town, including a note that "the great Poet" John Dryden had been set upon and beaten by three persons in Covent Garden ("Popish vengeance" suspected). At the bottom of the fourth column we find:

Advertisements

These are to give Notice That the Right Honourable the Lord Mayor, and the Commissioners of Surveyors for the City of London, and the Liveries thereof; have constituted and appointed Samuel Potts and Robert Davies, Citizens; to be the General Rakers of the said City and Liveries, and do keep their Office in Red Lyon Court, in Watling Street, where any Person or Persons that are desirous to be Employed under them, as Carters and Sweepers of the Streets, may repair from Eight a Clock in the morning till twelve a Clock at noon, and from two till six at night, where they may be entertained accordingly....

There is newly published a Pack of Cards, containing an History of all the Popish Plots that have been in England: beginning with those in Queen Elizabeth's time, and ending with this last damnable Plot against his Majesty Charles II: Excellently engraven on Copper Plates, with very large descriptions under each Card. The like not existent. Sold by Randal Taylor near Stationers-hall and Benjamin Harris at the Stationers Arms under the Royal Exchange in Cornhill.

The Milleners Goods that was to be Sold at the Naked Boy near Strand Bridge, are Sold at Mr. Vanden Anker in Limestreet.

Lost on Sunday night the 11 Instant in the Meuse, a pocket with
a Watch in a Single-Studded Case, made by Richard Lyons; also a
Bunch of Keyes, and other things; whoever brings them to Mr. Bently
in Covent-Garden, or Mr. Aiken at the Meuse Gate shall have 20 s.
Reward.[15]

This is not an untypical mix: in early advertising, commercial offers
sit among official and semiofficial promulgations, matrimonial proposals,
appeals for the apprehension of runaway slaves and deserters, change-
of-address notices, and any number of other offers, requests, inquiries,
warnings, and pleadings. We are familiar, of course, with the modern ana-
logues to this sort of advertising: classified and personal ads, but also birth,
marriage, and death notices, "calendar" listings, ride-share offers posted on
school bulletin boards, school snow closings scrolled across the television
screen, or even "people-finder" utilities provided on the Internet. Most such
practices, however, are no longer understood to be "advertising," and those
that are (chiefly "classifieds" and "personals") have little or nothing to do
with the language and logic of the broader culture of modern advertising.

With the steady growth of urban, regional, and eventually national
markets, commercial motives became evident in an ever-larger share of advertising space. Before the nineteenth century, however, advertisers generally
bowed to the *form* of the public notice even when their communicative objective was, quite straightforwardly, to persuade readers to buy something.
This disjunction between ostensive and actual meaning proves an abiding
characteristic of advertising, one that distinguishes it from most other broad
categories of human communication: news reports, political polemics, nov-
els or other narrative fiction, scientific findings, love letters, sermons, judicial
decisions—to give some random and intentionally eclectic examples. In all
of the latter, the form of the message is related in some fashion to the communicative intent of the message sender; both the form and the intent are
clearly signaled to the recipient. This is true whether the message is artful or
clumsy, true or false, inspired by generous motives or dishonorable ones. In
contrast, advertising often exhibits the formal characteristic of being something other than what it appears to be. It is as if one expressive form, with
its associated conventions and expectations, is overlaid by another. In attending to the first, the message recipient is in danger of being blindsided by
the second.

Consider this example, from the *London Daily Post and General
Advertiser,* March 15, 1740:

MARY SOUTHALL

Successor to John Southall, *the first and only person that ever found
out the nature of* BUGGS, *Author of the Treatise of those nauseous
venomous Insects, published with the Approbation (and for which he
had the honour to receive the unanimous Thanks) of the Royal Society,*

GIVES NOTICE,

THAT since his decease she hath followed the same business, and lives at the house of Mrs Mary Roundall, in Bearlane, Christ Church Parish, Southwark. Such quality and gentry as are troubled with buggs, and are desirous to be kept free from those vermin, may know, on sending their commands to her lodgings aforesaid, when she will agree with them on easy terms, and at the first sight will justly tell them which of their beds are infested, &c., and which are free, and what is the expense of clearing the infested ones, never putting any one to more expense than necessary.

Persons who cannot afford to pay her price, and is willing to destroy them themselves, may by sending notice to her place of abode aforesaid, be furnish'd with the NON PAREIL LIQUOR, &c.[16]

Mary Southall makes an argument here, but she does so within the form of a notice. Her case is made as an extended subordinate clause to the "public announcement" that she has succeeded her husband or brother and, at least in substantial part, inherited his credentials. There is nothing particularly secretive about this argument, but it is telling that she feels compelled to cast it in the form of an announcement.[17]

The separation between ostensive and actual form is most advantageous to the advertiser's objectives when it is unnoticed by the recipient of the message. ("Unnoticed" does not mean "unnoticeable" but something more like "not attended to" or "ignored.") With exposure over time, however, any "blindsiding" advantage that comes from the separation of ostensive and actual form tends to decay. The habit of deferring to the archaic form (in this case, the "public notice") itself becomes unnoticed and invisible. Advertising sheds the old form like a cocoon, and for a period at least, "what you see is what you get." Although these are evolutionary changes with long periods of overlapping conventions, the sense that persuasion must be wrapped in the cloak of "public notice" is largely gone by the turn of the nineteenth century. Artful advertisers found other ways to avert the eye of critical scrutiny, but in the case of many ads, "argument" was left to stand alone—a position that generally proved an awkward and vulnerable one:

For DISORDERS of the HEAD
The CEPHALICK SNUFF

WHICH has been found by long Experience a very grateful and effectual Remedy for most Disorders of the Head, especially the common Head-Ach. It removes Drowsiness, Giddiness, and Vapours; relieves Dimness of Sight; is excellent in curing recent Deafness; and has been of great service in hysterick and paralytik Complaints; as also in restoring the Memory when impaired by Disorders of the Head. Persons who visit the Sick, unhealthy Places, or Hot Climates, will find this Snuff an admirable preventive of Infection; and it is particularly serviceable in those Complaints of the Head which Painters, &c. are subject to. Those also who take much of the common Snuffs, may prevent their bad effects by mixing with them a proportion of this excellent Cephalick.[18]

We may feel reluctant to dignify quack hyperbole with the word "argument": the claims are just too wild, too extravagant, too implausible. But this is to affirm that they are, indeed, *claims* about the product. If the advertisement were not cast in propositional form, it would be less easy to dismiss as unconvincing and absurd. The most significant cost to the advertiser of shedding the cloak of public notice is, somewhat ironically, that it redirects the reader's attention to the product itself. In contrast, a public notice announcing the *availability* of Cephalick Snuff, a proposition we would have no reason to view skeptically, leaves claims about its wondrous properties just outside the spotlight. And this, it turns out, is exactly where the effective advertiser wants them to be: on stage, but just outside the focus of our attention.

Advertising in the industrial market economies of the nineteenth century quickly became a vastly more complex and variegated enterprise. Experimentation with stylistic devices for controlling attention and graphic elements designed to "catch the wandering eye" proliferated.[19] The development of new technologies for the mass reproduction of images, what Daniel Boorstin termed "the graphics revolution,"[20] opened the way to new avenues of attack. At mid-century, for example, chromolithography was quickly applied to trade cards as well as mass distribution of colorful calendars and decorative prints, many imprinted with commercial messages. By the last decades of the century, newspapers, which began printing halftone reproductions of photographs in 1880, followed the lead of magazines in publishing illustrated display ads spanning multiple columns. Nissenbaum may be right to argue that American consumer culture predates the turn-of-the century decades to which it is usually assigned,[21] but the transformations represented by automated production in manufacture and mass reproduction of images in communication during 1880–1920 surely provided the foundation for the development of modern marketing techniques. We find, in the 1920s and 1930s, the creation of a new language of commerce, one in which emphasis is shifted from text to image, from the attributes of the product to the hopes, fears, fantasies, anxieties, and emotional needs of the prospective consumer. By the end of the 1920s, we can see any number of examples of advertisements in which the habit of arguing for a product's merits sits as a kind of archaic residue next to an entirely different way of attaching consumer desire to products. Fifty years later, the "logic of image association" had become the norm: the expected way of presenting objects of consumption in any medium addressing national or even major urban markets.[22]

In a series of ads that begin in 1928, the American Tobacco Company promoted the health benefits of tobacco in terms nearly as shameless as those that had been employed by the purveyors of Cephalick. The primary thrust, motivated by a desire to expand the still small women's cigarette market, promoted smoking as a means of staying slender.[23] The other, which remained a theme in Lucky Strike advertising into the 1950s, suggested protection against throat irritation. In the 1930 ad "Pretty Curves Win," a trim and fashionable young woman on the back of a horse is seen vaulting over fence rails ahead of an overweight silhouette. "When tempted to over-indulge," the heading continues, " 'reach for a <u>Lucky</u> instead.' " A second slogan, "It's toasted," appears in equally large type at the bottom, along with a picture of a pack of Luckies. Slogans and an appealing image—typically having little or no direct connection to the product—are the marks of a message that speaks the language of image association. But the advertisement also includes a great deal of textual clutter that defers, awkwardly and, to the contemporary eye, somewhat absurdly, to the conventions of "argument." A paragraph set in small type reads: "Be moderate—be moderate in all things, even in smoking. Avoid that future shadow by avoiding over-indulgence, if you would maintain that modern, ever-youthful figure. 'Reach for a <u>Lucky</u> instead.' " And next to the word "shadow" there is an asterisk: this is an advertisement with a footnote! Following it to the bottom of the page, we find a judicious qualification: "We do not say smoking <u>Luckies</u> reduces flesh. We do say when tempted to over-indulge, 'Reach for a <u>Lucky</u> instead.' " The remaining copy takes up the other health theme, mimicking not just the forms and conventions of argument but those of scientific argument:

> <u>Lucky Strike</u>, the finest Cigarette you ever smoked, made of the finest tobacco—The Cream of the Crop—"IT'S TOASTED."
>
> <u>Lucky Strike</u> has an extra, secret heating process. Everyone knows that heat purifies and so 20,679 physicians say that <u>Luckies</u> are less irritating to your throat.

And to drive this point home, under the "It's toasted" slogan at the bottom: "<u>Your</u> <u>Throat</u> <u>Protection</u>—<u>against</u> <u>irritation</u>—<u>against</u> <u>cough</u>." The authority of science and scientific principles, an appeal to evidence, the testimony of medical professionals—and not just many, or even thousands, but precisely 20,679—all of this reads to most of us seventy years later like a zany jest: the report of a mad scientist who lives inside a cartoon.

How would a contemporary marketer handle the same assignment? We might expect two immediate suggestions: focus the message on just the primary theme, and banish any hint of explicit argument. Or, in what boils down to the same advice: drop the text. We do not need to imagine what the result would look like; we can see it in almost any popular women's magazine we might pick up. In one such ad, for instance, a slim young woman walking down a sun-drenched street looks back to give us an endearing smile. The air is clear, there is a light breeze, and she is smoking a slim cigarette. A brand name is specified (Capri, the island of light and clear air and beauty) and a product "model": Super Slims. But other than these and the text mandated by federal law, the advertisement has just eight words: "The dramatic look of a super slim. INTRIGUING." One incomplete sentence followed by a solitary word: there is no proposition, no assertion, no claim to anything. There is only oblique suggestion. And that very obliqueness makes it pointless even to awaken our critical faculties and contemplate the truth of the message. To say or think something like "No, the look is not dramatic" or even "What makes her, or it, or whatever, *intriguing?*" is to sound silly—even to ourselves.[24] So we do not say or think such things. We merely absorb the words and their connotations, along with the sunlight and the fresh air, along with the shades of rosy gray and orange brown and yellow, along with the youth and beauty, along with the slim figure and slim cigarette, along with our own memories and . . . and one or two seconds later, we turn the page.

This is the modern advertiser's preferred way of using words: sparingly, elusively, and floating free of any entanglement in propositional claims. Words generally serve the marketer best when used as images. Often, of course, words disappear altogether. The Parliament ad appeared over a number of years in several variations, both in magazines and on billboards. Its most stunning feature is its blue. The sea is close to cobalt, the pool is very slightly tinged with green, the sky is, well, sky blue, turning paler as it moves toward the horizon. The remainder of the photograph—with the exception of tanned skin and the "tall-dark-and-handsome" and "blond-and-beautiful" hair—consists essentially of shades of white. The sunlight is strong and sharp, the air pellucid. The language of image association is used impeccably: wealth, leisure, youth, beauty, sexual pleasure, health, purity, cigarettes. Translated into propositional logic, we have a message that is not so dissimilar from the pitch for Cephalick snuff:

> For DISORDERS of the BODY
> PARLIAMENT LIGHTS
> WHICH have been found by long Experience a very grateful and effectual Remedy for most Disorders of the Body, especially Unattractiveness and Disease. It removes Poverty and Aging; relieves Bodily Infirmities; is excellent in curing Impotence; and has been of great service in reducing social Anxiety and Nervousness; as also in ridding the Air of Smoke and Impurities of all kinds. Persons who visit the Sick, unhealthy Places, will never have to do so again; and any twinges of Guilt to which they may previously have been susceptible will be expunged by new Confidence in their own unerring sense of Style and general Sexiness.

Might we look forward to a future in which audiences, trained (if only by long exposure) to decode commercial messages couched in the language of image association with the same ease that makes advertising of the past so transparent and seemingly naive to ourselves, will find the Parliament ad similarly absurd? Let us hope so. What is certain is that the language of advertising, assuming, of course, that the practice retains its economic significance and vitality, will be at least one step ahead. We can already see, I think, intimations of another transition: from the logic of image association to a logic in which messages use expressive devices to secure a self-referential incorporation of audience-as-object into an audience-as-participant. These are deeply complicated and largely uncharted waters, and it makes no sense to try to navigate them within the framework of this essay. Since Christmas marketing has already moved in this direction, however, it seems necessary to give some hint as to what we should be looking for.

One last example from a tobacco merchant can serve the purpose. In "Viewer Discretion Advised," a 1998 advertisement for Camel Lights, an irreverent maid stands with an "I-could-care-less" expression and posture over a skillet that presumably holds part of the seriously late main course of the rich and very annoyed couple seen waiting at a table in the next room. She is smoking, and the overlong ash of her cigarette is just about to fall into the skillet while her eyes are turned away with a vacant "whoops, I didn't notice" expression. Every character is a caricature: rich man with ascot and club crest on his jacket, rich woman in satin and gold and bouffant hairdo, alarmed older butler in formal dress with high collar and lace-ruffled shirt, and the "saucy" mischief maker in short-skirted maid costume, meretriciously made-up. The text of the ad, set in a box that mimics film ratings labels, reads:

VIEWER DISCRETION ADVISED

This ad contains:

IR Idle Rich
ABR Abusive Bell Ringing[25]
PA Premeditated Ashing

At the bottom of the box is the phrase "Mighty Tasty!" which appears to invite simultaneous application (in different voices) to the cigarettes, to the ash-laced dish, and to the maid herself.

The ad is a joke, of course, but there is nothing innovative in that. Clever and irreverent humor was common enough in the advertising columns of the eighteenth century. This joke, however, is self-referential: it is cigarette advertising in the form of a joke about cigarette advertising. R. J. Reynolds had only recently ended its highly controversial "Joe Camel" campaign, accused by tobacco critics of targeting young people,[26] and the industry as a whole was under heavy regulatory attack, one aim of which was tighter controls over, or the outright ban of, cigarette advertising. At the beginning of the decade, Philip Morris had responded in part by sponsoring a fifty-state road tour exhibiting an original copy of the Bill of Rights. R. J. Reynolds responded (in part) with ads like this one.

Late-twentieth-century advertising, especially when it targets young adults, has increasingly adopted one or another variation on this tone. Practitioners of the trade and, more significantly, those who regard themselves as its savvy and experienced cognoscenti, look for the edgy, the irreverent, the seemingly subversive. Advertising, we are invited to presume, is something that only affects people who are less hip, less sophisticated, less culturally aware, less knowledgeable or levelheaded than we are. So we are amused at, and even impressed by, advertising campaigns that make fun of themselves, that knowingly undermine their supposed purposes, that invite us (with a wink and a nudge) to be complicit in this communicative act that unnamed others, but not ourselves, take seriously. Joe Isuzu, the fast-talking television salesman who promised "94 miles per gallon in the city, 112 highway!" while text at the bottom of the screen corrected his misrepresentation was, perhaps, an early example of this mode. The ABC "yellow" ad campaign at the end of the nineties ("TV is good." "Without a TV, how would you know where to put the sofa?") is another. During the 2000 Super Bowl, the premier annual advertising exhibition, most of the spots revolved in some fashion around a self-mocking or self-parodying premise. Twenty-five seconds of an amateurish and deliberately cheesy performing monkey is followed by two screens that say: "Well, we just wasted 2 million bucks" followed by "What are you doing with your money?"[27] Even simpler is an ad with no production values whatever: against a plain yellow screen with a child's uncertain and mistake-ridden rendition of "Chopsticks" as a soundtrack, a series of sentences in uneven courier type appear: "This is the worst commercial on the Super Bowl"; then "but it might be the best thing you see tonight." After identifying the company (Lifeminders.com) and its service in the same fashion, it concludes: "We're information experts (Geeks).... But we don't know diddly about making ads." Big production extravaganzas were equally self-referential. A visually stunning sequence shows a cheetah racing across what might be an African plain, while a bicycle rider chases after, and eventually catches him, in order to reach down the cat's throat and retrieve a can of Mountain Dew; advertising hyperbole is here, as often, at the center of the joke. Traditional pet food ads are spoofed by a talking dog endorsing Budweiser. In such cases, the advertisement calls attention to its own "ad-ness," inviting the viewer to identify as a participant in the project rather than as the object of its message. "Ads that parody other ads," remarked the *New York Times* advertising critic in his roundup on the Super Bowl, "have become a popular ploy for the new Madison Avenue because they give consumers credit for being in on the joke."[28]

Our "Festival of Commercialism"

The Super Bowl brings us back to the holiday season, our "annual midwinter festival of commercialism" in the words of the just-quoted journalist, "a sacramental moment that unites, momentarily, this meritocratic, hyperbolic, commercial nation" in those of political columnist George Will.[29] The Super Bowl is, of course, the most-watched television program of the year with an audience of more than one hundred thirty million in 2000—nearly half the entire population of the country. If the apex of the buying year comes in December, the apex of selling, or at least of the art of selling, comes in January. The Super Bowl concludes our midwinter festival of commercialism but it inaugurates the commercial year. In a certain symbolic sense, the seeds planted during the intervals between play at this sports event begin a new economic cycle that culminates in the retailer's harvest the following December.

Thirty years ago, members of ad agencies and business school marketing departments watched the Super Bowl (at least in part) for its advertising. Today, it seems, nearly the whole of the Super Bowl audience does. News media feed expectations ahead of the event with stories about things like the going rate for a thirty-second spot, and there is always extensive discussion afterward about what worked and what flopped, what viewers liked or disliked, what broke new ground technically or aesthetically. In the past, the phrase "informed consumer" was generally understood to imply familiarity with the characteristics of products; today it is probably better understood as implying familiarity with advertising. And the advertising that appears during the time we might call a retailers' harvest season is notable chiefly for its continuity with the forms, the themes, even the specific messages of the consumer advertising that appears year around. The festival of commercialism celebrates, and also normalizes, patterns of consumer behavior that are non-seasonal.

The traditional seasonal ad in which a standard product is wrapped in Christmas symbols has largely disappeared.[30] The Chesterfield-smoking Santa who recommended holiday-wrapped cartons as gifts has become an anachronism. Even when the editorial content of a magazine features Christmas themes, most of its major-account advertising is indistinguishable from any other issue. The cover of the December 1999 issue of *Gourmet,* for instance, announces a "celebrations" theme: Christmas, Hanukkah, New Year's Eve, and "11 Great Holiday Cookies." But of 133 full-page advertisements in the issue, only 11 make any reference to the holidays, and most of them do so in a minimal and understated way. The *New Yorker* of December 6, 1999, is fat with advertising (it has some 75 percent more pages than normal), but only one of the 69 full-page ads makes mention of or explicitly alludes to Christmas.[31] Even the two-page spread for RedEnvelope.com, whose business is "gifts online," shows only an office desk with a generic-ribboned gift box and the words: "A paycheck cannot always tell someone how much they're worth."

This sort of very muted seasonal reference, we may recall, also characterized the advertisement with which we began: the holiday season-opening message from Tiffany's in the *New York Times Magazine.*[32] It is, in fact, a splendid example of the magic wrought by image association: an expensive object is invested with the most powerful emotional significance by the context of images into which it is placed. Its price is part of what confers talisman status, but this is associated with some other leaps of "logic": that this is a man who can afford to give such a gift, that this ability testifies to his moral seriousness and depth of feeling, that she (given that she is loved by such a man and possesses so beautiful a face) must be comparably worthy. It is not that we think such thoughts explicitly; indeed, the moment they become explicit many people will feel entirely revolted. But I do think that they are implicit in the images, and that most viewers, especially within the target audience of the ad, absorb them—clearly, if not quite consciously.[33]

The target audience, by the way, is not the class of people who are looking for a $14,000 present for their wives. The line of descriptive text in this ad makes the most sense if we understand it to function as an image. The first, capitalized phrase, is perfect image-association-speak: "ABOVE ALL ELSE"—what does this say, and to what or whom does it refer? Many things, and nothing; I leave the parsing to you! But the remainder, what appears at first to be almost a catalog description, a straightforward piece of information, probably has a different significance altogether. There will not be a great many readers, even very wealthy ones, who are looking for precisely this descriptive detail, and those who might would be better served by something more closely approximating a catalog containing comparable descriptions and prices for other, similar bracelets from which they might choose. The description and the price are included to add value to the line above, the "brand name." Tiffany's is the place where men like him go to buy gifts like this to give to women like her. To the extent that a reader is moved ("convinced" is too propositional a word) by the message, Tiffany's offers the means by which to express love—even if a more modest selection is made.

It is significant that the impulse that pushes advertisers toward what I've termed "self-referential incorporation" and its attendant irreverence is evident even during what is usually regarded as the most conservative, the most "traditional," even sentimentally cliché-ridden season. As I previously indicated, traditional Christmas symbols (Santa, angels, snowy villages with trees, etc.) have receded in visibility, especially in upscale markets. When they do appear, moreover, it is often in the form of mild parody, self-mocking humor, or even edgy flirtation with the outer limits of respectability, as if to say: "Look, you and I are too sophisticated to take these images seriously." A 1999 Dunkin' Donuts television commercial shows two weary parents at the end of a long night of placing presents under the tree. As they finish, they look up in shock to see their children, eagerly descending the stairs in the classic pre-dawn Christmas morning rush. The parents suppress their initial dismay and stand in front of the tree with open arms and expectant faces, waiting for the little ones to run toward them and it. But just as the children come close, they swerve to the left and into the kitchen where they fall upon a plate of donuts—the real object of their Christmas morning excitement and desire. Some advertisers, even in what are considered highly respectable venues, appropriate classic Christmas imagery in ways that deliberately approach the outrageous. The "angel" on the cover of the 1998 Christmas catalog of major retailer Victoria's Secret, for instance, is no less this-worldly than the sexually provocative images that define the store's corporate identity throughout the rest of the year. During the 1999 season, an on-line jewelry retailer repeatedly placed an advertisement in the *New York Times* and elsewhere that might be described as a parody of the crudest sort of image-association advertising. For some, the ad is presumably edgy and amusing; for others, it is merely crude. A partially undressed woman pins a man to the floor while removing his shirt. Around her neck, and draped into his mouth, is the pearl necklace he has presumably just given her. The ad's text, evoking the phrase used by automobile dealers to refer to a model's gas mileage, reads "Actual results may vary." This advertisement ran repeatedly in the *Times,* both in a half-page and a quarter-page layout. Although small type at the bottom made the Christmas connection ("Christmas orders accepted through December 22nd"), the advertisement reappeared, identical in every respect save this line, shortly before Valentine's Day.

What, then, can we learn about Christmas by seeing its refraction in the language of commerce? First, there is reason to question whether it is still accurate to characterize Christmas as essentially or primarily a celebration of family values and domestic intimacy. If the holiday moved into the American household in the 1820s and 1830s, shutting the door to the outside world behind it, as Stephen Nissenbaum convincingly claims,[34] it has by the 1990s come back outside—or at the very least, it has opened the doors and windows. This is in part a simple expression of the fact that domesticity of the kind to which respectable American households aspired in the nineteenth and early twentieth centuries has itself been transformed by late-twentieth-century demographic trends: divorce and remarriage, single-parent households, dual-income households, and the physical mobility of family members. It also reflects the ways in which a national communication infrastructure—especially, but not exclusively, broadcast television—fed by highly centralized industrial producers of mass culture, has brought the public sphere into the home. But most of all, it has followed from the continuous and unrelenting pressure of commerce to "grow the Christmas market." Age, for example, is simply no longer "*the* axis along which gifts [are] given at Christmas";[35] it is but one (in dollar value a subordinate one) among many—both intra-familial and extra-familial. And children themselves, the central and in some ways defining element of the nineteenth-century household ideal, have themselves been "de-domesticated." Parents remain essential to gift exchange as bill payers, but negotiations regarding desires and the means of gratifying them are conducted directly with the commercial marketers as a result of the transformation initiated with Mattel's first advertisement on *The Mickey Mouse Club* in 1955 and extending to the Internet gift registries of 1999. Moreover, while Christmas continues to be an occasion for family gatherings, it is not dramatically more family-centric than many other holidays. Even the ostensibly civic celebration of national independence on the Fourth of July takes place primarily in family backyards rather than on the town common where communities gathered in the past. No holiday in the calendar has as many satellite celebrations outside the home as Christmas: in parties at work and school, at tree-lighting ceremonies, and spreading out to the even wider array of public celebrations described by Horsley.[36]

But if Christmas can no longer be considered a distinctively domestic holiday, neither has it simply reverted to the association with carnival that had, prior to the nineteenth century, sanctioned unruly behavior and the temporary turning of social relations of authority upside down. Elements of the tradition of "misrule" are, of course, still with us (and, it would appear from Nissenbaum's account, have never fully been expunged): the status-leveling informality of the office Christmas party, for example, or the annual complaints about Christmas tipping as a protection racket. But such examples weigh very little against the side of the Christmas scale that defers to and reinforces dominant relations of social power, not just in the distribution of the profits earned from Christmas business but in the distribution of Christmas "benefits." There is nothing democratic about the spirit of Christmas giving and, in spite of the holiday peak in charitable giving, little that is egalitarian either. The traditional spirit of carnival challenged or mocked power-holders, however insignificantly it actually undermined them. The spirit of giving as defined by the language of commerce does neither. The contemporary Christmas more closely approximates a groveling before images of wealth and power than it does the ridicule or even the questioning of them. This is most straightforwardly obvious in advertising that conveys what we might call the spirit of "Christmas at Tiffany's." But it is also evident in the style that presents itself as self-aware, cheeky, boldly irreverent: jewelry.com may mock sentiment, decorum, good taste, even advertising itself, but none of this diminishes its endorsement of the marketplace as the source and measure of value.

Both of the preceding points call attention to a third: that Christmas has come to play a role that is continuous with the commercial year as a whole. Both the domesticated and the carnivalesque Christmas represented, albeit in different ways, a kind of "break in the action" of social life: a time to withdraw into the intimacy of family and household or one in which social pressure is released by relaxing public constraints during a period safely bracketed off from the rest of the year. Contemporary Christmas, in contrast, is removed neither from public life nor from its norms. Christmas spending, which an American Express survey put at just over $1500 per person in the United States in 1999,[37] is the climax of annual consumption patterns but it is not an exception to them; it is more like a Sunday dinner than a wedding feast. Its importance to the economy is to be found not just, or even primarily, in the profits derived from Christmas sales, but in the

habits of consumption that are reinforced each year by the explicit association of commodities with the expression of fundamental human values. That
jewelry.com used the identical image for its Christmas and Valentine's Day
advertising might at first seem no more than a reflection of the character of
one company (cheap image, cheap advertiser). But precisely the same "one-
message-fits-all-occasions" assumption shapes the upscale market as well. In
the February 13, 1999, edition of the *New York Times Magazine*, the image
of Christmas at Tiffany's reappears as Valentine's Day at Tiffany's—and so
on throughout the year. The identical image, for instance, appears on the
back cover of the issue of June 28. The spirit of Christmas, the spirit of
giving, the *spirit of buying* lives on through the entire twelve-month cycle.

And this allows us to see why gifts and the spirit of giving are so very important to the health of commodity capitalism. Suppose that the message of
Christmas were something like this: "Buy a lot of stuff, consume or partially
consume as much of it as you can, fill your closets and basements with most
of what's left, and cart the rest—along with whatever you put in the closet
last year but had to remove to make room for this year's additions—to the
nearest landfill." This is not, unfortunately, a very inspiring message and
there is some risk that it might even lead some to put their resources to relatively unproductive uses such as feeding and housing the poor or otherwise
driving up labor costs.[38] But now let us redefine the commodity as an object chiefly significant not for its intrinsic characteristics, whether aesthetic
or utilitarian, but for its expressive power: it "says" you love her, it "tells"
him how much he is worth, it establishes that you are as "important" as
other children. If a commodity can be invested with the power not just to
express feelings but also to confer moral and spiritual worth, the problem of
getting products off the showroom floor will be greatly eased. Many of these
products, having served their expressive purpose but being unsuited to the
personal preferences of the recipient, will move expeditiously to the landfill.
Others will be retained and even treasured; yet a bracelet that said "I love
you above all else" last year does not keep talking; it is the giving, rather
than the gift, that counts (as we constantly keep reminding one other).

As Santa Claus recedes, one sort of mystification is replaced by another.
As Nissenbaum notes:

> Santa mediated magically between parent and child—between the
> buyer and the recipient of the gifts. His presence was what took the
> gift out of the realm of commerce—in the eyes of parents, perhaps, as
> well as children. To phrase this in a more contemporary fashion, we
> might say that Santa "mystified" consumption.[39]

But as we have seen, modern marketing has moved children and gift
giving squarely back into the realm of commerce. Yet in emphasizing the
non-material properties of commodities and associating them with the
psychological and emotional needs of consumers, modern marketing has
mystified consumption in a far more fundamental and, from its perspec-

tive, advantageous way. The change began awkwardly early in the century with advertisements that explicitly warned of the personal disappointment and social disapproval that would come from "that future shadow" or any number of other product-remediable shortcomings. By the end of the century, the problem-solving promise of commodities has been vastly extended and strengthened through the magic of image association, and skepticism further disarmed by self-referential incorporation.

This sort of mystification, of course, is a year-round phenomenon. But Christmas giving has a particularly crucial place in the process. It provides the occasion for both a huge, concentrated volume of spending that touches nearly everyone (even, perhaps especially, those who are excluded by poverty from participation) *and* a strong separation of the commodity from its utilitarian or aesthetic characteristics (since, after all, "It's the thought that counts"). To the extent that Santa "took the gift out of the realm of commerce," he proved a false friend of the capitalist economy! By reinserting it into this realm, twentieth-century retailers have discovered that Christmas helps to fuel sales all year long. Placing Christmas squarely in the realm of commerce, of course, does not automatically assure that it brings its seasonal moral resonance (love, depth of feeling, psychological affirmation, spiritual worth, etc.) along with it through the rest of the year. But some of the "Christmas magic" sticks. The festival of commercialism celebrates consumption, but it also nurtures the attitudes and assumptions that keep desire for commodities strong well after the Christmas season has come to an end. And it is this, and not just strong December sales, that make it so important for the economic system.

Christmas and Its Discontents

> I only caught the tag end of the conversation. A young woman waiting behind me in line at the drugstore shouted to her friend: "You know how much I hate Christmas!"
>
> This was an interesting if troublesome thought, and I couldn't resist asking the reasons for her Yulephobia. She replied with the crisp logic of a graduate student, which is what she turned out to be. "I hate the cold," she said. "I hate capitalism. And I don't like my family."[40]

Hating capitalism may not be an American commonplace, but hating the commercialization of Christmas certainly is.[41] As noted at the outset, Nissenbaum traces such complaints to the first half of the nineteenth century. But the picture I have described implies, I think, that we should not be too quick to turn away from such complaints with a sigh of resigned acceptance. For one thing, dismay at the relentlessness of the commercial colonization of Christmas runs wide and deep in contemporary culture: it deserves to be addressed. For another, there is reason to think that the depiction of Christmas commercialization as fixed and unchanging is itself deeply misleading.

We can accept Nissenbaum's assurance that, as something "commercial from its earliest stages, commercial at its very core,"[42] Christmas has not changed. But what has changed is the nature of commerce and commercial language itself. As a result, the affirmation that Christmas is "commercial at its very core" means something quite different at the end of the twentieth century than it did one hundred years ago. In the language of argument, the desirability of a commodity is assumed to lie primarily in material attributes (whether they be utilitarian or aesthetic). In the modern language of commerce, material properties are almost entirely subordinated to the commodity's power as a carrier of meanings that promise to confer status, validate emotions, relieve anxieties, gratify fantasies, express our inner selves. And the important point here—since objects have always functioned, to some degree, in this way—is that it is the advertiser, not the gift giver or the user, who writes, and rewrites, those meanings.

The use of objects (and, as we have seen, even words) as images undermines propositional logic. It would be entirely misguided to suggest that such uses are intrinsically manipulative or destructive. Image association is the primary language of the arts, and not just the visual arts; it has provided a vehicle for the expression, and thereby the recognition and understanding, of much of what makes us human. And, perhaps most significantly in the present context, it is our primary communicative means for reaching beyond the boundaries of propositional logic, for contemplating the transcendent or the sacred. Clifford Geertz's definition of religion, cited elsewhere in this volume by Horsley, is worth recollecting here:

> a system of symbols which acts to establish powerful, pervasive and long-lasting moods and motivations in men by formulating conceptions of a general order of existence and clothing these conceptions with such an aura of factuality [that] the moods and motivations seem uniquely realistic.[43]

With a few minor adjustments, this would do nicely as a description of the system of meaning created by modern advertising. But what distinguishes the symbol system of advertising from that of religion or other systems of meaning is its singular, overriding, and ultimately one-dimensional ulterior—but scarcely transcendent—motive: to sell. However beautiful, witty, moving, or uplifting the images of modern advertising, their validity is measured by their capacity to move merchandise. And that, of course, tends to undermine the authenticity of anything else they might say or be.

Yet it is advertising, more than any other system of meanings in our culture, that serves the functions that are provided in most societies by religion: "the establishment of personal and group identity, the embodiment of community, and the articulation of an overall meaning of life."[44] The language of commerce operates as a kind of faux religion, and it does so in a comprehensive and enveloping fashion only partially captured by the traditional concept of idolatry or even by Marx's commodity fetishism. The language of commerce is not the exclusive source of our sense of meaning, community, and identity, but it is the most important one. The Christmas market serves to confer a kind of moral authority on these values since at Christmas, commodities embody our better natures: they express our care for others, our capacity for deep emotional feelings, our attachment to family, our love of community. In giving fulsome expression to the spirit of giving, we bless and validate the spirit of consuming.

The breadth of Christmas discontent shows that while we may be powerfully constrained by this system of meanings, we are not entirely imprisoned within it. We participate, but we do not do so entirely willingly or without conflict. Our feelings at Christmas express, though perhaps more sharply, our relation to the advertising environment in general. At one level, we are completely captivated and controlled. As its defenders continually remind us, the unregulated market is an unparalleled instrument for the efficient allocation of profit-generating resources, and the business people who spend some $100 billion each year to purchase our attention are neither fools nor spendthrifts.[45] But with another part of our mind, we are perfectly aware of what is going on—our critical faculties are intact and our judgment is unimpaired. Advertising does not reduce its audience to a collection of unthinking zombies; indeed, this is not what the advertiser even wants (except insofar as that idea provides a straw man for the defenders of advertising culture to demolish). Both responses are alive within the same head;[46] our behavior is shaped and steered and delimited by advertisers, and we also make up our own minds.

So just as the problem of Christmas is embedded in an economic and cultural environment that extends throughout the entire year, so its solution requires that we rethink our options not just as holiday celebrants, but also as members of the broader polity. Commercial culture colonizes social and political life in ever more comprehensive ways. Advertising messages saturate the environment to a degree that would have been hard to imagine even fifty years ago, appearing, it sometimes seems, anywhere our senses might wander: shopping carts, ATM windows, telephone answering machines, university course registration booklets, the back of sales receipts, and on nearly every piece of publicly viewable real estate that is not protected by zoning or environmental regulation. Commercial slogans or logos identify our public buildings, accompany our personal electronic mail messages, decorate our clothing, provide content for the curricula of our elementary schools, and are a featured and prized attribute of our children's toys. Advertisers, not information-users, pay for our main informational media—nearly the entirety of network television and the largest share of newspaper and magazine revenues. Advertisements play the predominant role in educating citizens and supplying the resources they will use to decide how to vote. The language and the logic of advertising are evident in policy debate, in medical decision making, in the judicial process. Advertising provides, surreptitiously, much of the content of mass media in the form of product placement, news releases, pseudo-events,[47] cross-referencing,[48] and dozens of other examples that the ingenuity of the public relations industry continues to expand. The most significant new threats to individual privacy, ranging from supermarket scanning cards to Web "click-tracking," result not from government snooping but from the marketing efforts of private firms. The language and interests of commerce, in short, pervade much of public life. In so extending its reach, in exerting an influence that flattens distinctions between economic, political, cultural, and even religious life, the language of modern advertising is an extraordinarily powerful instrument for the advancement and protection of the interests of those with the means to employ it. In this sense it is a form of power more reminiscent of the monolithic integration of spiritual, economic, and political authority Horsley describes in ancient Mesopotamia[49] than anything that can be attributed to a "Big Brother" state.

In spite of all this, the expanding influence of advertising is generally viewed with little alarm. Advertising may be annoying but we comfort ourselves in the thought that, unlike inflation and taxes, it is something that does no damage to the pocketbook—where it "really" hurts; in fact, we assume, it gets us free stuff, like network television. Such comfort is illusory. From whose pocket, after all, does that $100 billion come? Even those who can claim with complete justification to be untouched by the advertiser's message still pay for it. In 1998, 11 percent of the price paid for a pair of Nike footwear went to advertising, 16 percent of the Mattel toy, 27 percent of the L'Oréal cosmetic.[50]

But as the complex and damaging effects of commerce on the celebration of Christmas make clear, out-of-pocket costs are the least of the problem. Modern advertising is a system of communication, a system of thought, that undermines authenticity and impedes the pursuit of truth. When modes of expression appropriate to a wide range of human communicative activity—including political discourse, journalistic investigation, scientific inquiry, spiritual reflection, aesthetic exploration, psychological self-discovery—remain vigorous and healthy, marketing can be dismissed as a relatively trivial part of the communication environment. But when the language and the logic of commerce threaten to dominate other domains, alarm is an entirely appropriate response.

The discontent of those who are troubled by the commercialization of Christmas is well-founded and a "been there, done that" response does nothing to address or resolve it. But as long as our concerns are packed up along with the lights and the tree decorations each January, it is unlikely that we will be able to understand them very clearly, let alone fashion a satisfying alternative. We need to look for opportunities to change not only our behavior between Thanksgiving and the Super Bowl, but also the way we do business from the Super Bowl to Thanksgiving. Even as we look for more appropriate, less damaging ways to celebrate this season of renewal, we must consider ways in which the invasive march of commerce might be slowed during the rest of the year. To suggest that measures like campaign finance reform, public funding for the arts, and the exclusion of corporate marketing from the classroom are necessary to the renewal of Christmas might seem to be both off-point and quixotic. I see no way to avoid the conclusion that it is neither.

Notes

1. He directs our attention, for instance, to the opening lines of an 1850 story by Harriet Beecher Stow: "Oh, dear! Christmas is coming in a fortnight, and I have got to think up presents for everybody! Dear me, it's so tedious! Everybody has got everything that can be thought of." Stephen Nissenbaum, *The Battle for Christmas* (New York: Alfred A. Knopf, 1996), 133–34.

2. This volume, p. 9.

3. Nissenbaum, *Battle for Christmas*, 318.

4. Ibid, xii.

5. The distinctive character of the "gift relationship" has been explored in an extensive literature flowing from both the social sciences and the humanities. To keep to my path, I plan to ignore those discussions here, but the interested reader should consult Lewis Hyde's fine book *The Gift: Imagination and the Erotic Life of Property* (New York: Vintage, 1983), which will, in turn, supply references to all the most important landmarks.

6. This volume, p. 171.

7. Cf. Nissenbaum: "The key, even more than the Christmas tree itself, is the element of surprise that accompanies it.

" . . . [B]ut even after the surprise was gone, the ritual would retain a lingering utility: It would continue to keep virtually total control of the gift exchange in the hands of the parents—control of the time and place, and of the knowledge of how many gifts there would be and what they were. . . .

"The difference between the ritual of crying out 'Christmas gift' and that of waiting for the 'Christmas Tree' is the difference between children playing the role of active agents in the gift exchange and their assuming the passive role of silent, grateful recipients. The Christmas-tree ritual, as it was introduced to [the] American reading public, was designed to render children completely passive participants in the process" (*Battle for Christmas*, 213–14).

8. Perhaps we might concede that Christmas advertising at mid-century represented a difference of degree rather than a difference of kind when compared to that described by Nissenbaum, *Battle for Christmas*, 134ff.

9. Cy Schneider, *Children's Television: The Art, the Business, and How it Works* (Chicago: NTC Business Books, 1987), 16. Figures for 1998 come from a database maintained by *Advertising Age* at http://adage.com/dataplace/archives/dp395.html (viewed July 31, 2000).

10. Quoted in Douglas Martin, "What's in a Name?: The Allure of Labels," *New York Times,* January 9, 2000, 2(4).

11. In 1998, total December retail sales (excluding automobiles) amounted to 10.26 percent of the annual total, i.e., some 23 percent higher than it would be if buying were steadily distributed with 8.33 percent of the annual total sold in each month. Stores selling general merchandise, apparel, and furniture sold 14.15 per-

cent of their annual total (70 percent above an average month) while jewelry stores sold 24.40 percent of their annual total (193 percent above average). From *Annual Benchmark Report for Retail Trade: January 1989 to December 1998*, Current Business Reports, Series BR/98-A (Washington, D.C.: U.S. Census Bureau, 1999), table 1, 2–3.

12. Nissenbaum, *Battle for Christmas*, 136.

13. See David P. Phillips and John S. Wills, "A Drop in Suicide around Major National Holidays," *Suicide and Life-Threatening Behavior* 17, no. 1 (Spring 1987): 1–12; Howard Gabennesch, "When Promises Fail: A Theory of Temporal Fluctuations in Suicide," *Social Forces* 67, no. 1 (September 1988): 129–45; Gert Jessen and Borge F. Jensen, "Postponed Suicide? Suicides around Birthdays and Major Public Holidays," *Suicide and Life-Threatening Behavior* 29, no. 3 (Fall 1999): 272–83.

14. This is not to say that efforts along the lines suggested by Richard Horsley at the conclusion of this volume should not be made; we need to do what we can to change or expand the language. It is only to say that the task is not an easy or straightforward one.

15. A facsimile of this issue of *Domestic Intelligence* is included in Henry Sampson, *A History of Advertising from the Earliest Times* (London: Chatto, and Windus, 1875). Christmas, as might be expected in a paper preoccupied with protecting "all good Protestants" from papist intrigue, goes unmentioned.

16. Cited in Sampson, *History of Advertising*, 185.

17. Something similar occurs when the public broadcaster says, "This program is made possible by the generosity of the Acme Corporation, specializing in the sale of . . . " and then spins that last, ostensibly subordinate, phrase into a message that undermines the authenticity of the first.

18. *Coventry Mercury*, February 14, 1791, reproduced in Gillian Dyer, *Advertising as Communication* (London: Methuen, 1982), 25.

19. The phrase is used by Sampson in his 1875 *History of Advertising*, 81.

20. Daniel Boorstin, *The Image: A Guide to Pseudo-Events in America* (New York: Atheneum, 1982).

21. Nissenbaum, *Battle for Christmas*, 338–39 n. 2.

22. I have leapt across a complex history here in the hope of bringing one issue into sharper relief. The reader who is interested in an appropriately detailed and nuanced picture of this transformation might begin with Stuart Ewen, *Captains of Consciousness: Advertising and the Social Roots of the Consumer Culture* (New York: McGraw-Hill, 1976), along with his *PR! A Social History of Spin* (New York: Basic Books, 1996); T. J. Jackson Lears, "From Salvation to Self-Realization: Advertising and the Therapeutic Roots of the Consumer Culture, 1880–1930," in *The Culture of Consumption: Critical Essays in American History, 1880–1980*, ed. Richard Wightman Fox and T. J. Jackson Lears (New York: Pantheon, 1983), 3–38, as well as his more recent *Fables of Abundance: A Cultural History of Advertising in America* (New York: Basic Books, 1994); and Roland Marchand, *Advertising and the American Dream: Making Way for Modernity, 1920–1940* (Berkeley: University of California Press, 1985).

23. The larger story of this campaign, which involved the "father of modern public relations," Edward Bernays, and his famous "Torches of Freedom" marchers in the 1929 New York Easter parade, is told in Larry Tye's *The Father of Spin: Edward Bernays & The Birth of Public Relations* (New York: Crown, 1998), 23–50.

24. Unless, of course, we are ad-makers. This, as we shall see, turns out to be a not insignificant qualification!

25. The rich woman is calling for service by ringing a small brass bell.

26. "Smooth" Joe Camel smoked regular Camels, not Camel Lights.

27. For E-Trade, an on-line broker.

28. Stuart Elliott, "Big Plays, Surprise Heroes, Shocking Defeats and Other Super Bowl XXXIV Marketing Memories," *New York Times,* February 1, 2000, 10(C).

29. Ibid.; George Will, "The Blessed Event Known as the Super Bowl," *Boston Globe,* January 29, 2000, 15(A).

30. As, indeed, has the commercial use of Santa himself.

31. One other, advertising a high definition television set, alludes to the Super Bowl ("the big one January 30th").

32. As the numbers in the preceding paragraph imply, traditional seasonal imagery does not disappear entirely; Tiffany & Co. itself provides an example in the December 12, 1999, issue, and the holidays are at least mentioned by eight of the forty-five other full-page advertisers.

33. There is much more to be said about the way in which gender power relations are expressed in this image and in the cultural conventions that support it. One of the significant ways in which modern commercial culture handles the contradiction between the need for a Protestant work ethic on one hand and a hedonistic culture of consumption on the other is by assigning them to different gender roles: the male exhibits, in dress and manner, the "austere simplicity" of the hardworking, frugal creator of wealth; his mate testifies to his success by displaying this wealth on her person, especially in the form of expensive jewelry that is understood to be most "meaningful" if it has been bestowed upon her by a man. This is a long story in its own right, but for a very insightful start see Stuart and Elizabeth Ewen, *Channels of Desire: Mass Images and the Shaping of American Consciousness* (New York: McGraw-Hill, 1982), 148ff.

34. See, for example, Nissenbaum, *Battle for Christmas,* 108, 172–73.

35. Ibid., 62 (my emphasis); cf. 110.

36. This volume, p. 113.

37. "Survey Says Holiday Spending Rose 36%," *New York Times,* January 18, 2000, 12(C).

38. This is not to say that a good marketer cannot rise to the challenge, as evidenced by the effectiveness of a huge category of advertisements that successfully trumpet variants of the "Indulge yourself" message. The phrase "Because I'm worth it" is a trademark of L'Oréal Paris.

39. Nissenbaum, *Battle for Christmas,* 175.

40. E. J. Dionne Jr., "Humbugs United," *Washington Post,* December 24, 1999, 15(A).

41. We won't touch the cold *or* the family!

42. Nissenbaum, *Battle for Christmas,* 318.

43. Clifford Geertz, "Religion as a Cultural System," *Anthropological Approaches to the Study of Religion,* Association of Social Anthropologists Monographs, no. 3 (London: Tavistock Publications, 1965), 79.

44. Horsley, this volume, p. 166.

45. According to *Advertising Age,* the 1998 measured media total was $92.352 billion. If AdAge estimates of unmeasured media (promotions, store displays, etc.)

are included, the total more than doubles to $201.594 billion. Data was found at http://adage.com/dataplace/archives/dp393.html (viewed July 31, 2000).

46. This is what Orwell meant (in *1984*) by "doublethink."

47. A term introduced in 1961 by Boorstin to describe events that take place only for the purpose of the publicity they will generate as items of "news" (*The Image*, 9ff.).

48. As when ABC "covers" parent company Disney's cruise ship or a novel is reissued with a promotional still from the film version on the front cover.

49. This volume, pp. 174–86.

50. Company averages, as found on the Advertising Age website: http://adage.com/dataplace/archives/dp395.html (viewed July 31, 2000). It may be objected that Nike's advertising so increased sales as to allow you (who were not influenced by the ad) to benefit from economies of scale, a point that, even if granted, fails to sustain the claim that advertising has no effect!

Part 3

Saviors and Messiahs, Biblical and Other

Chapter Six

The Gospel of the Savior's Birth

Richard Horsley

Imagine a complex multicultural society with a great, elaborate festival that lasted not simply for a few days but for several weeks:

- a great festival celebrated in honor of the birth of the Lord and Savior of the world, the Prince of Peace, a man who was also worshiped as divine;
- a great festival celebrating not only the beginning of the New Year, but also the beginning of a new era, which began with the Savior's birth;
- a great festival celebrating abundance, with indulgence in feasting, drinking, and gift giving;
- a great festival during which the poor were recipients of the philanthropy and generous giving of the rich, so that they could enjoy festive food at least once a year, when all feasted on sumptuous fare;
- a great festival whose presence virtually pervaded public space, visually and otherwise;
- a prolonged festival filled with a surfeit of public entertainments in song, dance, theater, and athletic games;
- a prolonged festival during which local political and religious leaders presided over various rituals and ceremonies;
- a prolonged festival in which the very wealthy people of a city sponsored parades and lavished public displays that both entertained the masses and brought their own names to public attention;
- a prolonged festival in which sales of goods and services flourished as at no other time of the year;
- a great festival that brought a sense of unity to the civic community while honoring the Savior.

These are all important aspects of "the holidays" in America, the prolonged festival that lasts from Thanksgiving through Christmas and New Year's Day—and now through the Super Bowl. However, they are also key features of the great society-wide festival of the Roman emperor as Savior of whole world, a festival that began to be celebrated throughout the

Roman Empire right around the time of Jesus' birth. Many, perhaps most Americans think that Christmas is primarily about the birth of Christ. But historically there was never any society-wide festival like the American holidays that celebrated the baby "wrapped in swaddling clothes and lying in a manger." At the time Jesus was born, however, there was indeed an elaborate society-wide festival celebrating the birth of the Savior of the world, only that savior was not Christ but Caesar. And it is that festival, honoring the Roman emperor for bringing peace and prosperity to the empire, which bears such a remarkable resemblance to the elaborate American Christmas holiday festival.

There were thus two saviors in the early Roman Empire. The one, having "pacified" other peoples with the unprecedented military strength at his disposal, brought unprecedented prosperity to the great metropolitan centers of the empire, importing goods from the far corners of the empire for the "bread and circuses" enjoyed in Rome itself and in other imperial cities. The other was born in a manger when his parents had to register to pay the tribute that supplied the "bread and circuses" for Rome. He had to flee to Egypt when the military death squads were sent out to massacre children. And he grew up in a village where the Roman military had enslaved the people because they resisted the Roman savior and his peace.

The gospel of both saviors is preserved in sacred writings. We have long known the stories of Jesus' birth from the beginning of the Gospels of Matthew and Luke, although most of us never read them carefully. We have only recently discovered the gospel of the imperial savior, which is chiseled on numerous monuments, shrines, and temples at the centers of ancient cities where the Roman emperor was honored as a god and his birthday celebrated as the beginning of a whole new era. A closer look at both gospels will reveal that the one about the savior born in a manger is diametrically opposed to that of the imperial savior. Indeed, a careful reading of the story about the birth of Jesus in Luke 2:1–20 will suggest that the "salvation" offered by Caesar is oppressive for people subjected to the imperial order.

First, however, it may help to inquire why we only recently came to recognize the presence of the imperial savior and how the gospel of his birth, and not that of Jesus' birth, was celebrated in the elaborate festival that so resembles the American holidays. There are three main reasons for the failure of modern theologians and religious historians to recognize that the emperor cult was the dominant religious festival of the Roman Empire. The first reason is the modern Western individualism that severely limits our historical understanding. In modern Western societies, especially in the United States, religion is understood mainly as individual faith, especially the personal faith that results in salvation and/or strength and guidance through the crises of life. This narrow understanding of religion excludes much of the rich cultural heritage, social forms, and important social activities that would be understood as integral aspects of religion in most other societies. In non-Western and historical societies, the significant religious forms are social and the significant religious activities are communal—carried out by whole groups of people such as families, tribes, and village or city communities. Modern Western individualism also obscures the importance of the natural, social, and even spatial environment for personal and communal identity, social structures, and patterns of meaning. Western Christian scholars have therefore missed the importance of the collective representations and rituals that pervaded public space and structured the annual cycle of life in the cities of the Roman Empire.

Second, a methodological voluntarism often accompanies this methodological individualism—an assumption that people have a choice about participating in the already institutionalized festivals of their village, city, and society. But people are born and socialized into those festivals. If the elite that effectively controls the city or society successfully sponsors adaptation and transformation of those festivals, individuals have little choice but to go along with the transformed festival; they are simply swept along in the cultural stream. In the cities of the Roman Empire, involvement in the emperor cult was not voluntary, just as in modern Christmas an individual has no choice about being involved. When we go downtown or to the mall, we see the Christmas decorations and smell the aromas. When we turn on the radio during the holidays, we hear the holiday music, even on state-supported public radio. Everywhere, attacking all our senses, is the multimedia marketing of goods. The people we are closest to are socialized into the holidays and have expectations of us as members of families and neighborhoods. Since the presence of the emperor pervaded public space and imperial celebrations were embedded in the calendar of public life, subjects of the Roman Empire had no choice but to participate, however ambivalently they felt about it.

The third reason we have failed to recognize how important the Roman imperial festival was is the peculiar Western separation of church and state, of religion and political-economic life. Christian theologians and biblical scholars have simply dismissed the elaborate rituals and festivals of the imperial cult as exercises in political loyalty, even as empty forms of flattery. Closely related is the peculiar Christian definition of the sacred and the secular. Since Christianity is the only true religion, other rituals and loyalties must be secular. This dichotomy may even have originated partly as a defensive maneuver against the emperor cult. Ancient Christian theologians (such as Origen) distinguished between religious and secular honors. To drive a wedge between honoring the true God and honoring false gods and the emperor, while claiming that Christians were model citizens of the empire, Christian theologians claimed that the emperor cult was more a matter of politics than religion, an expression of political loyalty, more a matter of honoring the emperor, not true religious worship. For the subject of the Roman Empire, however, the great, prolonged festivals honoring the imperial savior were the most important and virtually unavoidable religion of the imperial society.

The Great Festival Celebrating the Gospel of Caesar
as Savior of the World

In contrast to the separation of church and state in modern Western societies, religion and politics and economics could not be separated in the
ancient Roman Empire any more than they could be separated in any traditional society. The most obvious case of all would be the emperor cult.[1]
Just as the modern Christmas constitutes the climax of retailing in the annual economic cycle and holds a diverse American society together, so the
emperor cult held the empire together; it integrated the Greek cities and,
via the patronage system, their economies into the overall Roman imperial
order centered in the emperor, the divine savior of the world. To understand
this we can investigate how the imperial festivals constituted imperial power
relationships and what interests they served.

The following declaration of faith in the divine lord and savior, which
bears striking resemblances to later creeds and declarations of faith in Jesus
Christ, illustrates a number of respects in which the emperor cult must be
taken seriously as the dominant religious expression of Roman imperial
society:

> The most divine [Lord]...we should consider equal to the Beginning
> of all things. For when everything was falling into disorder, he re-
> stored order once more and gave to the whole world a new aura.
> Caesar, the common Good Fortune of all,...[t]he beginning of life
> and vitality...[A]ll the cities unanimously adopt the birthday of the
> divine Caesar as the new beginning of the year.... Whereas the Prov-
> idence which has regulated our whole existence...has brought our
> life to the climax of perfection in giving to us the emperor Augustus,
> whom Providence filled with virtue [power] for the welfare of human-
> kind and who, being sent to us and our descendants as our Savior, has
> put an end to war and has set all things in order; and whereas, hav-
> ing become god-manifest, Caesar has fulfilled all the hopes of earlier
> times...in surpassing all the benefactors who preceded him...; and
> whereas the birthday of the god [Augustus] has been for the whole
> world the beginning of the gospel concerning him, [therefore let a new
> era begin from his birth].[2]

Before the birth of Jesus and the development of Christian theology, this
statement of faith in the imperial divine lord and savior attributed to Caesar
many of the principal functions or roles that later Christian creeds (theological statements of faith) attributed to God and Christ. Caesar was viewed as
the originator and orderer of all things, just as the Judeo-Christian God was
understood as the creator of all things. Similarly, in guiding and regulating
human affairs Caesar was the force of Fortune or Providence, whose role was
also to bring human affairs to "the climax of perfection," the fulfillment of
human aspirations for the good life. But Caesar was also, like Christ, sent as

the savior of the world, the very manifestation of God, fulfilling "the hopes and fears of all the years" (to quote a later Christian carol). Therefore not only was the annual calendar rearranged to begin with his birth, but a new historical era began with his birth.

The elaborate imperial festivals of Caesar as the lord and savior of the world were celebrated throughout the Roman Empire, in every town and city of significance. In this regard the Roman imperial cult contrasts with much royal ritual. In many kingdoms, royal rituals such as coronations and ceremonies of the court were centralized, concentrated in the court and the royal capital, with little representation of the monarch outside the center. Related to this is the observation in recent studies of kingships and aristocracies that ceremonies of rule are performed primarily for the benefit of the ruling circles themselves. In the Greek cities of the Roman Empire, however, the institutionalized emperor cults were performed on a regular basis for the emperor in his absence.[3] In these festivals and in all the rituals and constructions and decorations that went with them, the Greek cities represented the emperor to themselves. They ritually and monumentally constituted the presence of the (absent) emperor in their communal urban, that is, political life.[4]

Like the American Christmas, the imperial festivals in the various cities were based on earlier religious practices. Just as the American Christmas developed out of local practices of displaying an evergreen tree in German areas of Pennsylvania and of Santa Claus giving gifts to children of aristocratic New York families, so the emperor cult was built on the traditional religious practices of Greek cities, such as sacrifices to local gods and the celebration of regional games.[5] The representations of the emperor and the ceremonies by which his power and presence were celebrated were not foreign imports imposed on the Greek cities from the outside. Rather,

> the visual representation of the emperor was incorporated into the regular life of the communities through public celebrations. Long established festivals...had an imperial element added to them; they were now also called *Sebasta* [i.e., dedicated to *Sebastos*=Augustus, the emperor]. Separate festivals were also founded, where sacrifices were offered and the whole community was involved either in processions or as the recipients of donations from members of the elite, often acting as imperial priests. The honors, temples, priests, festivals, and sacrifices were curiously close to the honors given to the traditional gods. Indeed, these honors were designed to display quite explicitly "goodwill and piety to the god [Augustus]."[6]

"Whatever Greeks in the time of Augustus may have thought or experienced in a sacrificial procession in honor of the emperor, such rituals were linked with parades, public meals, and lavish games." The imperial festival became the climactic high point of the entire year, when the people could experience a sense of community. "As part of the excitement, people streamed in from neighboring towns, markets were held, and self-important embassies came from distant parts. An imperial feast day was also a bright spot in the lives of the poor. Rituals performed for the emperor, who remained in faraway Rome, blended with high spirits and pride in one's own city. For prominent citizens, it was an opportunity to show off their own status and how much they could afford to lavish on honors for the emperor and enjoyment of their fellow citizens."[7]

In the same way as local or regional and eventually international corporations took the lead in sponsoring and shaping Christmas festivals such as Macy's Thanksgiving Day parade in New York City, so the political-economic elite in the ancient Greek cities, who with their patronage networks were the equivalents of modern corporations, sponsored the imperial cults and celebrations. The sponsors were thus assured of continuing prestige by the inclusion of their descendants in the festival procession or dedicatory inscriptions on the temples to the emperor (like the sponsors of Christmas parades, Macy's, and New Year's bowl games). The imperial priests (who were the sponsors economically) were the local elite,[8] just as the priests (sponsors) of Christmas are local and now national elite corporations such as Macy's. Like the American holidays, the Roman imperial festivals constituted the climax of the economic cycle for far more than just the economic elite who controlled the local and regional economy. This can be seen in Dio of Prusa's comments that the centers of imperial festivals "bring together a huge throng of people, litigants, jurors, orators, governors, attendants, slaves, pimps, muleteers, tinkers, prostitutes, and craftsmen. Consequently those who have goods to sell get the highest price and there is no lack of work in the city, either for the transport or houses or women" (*Orations* 35.15).

Abundantly evident is the way in which powerful families embody and consolidate their positions in the imperial order—again demonstrating the inseparability of the civic and economic functions from the religious functions of the festivals. On the one hand, the local elite expresses its generosity in forms beneficial to ordinary people, funding feasts, providing meat, and distributing wine. On the other hand, rituals such as organized feasting and public ceremonies "recapitulate an ideal version of the local social hierarchy. Religious celebrations provide a privileged context within which a certain notion of community can be evoked: all are united in general gratitude" to the local magnates. Their wealth is almost certainly derived from their dominant roles in reproducing the very social relations that their activity as philanthropists serves to veil.[9] Just as modern-day local and national corporations sponsor holiday events, charities, and performances, so the urban elite of the Roman Empire consolidated their position by sponsoring the elaborate imperial festivals:

> The nature of what is given, the distribution of food, wine, oil and
> money, the buildings, the art products, the silver goods for rituals, the

foundations and orphanages, construct an image of what is needful to the community, an idea constructed by the elite in terms of its own judgments of value. Lavish goods for the gods are set side by side with necessaries for orphans. Just as the elite takes responsibility for the community it takes responsibility for the gods. It thus sets itself up as the major carrier of central values in the community. At the same time the community becomes dependent upon the elite for the means of worshiping "piously," that is, equipped with suitably lavish items of religious paraphernalia: the elite inserts itself surreptitiously into the communication between here and the other world, not by claiming some special mediatory status but by means of the provision of the agencies of worship.[10]

Like the American holidays, the Roman imperial festivals restructured the very temporal order of life. Although it began as a few days of raucous wassailing by the poor in the mansions of the rich and a few sweets or books or toys as gifts for the children at the time of the winter solstice and New Year's Day in the early 1800s, Christmas developed into a festival of consumption and indulgence that lasts from Thanksgiving to New Year's Day (or from Halloween to Super Sunday and the Super Bowl). Similarly, the emperor cult altered the very structuring of time in the early Roman Empire. The beginning of the year was now the celebration of the birthday of the emperor. And the months took on such imperial names as "Caesarian" or "Tiberian" to mark the celebration of an imperial festival. Whereas before there was a variety of local calendars and celebrations, the celebrations of the imperial cult and festivals now determined local calendars.[11]

The Roman imperial festivals also filled and restructured the very environment in which people lived, as the presence of the emperor came to pervade public space, much as the American holidays have come to pervade the entire environment of public and domestic life during the holiday season. Significant changes were made in civic space in the early imperial period. "Imperial temples and sanctuaries were generally located in the most prominent and prestigious positions available within the city.... The larger cities were able to place their imperial temples in preeminent positions."[12] At Ephesus, the richest city of the province of Asia (western Asia Minor)—and site of a prolonged mission of the Apostle Paul, during which he wrote most of his letters—the whole upper square was redesigned during the reign of Augustus. Two small imperial temples were built between the magistrate's building, which contained the sacred hearth and the city council chambers. In front of these was the large public space, the "royal portico" dedicated to Artemis, Augustus, and Tiberius, in the middle of which stood a large temple of Augustus. Later in the first century, a temple to Domitian was built in the open space adjacent to the royal portico. A contemporary decree refers to "the new grandeurs of the imperial works," which were matched by the renovation of old buildings. The emperor was given preeminence in the central structure of the city. It was thus literally true, in the rearrangement of space, that the emperor was permanently constructed into the heart of the city of Ephesus.[13]

The presence of the emperor in public space was embodied in several forms. The emperor was usually installed into the temples to the gods (of the city), his name was added in the dedication to the god, space for honoring the emperor was created at the entrance or deeper inside, and statues of the emperor were placed inside. Temples were built devoted solely to the emperor; "the most elaborate...were large and expensive buildings with columns all the way round, which were externally identical to a standard temple of the gods."[14] The Jewish philosopher Philo observed diplomatically in his appeal to Caligula, "In cities old and new, they build temples, propylaea, sacred precincts, and colonnades for him" (Philo, *On the Embassy to Gaius* 149–51). "These new sanctuaries for the emperor were often larger and grander than those of the traditional gods."[15] Just as the pervasive holiday music, decorations, entertainments, and advertisements constantly remind contemporary Americans of their obligations to buy gifts and participate in holiday festivities, so all the shrines, statues, temples, and festive games in the ancient Greek and Roman cities constantly reminded ancient city-dwellers of the importance of worshiping the emperor. "Every day of the year, a permanent architectural stage set, against which people played out their lives, was a constant reminder of the emperor."[16]

Close examination of how the Roman Empire held together suggests that in areas such as Greece and Asia Minor, what we usually think of as political institutions and functions played little or no role.[17] Virtually no military forces were stationed in the Greek cities. And the emperor maintained minimal administrative structure (just a governor with a minimal staff) in those areas. Thus we simply cannot continue to pretend that the emperor cult was an ancillary institution that served only to "legitimate" imperial power that otherwise operated in political institutions such as military forces or an administrative bureaucracy. Since there were no such political institutions to legitimate, we must recognize that the imperial system in the Greek cities was constituted by, as well as embodied in, religion—by the imperial cult, rituals, and the sustained weeks-long imperial festivals. For example, there was virtually no such thing as diplomacy separate from the imperial cult. Religious language was used in approaches to the emperor. "Offers of cult were sometimes made in association with requests concerning privileges and other matters. Ambassadors to the emperor were frequently also imperial priests.... Ambassadors from Mytilene...were to address Augustus as one who had attained the eminence and power of the gods, and were to promise further divine honors which would 'deify him even more.' "[18] The very actions of the greatest among the powers that determined the lives of the inhabitants of the Roman Empire were portrayed in blatantly religious terms. "In his images, Augustus was thus manifest as both god and man, corresponding precisely to his special status in the imperial cult."[19] Similarly, the actions of his later successors Gaius and Hadrian are presented as the work of "such a great god."[20] What held the Roman Empire together was not so much the political institutions of the Roman legions, which were stationed only on the frontiers, or the imperial bureaucracy that was minimal anyhow, but the elaborate imperial festivals celebrated for weeks in every city of the empire focused on the birthday of the lord and savior of the world.

The Other Savior's Birth: "Good News of Great Joy for the Whole People"

The Gospel of the Savior born in a manger is the opposite of that of the imperial savior. Indeed, if we listen carefully to the story about the birth of Jesus in the Gospel of Luke 2:1–20, his Gospel is proclaimed in opposition to the imperial order and how oppressive it is for those subjected by the empire. Having sequestered the stories of Jesus' birth safely in the sphere of religion, separated from political-economic matters in the real world, modern Christian interpreters find no conflict between Christ's birth and the imperial order celebrated in the lavish festival of the imperial savior. Caesar and his census are merely incidental to the story of Jesus' birth, unimportant in themselves. Caesar's census is merely a literary device to get Joseph and Mary to Bethlehem, the city of David, where the Messiah, son of David, is supposed to be born. Caesar Augustus, although widely celebrated as "savior of the whole world" after "pacifying" it, provides a "chronological framework" and "ironically . . . [simply] serves God's plan." Far from "denying the imperial ideals," the story of Jesus' birth merely presents "an implicit challenge to the imperial propaganda."[21]

Such interpretations, however, impose the modern separation of church and state, of religion and politics, onto the story of Jesus' birth and its historical context. Caesar and his census were hardly innocuous for the people of Nazareth and Bethlehem or for those who told this story. To say that Caesar was incidental to the story of the birth of Jesus would be like saying that George III was incidental to the Declaration of Independence and the American Revolution or that British imperialism was incidental to Gandhi's movement of non-violent resistance. If we listen to the story of Jesus' birth in Luke 2:1–20 in the context of the realities of the Roman Empire, the Gospel of the Christ child stands in stark opposition to the Roman Empire and its savior in four interrelated ways:

1. The Galilean and Judean people among whom Jesus was born and worked and who told stories about him were subject to repeated military violence by the Romans because they had the audacity to resist Roman imperial rule, an aspect only implicit in the story's mention of "Caesar Augustus."

2. The people subjected by the Romans were being economically exploited by the Romans and their client kings like Herod, an aspect
that dominates the first part of the story in Luke 2:1–5.

3. The Gospel of the Savior in the manger was specifically for the impoverished people subjected to the Roman imperial order who were
yearning for liberation, as seen in the response of the shepherds to the
"good news" (Luke 2:8–18).

4. Jesus was born as God's designated figure to represent and lead liberation from the Roman imperial order, as announced in the titles
"Messiah" and (anti-imperial) "Savior" (Luke 2:11).

1. Caesar

The *pax Romana* was imposed by military violence.[22] The peace that Augustus and his successors brought to the world was literally the flip side of
a coin, the other side of which was military victory. On numerous imperial coins, the head of the goddess Pax appears on one side, with Augustus
in military garb with a spear in hand on the other. The Romans militarily subjected city after city, people after people, around the Mediterranean.
Their military conquest was bloody and brutal, particularly when people
had the audacity to resist. They destroyed the city of Corinth in 142 B.C.E.,
then colonized the area a century later. In Germany in 14 C.E., Germanicus
"wasted the country with sword and flame for fifty miles around. Neither
age nor sex inspired pity. Places sacred and profane were razed indiffer-
ently to the ground" (Tacitus, *Annals* 1.51.1). The principal Roman tactics,
however, were not to destroy but to terrorize subject peoples into submission by enslaving the able-bodied, slaughtering others, and crucifying a few
hundred "rebels" for the "demonstration-effect" on what remained of a conquered people. As Augustus himself declared in his *res gestae* (his imperial
"resumé"), prominently inscribed on public monuments: "Foreign peoples
who could safely be pardoned I preferred to spare rather than to extirpate."

As a by-product of the violent Roman subjugation of other peoples, the
Roman plebeians themselves were impoverished. Deeply indebted because
they had been away from their land while serving in the conquering legions,
Roman and other Italian peasants were forced off their land by the patricians
who were also their commanding officers. The peasants thrown off their own
land were replaced by slaves brought in to farm the aristocrats' burgeoning
latifundia (the ancient Roman version of "agribusiness"), in other words,
by the very conquered people they had helped enslave during their service
in the legions.[23]

Once the savior of the world had conquered subject peoples with such
terrorizing violence, he then maintained the "Roman peace" with further
violence and techniques of terrorization. Subject peoples had no need of political activity since, under the *pax Romana*, all war had ceased. As the great
biographer Plutarch put it in a treatise on *Precepts of Statecraft* (32), "Of

liberty the people enjoy as much as our rulers allot them, and perhaps more would not be better." Subject peoples were expected simply to accept and obey Roman rule, to "preserve mutual goodwill with peace and concord and friendship" (Seneca, *De Clem.* 1.1, 2). If local unrest erupted here and there, a cohort or legion of the Roman army was dispatched, "the terrors of which, along with a few executions, restored things to concord" (Tacitus, *Annals* 13.48). Subject peoples were well-advised to acquiesce in their "pacification." As the historian Tacitus has a Briton chieftain say to his people: [The Romans] are the plunderers of the world.... If the enemy is rich, they are rapacious, if poor, they lust for dominion. Not East, not West has sated them.... They rob, butcher, plunder, and call it 'empire'; and where they make a desolation, they call it 'peace' " (*Agricola* 30).

Of all peoples subjected by Rome, the Galileans and Judeans mounted the most sustained resistance. The Romans conquered or reconquered Palestine four times in the course of two centuries before the people finally acquiesced under imperial rule. The initial conquest lasted nearly a generation, from Pompey's capture of Jerusalem in 63 B.C.E., including his attack on priests engaged in sacrifice at the altar of the temple on the Sabbath, to the Roman imposition of their client king Herod in 40 B.C.E. Crassus plundered the temple again in 54–53 to fund his war against the Parthian empire to the east. And Cassius, in another war against the Parthians, enslaved thirty thousand people in and around the town of Magdala (Josephus, *Jewish War* 1.179–80; *Jewish Antiquities* 14.105, 120), leaving the mark of Roman terrorization indelibly imprinted on the memories of families such as that of Mary Magdalen. After he was appointed "king of the Judeans" in Rome, it took Herod three years before he could finally force the Judeans and Galileans into submission with the help of Roman troops.

The second major Roman conquest of Galilee and Judea came in response to widespread popular insurrections in every major section of Palestine at the death of the hated tyrant king Herod, 4 B.C.E., right around the time Jesus was born. Several movements of Judean and Galilean peasants, led by popularly acclaimed "messiahs," simply asserted their independence in certain areas. The punitive Roman retaliation again wrought slaughter and enslavement in Palestine, significantly in places associated with Jesus and his followers. In the area around Nazareth, where Jesus supposedly grew up, the Roman troops "captured and burned the city of Sepphoris [and/or the villages nearby] and reduced its inhabitants to slavery." The whole district of northwest Judea "became a scene of fire and blood ... Emmaus [cf. Luke 24], the inhabitants of which had fled, was burned to the ground," after which the Romans rounded up "rebels" from around the countryside and crucified about two thousand (*Jewish War* 2.68–75; *Jewish Antiquities* 289– 95). Memories of the rebellion against Roman and Herodian rule and of the devastating Roman reconquest would have been fresh in the minds of the first followers of Jesus.

Seventy years later, about the time the stories of Jesus' birth were taking their distinctive shape, Galileans and Judeans again rose in rebellion against Roman imperial rule. Having been effectively driven out of Palestine by widespread popular insurrections, the imperial legions had to mount a major military mobilization for their reconquest. In the countryside the Romans implemented a "scorched earth" policy, destroying village after village and slaughtering the inhabitants, followed by "search and destroy" cavalry missions to hunt down those who had fled. In the village of Japhia, a few miles from Nazareth, in a full day of devastation, "the more efficient combatants were at length exterminated, and the rest of the population was then massacred in the open or in their houses, young and old alike. For no males were spared except infants; these along with the women the Romans sold as slaves" (*Jewish War* 3.304–5). After a prolonged siege, the Roman legions finally captured Jerusalem, destroyed the temple, and killed or enslaved the remaining defenders. Vespasian, whose prosecution of the war in Galilee and Judea positioned him to become the new emperor, celebrated his great victory over the intransigent Judean and Galilean people in a grand triumphal procession in Rome with lavish display of military power and destruction. As Josephus, the Judean historian who had deserted to the Romans, writes:

> The war was shown in numerous representations.... Here was to be seen a prosperous country being devastated, there whole battalions of the enemy slaughtered; here a party in flight, there others being led into captivity;... an area deluged in blood,... houses pulled down over their owners' heads; and, after general desolation and woe, a country still on every side in flames.... (*Jewish War* 7.122–56)

At the climax of the triumphal procession at the Roman forum, the victorious emperor presided over the ceremonial execution of the enemy general, Simon bar Giora, the "king of the Jews," who had led the revolt as a popularly acclaimed king.

The final Roman reconquest of Judea came in 132–35 C.E. Again the revolt was led by a popularly acclaimed "king" of the Judeans, and again the Romans devastated both land and people in a prolonged war of attrition.

Framed by the popular revolts and Roman reconquests of 4 B.C.E. and 66–70 C.E., the first half of the first century—the period of Jesus' life and the first generation of the Jesus movements that would have told stories about the birth of Jesus—was a long history of conflict between the Galilean and Judean people and their Roman imperial rulers. Tensions were high throughout seventy years leading up to the great revolt in 66. Provocations by insensitive governors such as Pontius Pilate repeatedly led to massive protests against Roman rule by Judeans. Tensions were particularly high during the Passover celebration centered in Jerusalem. Anticipating trouble at this festival of deliverance-from-bondage-under-foreign-rulers, the imperial governors regularly stationed troops on porticoes of the temple. But this only escalated the tension, often to the breaking point, as under the governor Cumanus. The emperor Caligula almost induced a full-scale rebellion among both Judeans and Galileans by his order to place a statue of himself in the temple for appropriate divine honors. Masses of Galilean peasants, contemporary with the first generation of Jesus' followers, mounted a massive strike, refusing to plant the fields, which would have denied the Romans and their client rulers the revenues from tribute and taxes.

Modern Christian scholars may be able to avoid awareness of the Roman imperial presence in ancient Palestine, but the followers of Jesus who told stories about his birth had no such luxury. Memories of the mass enslavement at Magdala and Sepphoris and the experience of strikes and demonstrations against provocations by Roman rulers blocked any denial of the political-economic-religious realities of their lives. Some of the slaves who farmed the estates and served the personal needs of the wealthy imperial urban elite—those who sponsored the festival of the imperial savior—were Galilean and Judean peasants enslaved in Rome's wars of conquest and reconquest. Caesar was not incidental to the stories of Jesus' birth!

2. Caesar's Census

The story of Jesus' birth opens with Caesar's decree that all the world should be registered for tribute. The story may well explain narratively that Jesus, known to be from Nazareth, had actually been born in Bethlehem, where the Messiah was supposed to be born. But Augustus's decree of enrollment for the tribute is far more than "a purely literary device" to bring Mary and Joseph to the city of David.[24] The "elaborate setting" of the census in Luke 2:1–5, which is much longer than the description of the birth of Jesus itself in 2:6–7, indicates that the census itself is of significance in the story. This is confirmed by the importance of the issue of the tribute to Rome toward the end of Luke's Gospel. In Luke 23:2, 5, Jesus is accused of "forbidding us to give tribute to Caesar" as well as of claiming to be "Christ a king" and of "stirring up the people," accusations that are clearly true, given Luke's presentation of Jesus' teaching and actions.[25] We must take more seriously the concrete as well as the christological implications of Luke 2:4–5: "Joseph also went... to Judea, to the city of David called Bethlehem, because he was descended from the house and family of David,...to be registered with Mary, to whom he was engaged...." We must obviously ask what the tribute would have meant for Mary and Joseph, the shepherds, and the hearers of this story.

The very purpose of ancient empire, of course, was to control economic resources. None was more aggressive than the Roman Empire. After they plundered temples and palaces for booty and villages and towns for slaves, the Romans then placed subjected peoples under tribute. The tribute was a way of generating revenues to support the imperial apparatus—as well as a way of demeaning a conquered people. The conqueror's prerogative was articulated by a Roman general to the Gauls: "Though often provoked, we have used the right of conquest to burden you only with the cost of maintaining peace"—in other words, supporting the army with the tribute (Tacitus, *Historiae* 4.74). Directly or indirectly, moreover, tax-farmers, governors, and senators also added to their great wealth from the tribute. From the time of Julius Caesar, Judean peasants rendered up 12.5 percent of their crops annually (except for sabbatical years), while continuing their traditional tithes and offerings to the temple-state in Jerusalem. Partly because the tribute was a symbol of subjection, the Romans regarded nonpayment as tantamount to rebellion, and mounted punitive military retaliations to enforce their demands. Fifty years before Jesus' birth Judeans had experienced the Romans' wrath in this regard. During the Roman civil war, Cassius had laid Palestine under extraordinarily heavy tribute. When areas of Judea were slow to deliver, he ordered the males of four principal district towns (Gophna, Emmaus, Lydda, and Thamna) sold as slaves (*Jewish Antiquities* 14.271–76; *Jewish War* 1.220–22).

Judeans and Galileans, however, would have faced an unusual struggle over the tribute to Rome, for "rendering to Caesar" would have been tantamount to disloyalty and disobedience to their God. The first commandment of the covenant between God and Israel, mediated by Moses on Mount Sinai, required exclusive political-economic-religious loyalty to God, who was understood not simply as a spiritual force but as their king, literally as the ruler of the people. Thus any payment of tribute to a human ruler was against the will of God as articulated in the Torah. Even the great King David, the prototype of the messianic king, had been severely punished by God when he conducted a census for tax purposes (1 Sam. 24:1–14). Insofar as the tribute to Rome symbolized submission to the alien rule of Caesar (who also posed as god), rendering up payment to Caesar constituted disloyalty to God.

It is not surprising that when Augustus imposed direct Roman rule on Judea and again laid Judea under tribute in 6 C.E., ten years after Herod's death, a serious movement of resistance emerged. The teacher Judas of Gaulanitis and the Pharisee Saddok, leaders of what Josephus calls "the Fourth Philosophy," militant activists who agreed basically with the views of the Pharisees (that the people must adhere to the covenant law), urged the people "not to consent to the tribute to the Romans and not to tolerate mortal masters, since they had God as their lord" (*Jewish War* 2.118). They insisted "that God alone is their leader and master" and that they should submit to torture and death rather than be subjected to any man as master" (*Jewish Antiquities* 18:23). The high priest Joazar, who energetically advocated submission to the assessment for the tribute on behalf of the priestly aristocracy that was responsible for its collection, was later "overpowered by the multitude" (*Jewish Antiquities* 18.26). This suggests that the resistance to the tribute was a significant movement that posed a serious threat to Roman rule in Judea. Resistance to the tribute again gained momentum in the steadily deteriorating economic and political conditions that led to the outbreak of massive popular revolt in 66 C.E. When the Herodian king of eastern Galilee, Agrippa II, admonished the people to pay the tribute, which was seriously in arrears, they drove him out of Jerusalem and proclaimed his banishment from the city (*Jewish War* 2.345–404).

The two references to the tribute to Caesar in the Synoptic Gospels must be understood in precisely this context of the Israelite biblical tradition informing Judean and Galilean resistance to Roman imperial rule. The standard modern interpretation of "Render to Caesar the things of Caesar and to God the things of God" in Mark 12:14–17 (and parallels) in terms of separate material and spiritual dues imposes the separation of church and state, of religion and politics, onto the biblical texts. But as noted above, this distinction is peculiar to modern Western societies and inapplicable to the Roman Empire or to Israelite biblical tradition. Jesus' shrewd reply to the Pharisee and Herodian attempt at entrapping him with the question "Is it lawful to pay the tribute to Rome?" left no doubt in the minds of those informed by biblical tradition that for them precisely nothing belonged to "the things of Caesar," because all belonged to "the things of God," their sole ruler and lord.[26] Similarly, in the story of Jesus' birth, the registration for the tribute to Rome was by no means incidental. It was rather a hated symbol as well as a heavy material burden of the people's subjection to Caesar, whose "peace" had meant devastation and enslavement for them.

One reason that the enrollment for the tribute has been dismissed as incidental is the failure to discern why Joseph and Mary were required to undertake the long journey from Nazareth, where they lived, to Bethlehem, Joseph's ancestral home. In a traditional agrarian society such as ancient Judea and Galilee the usual pattern would have been for peasant families, which constituted the vast majority of the population, to live on the land of their family inheritance. This was particularly true in a society such as ancient Israel, in which there were strong traditions of inalienable family inheritance of land as a gift from God. In order to keep families economically viable on their land and thus productive members of village communities, the people were supposed to strictly observe certain economic mechanisms, such as cancellation of debts and release of debt slaves every seventh year. It is not the normal situation, therefore, to find Joseph living (and engaged) in the Galilean village of Nazareth, far from his ancestral home in the Judean village of Bethlehem. According to the tradition in Mark 6:3 and Matthew 13:55, moreover, Jesus was a builder (carpenter), son of a builder. That suggests that his family was "downwardly mobile," that they had somehow been forced off their ancestral land. Joseph or his father had been forced to "hit the road" in search of day labor as a means of support.

Both at the time Jesus was born and at the time the stories of his birth were being told, Judean and Galilean peasant families were being forced off the land by a number of factors in the Roman imperial order. Virtually a whole generation would have been decimated in certain areas by the devastation, slaughter, and enslavement during the repeated Roman and/or Herodian conquests. Military raiding parties sent into the countryside for provisions would have left some families or even whole villages destitute of provisions and the seed grain and draft animals necessary to begin their recovery. The structure of multiple layers of rulers in the imperial situation would have forced many to borrow at interest from wealthy creditors in order to make it through to the next harvest after rendering to the temple and Herod as well as to Caesar. Severe drought and famine struck in the middle of Herod's long, tyrannical reign, with the people clamoring for reduction of the tax revenues Herod used to underwrite the huge cost of his elaborate court and his massive building projects (*Jewish War* 2.4; *Jewish Antiquities* 17.204). The large number of workers utilized on his massive rebuilding of the temple in Jerusalem and other vast building projects indicates that creditors taking advantage of the peasants' spiraling indebtedness had probably already displaced many from the land.

Circumstances only became worse in the first generation of the first century c.e., whether under Herod Antipas's taxation to build his capital cities in Galilee or under the Roman tribute and dues to the temple-state in Judea. In mid–first century the escalating banditry and the large numbers of people prepared to abandon their homes to join one of the popular prophetic movements suggest that the economic viability of peasant families on the land was seriously threatened. The teachings of Jesus, including the Lord's Prayer, clearly address people who are hungry and in debt (e.g., Luke 6:20–21; 11:2–4). One of the principal acts of the rebels who took control of Jerusalem at the outbreak of revolt in 66 was to burn the public archives where the records of debts were kept (*Jewish War* 2.427). Therefore, whether Joseph's and Mary's journey from their home in Nazareth to his ancestral home in Bethlehem reflects some memory of Joseph's background or a typical situation of debt and displacement of peasant families at the time the story was formulated, it would have had significant resonance with the listeners' experience of spiraling debt and displacement from their ancestral lands.

But why did Joseph and Mary have to make such an arduous journey, particularly when she was expecting her baby's birth at any moment? Why did they have to move from Galilee, which was ruled and taxed by Herod Antipas, to Bethlehem in Judea, where the registration was being conducted following its placement under direct Roman rule in 6 c.e.? Although evidence for tribute and taxation from Palestine itself is scarce, papyri from Egypt shed some light on this aspect of the story of Jesus' birth. In connection with the enrollment conducted in Egypt in 103 c.e., a prefect had issued the following decree:

> The house by house census having begun, it is necessary that all persons who for any reason whatsoever are absent from their home districts be alerted to return to their own hearths, so that they may complete the customary formalities of registration and apply themselves to the farming for which they are responsible. . . . Those who show their presence to be necessary [in the city of Alexandria] will receive signed

permits.... All others are to return home within thirty days. Anyone who thereafter is found lacking a permit will be punished without moderation. (London Papyrus no. 904)

Palestine was surely not as strictly regulated as Egypt. Yet as indicated by this papyrus, the Roman imperial regime expected people to remain tied to their ancestral homes precisely in order to produce crops to be rendered up in the tribute. Ironically, such papyri indicate that large numbers of peasants were absent from their ancestral homes and lands, apparently because they could not support themselves as well as raise the tribute. Not to be deterred by economic realities, however, the Roman authorities held the economically destitute peasants responsible for their portion of the local assessment and even rounded up fugitives whom they forced back into their old villages for the requisite agricultural productivity. Caesar's decree of enrollment for the tribute that forces Joseph and Mary to return to his ancestral home in Bethlehem represents precisely the irony and absurdity of Roman rule. Besides forcing the people into disloyalty to their God, the registration for the tribute forced them back into an economic situation that had already proven unviable. Because of such factors as the tribute, they were no longer able to "make it" farming on their ancestral land, but they were forced to return precisely in order to raise the tribute. As representatives of the thousands of rootless people cut loose from their lands yet forced back into impossible situations by the oppressive and unrealistic Roman demands, Joseph and Mary also represent the ways in which the imperial Roman system threatened the lives of ordinary people in general.

With regard to Caesar's census as with regard to his conquests, the Gospel of the Savior laid in the manger was diametrically opposed to the system headed by the imperial savior. The festivals honoring the emperor as divine savior were funded by the produce expropriated from subjected peasantries around the empire, either as rents in the case of more "civilized" areas or as tribute by subject peoples such as the Galileans and Judeans. "Bread and circuses" provided for the urban masses in the imperial metropoles—Italian or Greek peasants previously displaced from the land to make room for the ancient equivalent of agribusiness—was provided from the tribute taken by the imperial savior from the subjected Egyptian and Syrian peasants. Ironically, the empire still expected the peasantry to produce despite the fact that many overtaxed and heavily indebted peasants could not feed their families after rendering to Caesar. The people who produced and recited the story of Jesus' birth apparently knew well that the desperate plight of a couple like Joseph and Mary was due to the demands of Caesar.

3. Shepherds Receive the Good News for All the People

Judging by the relative amount of coverage, the story of Jesus' birth empha-sizes the announcement of its significance to the shepherds, their visit to the

newborn child lying in the manger, and their spreading the good news to
the rest of the people (Luke 2:8–20) more than the birth itself (2:6–7).

The shepherds have been overinterpreted, either as symbols of an ideal
pastoral existence or as despised and degraded outcasts from the society[27]
on the one hand, and underestimated, along with the manger, as merely bits
of local color in a story centered on Bethlehem, on the other. The shepherds
are not just one more type of lowly people for whom Luke the author has a
special predilection.[28] Nor are the shepherds inserted as a springboard to a
christological point based on the ancient Near Eastern image of the established king or emperor as the shepherd of the people. Such an interpretation
would appear to turn the story into its opposite, to place Jesus on the same
level with the imperial savior Caesar Augustus.[29] That the "good news" is
announced by the messenger of the Lord to the shepherds stands in pointed
contrast with the decree by the Emperor Caesar Augustus that all the world
should render tribute. The principal effect of the story as a whole is to juxta-
pose the powerful Roman emperor who lives in luxury with subject people
whom he forces to render tribute, featuring the most destitute of his peasant
subjects, the shepherds.

While sheep herding was held in disrepute by kings, according to the
Jewish philosopher Philo (*On Husbandry* 61), and viewed as a despised occupation by later Jewish rabbis (*tractate Sanhedrin* 25b in the Babylonian
Talmud), shepherds were basically the lowest-status peasants, the most marginal producers eking out an existence on the most marginal land. Around
Bethlehem, which was shepherd country because the rainfall was insuffi-
cient for extensive cultivation of the soil, shepherds were the equivalent of
farmers elsewhere, except more destitute. There is reason to believe that
shepherds around Bethlehem, like Joseph, may well have been alienated
from their ancestral lands. With the expansion of the sacrificial system in
the temple as rebuilt by Herod, the demand for local livestock production
had intensified, and the land in the villages such as Bethlehem in the en-
virons of Jerusalem may have come under the control of the increasingly
wealthy high priestly families in Jerusalem. So shepherds around Bethlehem
and other such villages may have been working on large estates helping
supply sacrificial animals. They would then, like Joseph, have represented
people whose livelihood, social standing, and traditional way of life were
increasingly threatened by Caesar's census and the imperial system generally.
The story states explicitly that as recipients of the good news the shepherds
are representatives of "the whole people" (2:10). In portraying the peasants
as the representative figures, however, the story pointedly focuses attention on the poorest of the poor, the most destitute of the always marginal
peasantry, subject to the imperial savior and his debilitating tribute.

That the child was laid "in a manger," which is pointedly stated at
three crucial steps in this brief story, draws the hearers into an unavoidable recognition that Jesus was born among the poorest of the peasantry.
The traditional English Bible translation of the story, that Mary laid Jesus

in a manger "because there was no room for them in the inn," can be misleading. It suggests that the child is set apart from ordinary people, who stay
in the inn, or even "hotel," in some translations. (The ox and ass that have
become standard in visual and musical representations of the stable scene,
but are absent from the story itself, may reinforce this impression of Jesus'
birth as set apart from the people, who stay in the inn.) But Luke uses a very
different Greek word for "inn" (*pandocheion*) in the parable of the Good
Samaritan (10:34). The Greek terms here in 2:7 (*katalyma*, 2:7) is more
a simple "lodging," a sort of caravansary or khan where several travelers
might find shelter under one roof. Thus the manger is not contrasted with
but is an integral part of the larger scene at such a simple lodging or khan
where poor travelers might stay the night. Because there was no room left
in the place where the rest of the travelers were staying, Mary had to lay her
child in the feeding trough for the animals. The humblest of births, among
the poorest of the poor.

That the shepherds "will find a child wrapped in bands of cloth and lying
in a manger" is declared to be "a sign" for them that a savior, who is the
Messiah, has been born in the city of David (2:12). A sign in biblical history
is often misinterpreted as merely an authenticating proof of a message or
promised future event. A sign in biblical history is rather an occurrence
that bears out or exemplifies a message of a future event and it usually
impinges directly on the people addressed in the message. While it may not
be satisfying to urbane theologians keen on sophisticated higher levels of
meaning, the sign in this story, as stated explicitly in 2:12, is the simple fact
that Jesus is laid in a manger. That the child is laid right there in the manger
in their midst, as one of them, exemplifies and bears out the message that a
savior-messiah has been born for them and for the whole people. That the
babe is laid in a manger is the sign for them; furthermore, it bears a credible
historical verisimilitude. Although modern readers recognize that the story
is legendary, its portrayal of the Messiah as born among the poor peasantry
fits what we know of other popular leaders of deliverance. Those figures
who were acclaimed as popular kings/messiahs and heard as prophets by
crowds were not from either scribal circles or the priestly elite, but were
from among the people themselves, whether Athronges, a lowly shepherd,
Judas son of Hezekiah, the brigand-chieftain, or Jesus son of Hananiah, a
"crude peasant."[30]

Just as the child is born among the peasantry, represented by the shepherds, so the shepherds act as representatives in the story. First they receive
the good news of great joy which is "for all the people" (2:10). Then they
immediately and "with haste" go to "check it out" (2:15–16). And finally,
when they have seen the child laid in the manger as the sign of the birth of
their anointed deliverer, they spread the message they had received to the rest
of the people, who were amazed at the good news (2:17–18). The shepherds
in this story are representatives of "the whole people," to whom the good
news, the birth of their deliverer, is directed. The "salvation" or "peace and

security" (1 Thess. 5:3) established by the imperial savior was indeed "good news" for the wealthy and powerful elite of the Roman Empire. It secured their positions of power and privilege. The Gospel heard and broadcast by the shepherds in Luke 2:8–20 was for "all the people" who were subjected and exploited by the denizens of empire, people eager to hear what for them would be "good news," in opposition to the imperial order.

4. "To you is born... a Savior, Who is the Messiah, the Lord"

Finally we come to the crux of the matter, which is the content of the "Gospel" which is for all the people. As seen in the discussion of the Roman emperor cult above, "gospel" or "good news" was the "loaded" term used for the message that the emperor Augustus, the savior, had brought peace and security to the whole world. "Savior" as one of the principal titles of Caesar, "Lord" as another of his titles, and "peace" and "salvation" as the principal symbols of what the divine savior had brought to the world, were all similarly "loaded," fraught with resonance throughout the Roman imperial order—negative or positive, depending on the audience. In the story of Jesus' birth, the messenger announces to the shepherds a Gospel that is diametrically opposed to the imperial savior and his gospel. Contrary to what may often be assumed, the title "Savior" is seldom used for Jesus. This is the only occurrence in all of the Synoptic Gospels (Matthew, Mark, and Luke)! In the seven genuine letters, Paul uses it only once, in a way that contrasts pointedly with the Roman emperor as savior (Phil. 3:21). We can only conclude that "Savior," used here for the newborn Jesus, is in opposition to Caesar as the imperial savior. In the context of this blunt opposition to the imperial savior, the occurrence also of the title "Lord" and the advent of peace on earth—along with the birth of the deliverer among the people—also carry the message of an alternative. This new Savior is presented in opposition to the imperial savior whose "peace" devastates the people's lives and whose decree of tribute disrupts what is left. This newborn child is a Savior for "the whole people" who have been devastated by the savior whose gospel is proclaimed and whose divinity it celebrated in festivals sponsored by the wealthy and powerful elite of the cities of the empire. This is a Gospel for "the whole people" who have been subjected militarily and whose taxes and tribute provides the economic support on which Caesar and the imperial elite enjoy their privilege and power.

That the story sets the newborn Jesus as Savior in political-religious opposition to the imperial savior is confirmed by the other title used in the Gospel, "Messiah," especially in combination with his birth in "the city of David." It has been recognized for over a generation now that there was no standard Jewish expectation of "the Messiah" at the time of Jesus,[31] nor was there a standard concept that the followers of Jesus could draw upon to interpret Jesus. It is difficult to discern in New Testament literature any standard Christian synthetic concept of "the Messiah." Similarly, there is no evidence for some sort of spiritual messiah as different from a political or military messiah. Such a misconception is a construct of the modern separation of religion and politics. But in antiquity, there was no such separation of the religious and the political. Just as the power relationship between Caesar the imperial savior and the people of the empire was inseparably religious and political, so also an anointed leader in the Israelite biblical tradition was inseparably religious and political.

Even more significant for the story of Jesus' birth in Luke 2:1–20, there are few *texts* from the time that attest to any expectation of a messiah. That is, the scribal circles that produced literature were not particularly interested in messianic leaders or the renewal movements they might lead. Perhaps the most significant "messiah" text from the time of Jesus, Psalm of Solomon 17, looks for an anointed son of David who will restore the tribes of Israel on its land and judge oppressive foreign rulers, but through the word of his mouth, like a sage or scribe, and not by the sword or with war chariots. The several references to anointed figures in the Dead Sea Scrolls are not all that impressive considering how infrequent they are in the vast new literature produced by the Qumran community.[32]

This relative lack of interest in a messiah among the scribal elite (except perhaps at Qumran) make it all the more significant that the most solid evidence for interest in a messiah comes from concrete movements that emerged among the Judean and Galilean peasantry just at the time Jesus was born and again about thirty years after Jesus' own activity.[33] According to the Jewish historian Josephus, when the hated tyrant and Roman client king Herod the Great died in 4 B.C.E., in every major district of his kingdom there arose sizeable popular movements in which the people acclaimed one of their number as "king." If we translate Josephus's Greek-style historiography into Israelite idiom, these were "messianic" movements, patterned after the great historical prototypes of earlier movements of Israelite peasants who acclaimed first Saul and then David as "messiah" (see especially 1 Sam. 2:1–4; 5:1–4). Just as the historical prototypes were formed in resistance to oppressive foreign rule, so also the movements led by popular messiahs at the time of Jesus were formed to reclaim self-rule against the rule of the Romans. These movements were even successful for awhile, before the Romans finally mounted sufficient military forces to "search and destroy" them from their base in Galilean and Judean villages.

The leaders and location of these movements are also significant for our understanding of Jesus of Nazareth and stories about him. The movement in Galilee, led by Judas, the son of a brigand-chieftain named Hezekiah, arose in the area surrounding Nazareth where Jesus supposedly grew up, and attacked the royal fortress and storehouse in Sepphoris. The most extensive movement that emerged in the hill country of Judea was led by

> Athronges, a man whose importance derived neither from the renown of his forefathers, nor from the superiority of his character, nor the extent of his means. He was an obscure shepherd, yet remarkable

for his stature and strength. . . . He also had four brothers. . . . Each of
them had an armed band, for a great throng had assembled around
them. . . . Athronges held council on what was to be done. . . . He held
power for a long time, having been designated king. (*Jewish Antiquities*
17.278–81; cf. *Jewish War* 2.60–62)

These popular messianic movements contemporary with Jesus' birth indicate that Galilean and Judean peasants, including shepherds, were ready
to form movements directed against Roman and Herodian rule and led by
a king from among their ranks. This is very close to what the messenger
announces to the shepherds in the Gospel for the whole people in Luke 2:8–
20. In comparison with these popular messianic movements, the story of
Jesus' birth has remarkable "historical verisimilitude" as a representation
of another anti-imperial movement formed among the Galilean and Judean
people. The Gospel that God's messengers announce to the shepherds, who
made it known to the rest of the people, was that the child in the manger
was an anti-imperial Savior and Messiah who would lead their liberation
from the Roman imperial order headed by the savior whose salvation for
people of power and privilege meant only oppression for them.

The anti-imperial agenda of the story in Luke 2:1–20 is paralleled earlier
in the Lucan infancy narrative in the psalms recited by Mary and Zechariah.
These are striking for their political as well as religious thrust, particularly
their explicit articulation of God's militant deliverance of the poor against
their wealthy and powerful rulers and deliverance of Israel from enemy
forces who would subject it. As a not so "gentle Mary, meek and mild"
prays in the Magnificat,

> He has brought down the powerful from their thrones, and lifted up
>   the lowly. . . .
> He has helped his servant Israel. (Luke 1:52–54 NRSV)

Or, as John the Baptist's father, Zechariah, declares:

> He has raised up a horn of salvation for us in the house of his servant
>   David. . . .
> That we would be saved from our enemies. (Luke 1:69–71 RSV)

The new anti-imperial Gospel that "to you is born this day in the city of
David a Savior, who is the Messiah," is precisely that "horn of salvation in
the house of David." And he is apparently expected to be the people's leader
through whom God will again "bring down the powerful from their thrones
and lift up the lowly . . . his servant Israel," just as he had done many times
previously in the history of Israel.

The traditional and somewhat vague reading of "the multitude of the
heavenly *host*" in Luke 2:14 has obscured just how militant the anti-imperial
Gospel is that the messenger announces to the shepherds. The word in Greek
is "army" (*stratia*). What the shepherds hear is not a bunch of innocuous

angels singing of God's glory, but the heavenly *army* of God. The shepherds
in the story experience God's anticipated deliverance in terms of a lively and
long-standing Israelite biblical tradition, that God liberates his people Israel
by means of a heavenly army. Indeed, in biblical passages speaking of such
liberation, God is referred to as Yahweh of hosts, the LORD of the heavenly
armies. Far from being dormant at the time of Jesus, the heavenly armies
were a prominent feature in contemporary apocalyptic literature (e.g., the
War Scroll from Qumran, 1QM). And God's heavenly armies of angels figure
prominently at points in New Testament literature, as when Jesus says at his
arrest that God could easily send "twelve legions of angels" to his rescue
(Matt. 26:53). Luke may well be addressing people of some means in his
Gospel, whom he has Jesus ask to give half of their goods to the poor,
and he may be portraying Christians in the book of Acts as not threatening
to the imperial order. But he has done little to veil or obscure the anti-
imperial Gospel announced in the anti-imperial story of Jesus' birth or the
anti-imperial songs sung by Mary and Zechariah.

It is difficult to imagine or comprehend two such different saviors as Caesar Augustus and Jesus and the dramatically different societies and values
they represent. The first stood at the apex of a "worldwide" hierarchical political-economic-religious system in which the prolonged festivals
celebrating the savior's birth and the salvation he provided both ritually constituted the hierarchical imperial power relationships and consolidated the
political-economic-religious positions of the power brokers who sponsored
the festivals. The newly born Messiah of Israel, laid in a feeding trough, was
the very opposite of a symbol of power that determined people's lives. He
represented the hopes and aspirations of a subject people to be free from
the exploitative imperial system that controlled their lives and drained away
the produce of their labor that they needed to support their families and
maintain their community life.

   It seems ironic that the bishops of the Christian church that came to worship Jesus Christ as their Lord and Savior—in an effort to displace or replace
the worship of Caesar as savior with the worship of Christ—established
Christmas as the holy day honoring Jesus' birth at the time of the winter
solstice, which had become the standard season for the imperial festivals.
For most of Christian history, however, Christmas remained a modest celebration compared to the great festivals celebrated in honor of Caesar in
the Roman Empire. Two millennia after both Caesar and Jesus were proclaimed saviors, Christians and others are only beginning to puzzle over
the implications of what has happened in the course of the last century in
America. Beginning little more than a century ago—after the distinctively
American combination of commercial gift giving and solstice—New Year's
celebration had developed into a fairly elaborate society-wide festival that
had little or nothing to do with Christian observance of the birth of Christ:

merchants began to include scenes from the stories of Christ's Nativity in their window displays to attract customers. Wanamaker's giant department story in Philadelphia was transformed into a Christianized cathedral of consumption, replete with pipe organ and caroling choruses for the "season." A few decades later, jealous for their faith and perhaps unaware that the American Christmas had never focused much on Christ's birth, the Knights of Columbus in Milwaukee and others began displaying seasonal billboards with the message "Put Christ Back in Christmas." Only in the twentieth century did most mainline Christian churches embrace the holiday festival. Perhaps Americans, while scurrying about purchasing gifts made by low-paid labor in third-world countries, can take some consolation in knowing that the combination of Christ with the elaborate holiday festival also called Christmas has indeed been "made in America." If and when Christians read Luke's story of the child born in the manger because his parents had to register to pay tribute to Caesar, it would not be surprising if they questioned just how appropriate it is to "keep Christ in Christmas." The great American Christmas festival seems more appropriate to the gospel of the savior who decreed that all the rest of the world should render tribute to support the "bread and circuses" in the imperial metropoles.

Notes

1. S. R. F. Price, *Rituals and Power: The Roman Imperial Cult in Asia Minor* (Cambridge: Cambridge University Press, 1984); selections repr. in Richard A. Horsley, *Paul and Empire: Religion and Power in Roman Imperial Society* (Harrisburg, Pa.: Trinity Press International, 1997), 51.

2. *Orientis graeci inscriptiones selectae*, vol. 2, ed. W. Dittenberger (Leipzig, 1903–5), no. 458.

3. Price, *Rituals and Power*, in *Paul and Empire*, 47.

4. The Greek word for the city-state was *polis*, from which we derive "political," and the Latin words were *urbs* and *civis*, from which we derive "urban" and "civil."

5. As explained by Stephen Nissenbaum, *The Battle for Christmas* (New York: Alfred A. Knopf, 1996) and Price, *Rituals and Power*, respectively.

6. Price, *Rituals and Power*, 49.

7. Paul Zanker, *The Power of Images in the Age of Augustus* (Ann Arbor: University of Michigan Press, 1988), selection reprinted in *Paul and Empire*, 74.

8. Price, *Rituals and Power*, 55.

9. Richard Gordon, "The Veil of Power: Emperors, Sacrificers and Benefactors," in *Pagan Priests: Religion and Power in the Ancient World*, ed. Mary Beard and John North (London: Duckworth, 1990), repr. in *Paul and Empire*, 134.

10. Ibid., 135–36.

11. Price, *Rituals and Power*, 59. Cf. the Presidential decree making Thanksgiving Day the Thursday four weeks before Christmas at the behest of corporations so that the retailing season would be sufficiently long.

12. Ibid., 61.

13. Ibid., 62–64. Anthropologists have recognized that the ordering of space

serves both as a representation of social ideas and as part of the very fabric of reality. The reordering of space reflects and constitutes political and social changes.

14. Ibid., 64–65.

15. Zanker, "The Power of Images," 73.

16. Ibid., 74.

17. Price, *Rituals and Power,* 66.

18. Ibid., 69–70.

19. Zanker, "The Power of Images," 74.

20. The emperor, said Seneca in a soliloquy to the youthful Nero, had "been chosen to serve on earth as vicar of the gods" and was "the arbiter of life and death for the nations" (*Clem.* 1.1, 2). There was no question about the power exercised by the emperor: "Like one continuous country and one people, all the world quietly obeys. Everything is carried out by command or nod. . . . The constitution is a universal democracy under the one man that can rule and govern best" (Aelius Aristides, *To Rome* 30, 60).

21. Joseph A. Fitzmyer, *The Gospel According to St. Luke,* 2 vols., Anchor Bible (Garden City, N.Y.: Doubleday, 1981–85), 1:393–94; Raymond E. Brown, *The Birth of the Messiah* (Garden City, N.Y.: Doubleday, 1977), 414–15.

22. The ensuing discussion of Caesar and the census are dependent on the more extensive discussion in Richard A. Horsley, *The Liberation of Christmas: The Infancy Narratives in Social Context* (New York: Crossroad, 1989), chapter 2.

23. Keith Hopkins, *Conquerors and Slaves* (New York: Cambridge University Press, 1978).

24. Fitzmyer, *Luke,* 1:393. Scholarly preoccupation with Luke's apparent chronological confusion, which correlates Jesus' birth with the date of the first enrollment in Judea for the tribute to Rome, has diverted attention from what the tribute would have meant concretely to the people subjected to it.

25. See further Richard A. Horsley, *Jesus and the Spiral of Violence* (San Francisco: Harper & Row, 1987), 162–63, 306–17.

26. More fully discussed in Horsley, *Jesus,* 304–17.

27. Joachim Jeremias, *Jerusalem at the Time of Jesus* (Philadelphia: Fortress, 1969), 303–12. See the fuller critical discussion of the shepherds in Horsley, *Liberation of Christmas,* 100–106.

28. Against Fitzmyer, *Luke,* 1:392, whose only good proof text illustrating that the shepherds are lowly is from the clearly pre-Lucan Magnificat, Luke 1:52. Because of the distinctively Semitic language and other stylistic features, it would be arbitrary to decide that Luke himself composed the story of Jesus birth.

29. It would be comforting theologically to be reassured that the condition of the Christ-child was regal and secure, as argued by Fitzmyer, *Luke,* 1:394–96, and Brown, *Birth of the Messiah,* 419–20; but such an interpretation runs counter to the thrust of the story and its key features.

30. Discussed at length in Richard A. Horsley with John S. Hanson, *Bandits, Prophets, and Messiahs,* new edition (Harrisburg, Pa.: Trinity Press International, 1997).

31. Among the works to address this question are Richard A. Horsley, "Popular Messianic Movements around the Time of Jesus," *Catholic Biblical Quarterly* 46 (1984): 471–95; Jacob Neusner, W. D. Green, and E. Frerichs, *Judaisms and Their Messiahs at the Turn of the Christian Era* (Cambridge: Cambridge University

Press, 1988; and James H. Charlesworth, ed., *The Messiah: Developments in Earliest Judaism and Christianity* (Minneapolis: Fortress, 1992).

32. On the other hand, John J. Collins, in *The Scepter and the Star: The Messiahs of the Dead Sea Scrolls and Other Ancient Literature* (New York: Doubleday, 1995), argues that the references to anointed ones and related figures in the Dead Sea Scrolls, taken together, appear to be moving toward a synthetic image of eschatological leader-figures.

33. The following discussion depends on the fuller analysis in Horsley, "Popular Messianic Movements," and subsequent publications, such as *Bandits, Prophets, and Messiahs,* chapter 3.

Chapter Seven

Messiah, Magi, and Model Imperial King

Richard Horsley

Christmas pageants and Christmas crèches do not tell the whole story about the birth of Christ. Similarly, theological interpreters of the Christmas story do not explore the whole story. While revealing and reveling in partial truths, they hide or distort important aspects of the truth told in the story of Christ's birth—in four interrelated and overlapping ways.

First, they portray the parts of the Christmas story that make us feel good, like the wise men bringing gifts to the child. Pageants, crèches, and scholars all seem to tailor the Christmas story to fit our domestic celebration of Christmas. But they leave out the horrible parts, such as King Herod sending out the death squads to brutally massacre all the children in Bethlehem, forcing Mary, Joseph, and Jesus to become homeless refugees in Egypt.

Second, they pretend that the Christmas story is only or primarily religious. More particularly, they assume that the story of Christ's birth is about the origin of Christianity insofar as Jesus, who was born as the Jewish Messiah, was rejected by his own people, the Jews, and accepted by the Gentiles, whose belief in Jesus as the Christ (=Messiah) resulted in a new, universal, and truly spiritual religion. So, in Matthew's Gospel, Herod and "all Jerusalem" are understood as representative of the Jews' rejection of Jesus as the Messiah, while the Magi are seen as representative of the Gentiles, who honor and accept the Messiah. This portrayal of the story of Herod, the Magi, the newborn baby, and the massacre of the children, however, is simply an application of a Christian theological scheme that perpetuates a long history of Christian anti-Judaism.

If the story in Matthew 2 is read without imposing that theological scheme, it is clearly not about spiritual salvation, but about political struggle. The Magi come following the star in search of the child who has been born *king of the Jews,* a political leader. But there is already a king of the Jews, Herod, who, along with the rest of the ruling apparatus in Jerusalem, is understandably frightened that a revolution against his power and privilege is afoot among the people in such villages as Bethlehem, from which it had been prophesied that God's messiah ("anointed one") would come as "a [political!] ruler who is to shepherd my people Israel." There are religious aspects to the story, but they are only secondary touches. The Magi were specialists in studying the divine heavenly bodies and their implications for political affairs. The chief priests and scribes were specialists in interpreting sacred scrolls. And Joseph received repeated communications from messengers of the Lord in his dreams. But the story in Matthew 2 as a whole is one of a life-and-death political struggle between the newborn "king of the Jews," who is to become shepherd-ruler of the Israelites in fulfillment of prophecy, and the reigning king of the Jews who "killed all the children in and around Bethlehem" in a desperate preemptive strike against the rebellion before it could take hold.[1]

Third, crèches and especially theological biblical interpreters focus narrowly on the Christ(-child) and attempt to extract a "christology" from the narrative as a whole. A classic Christian theological formula is that the genealogy and the announcement of Jesus' birth in Matthew 1 are about the "person" of Christ, while the story in Matthew 2 is about the "work" of Christ. The story of Matthew 2 as a whole, however, is about far more than the birth of Christ. As already noted, the story focuses on a political struggle in which the reigning king of Judea plays the dominant role. The story is also about the Magi and about Joseph, who takes the necessary actions to keep the child alive after being instructed by the messengers of the Lord. And the story features the fulfillment of one prophecy after another.[2]

Beyond the principal actors in the story, however, are the striking parallels it exhibits with the biblical story of Moses and Israel's exodus from Egypt.[3] In some cases, the Matthean story even uses words and phrases found at parallel points in biblical accounts of the Moses/exodus story. The harsh reigning king threatens the life of the child. Herod, like Pharaoh, orders all male children killed. Jesus, like Moses, is rescued by actions of his family. Joseph with Mary and the baby "went away" (*anachoreo;* Matt. 2:13–14) just as Moses "went away" (Exod. 2:15). In citing the prophecy (Hos. 11:1) "Out of Egypt I have called my son," Matthew 2:15 makes Jesus recapitulate the exodus of Israel (God's "son") from foreign rule in Egypt. The word used for Herod's death in Matthew 2:19 is the same as used for that of Pharaoh in Exodus 2:23 in the Greek Jewish Bible, the Septuagint. The language used in Matthew 2:19–20 is influenced by that in Exodus 4:19. The Magi in Matthew 2 bear resemblances to the way the Jewish philosopher Philo portrays Balaam as a *magos* from the East who prophesies a king of Israel, symbolized by the "star coming forth out of Jacob," who will come from out of Egypt (Philo, *On the Life of Moses* 1.276–78). In consideration of all these parallels, we can only conclude that the story in Matthew 2 portrays the origin of Jesus as the ruler to shepherd Israel as a recapitulation of the origin of Israel itself under the leadership of its representative figure, Moses.

Fourth, both crèches and theologians domesticate the story, yielding to its magical and fairy-tale motifs and effects: the "three kings" following the star and bringing costly gifts to the Christ-child. For all its apparent fictional or "mythical" elements, however, the story has a remarkable historical verisimilitude in its representation of harsh historical realities—and they may be the most difficult for us to approach by historical analysis and interpretation. Before they were domesticated by bourgeois interpreters such as the Brothers Grimm and sold as "fairy tales" for American children's bedtime stories, folktales were full of realistic portrayals of the harsh realities of life and political protest. Similarly, the story in Matthew 2 presents a realistic historical picture of life under King Herod, even if the "massacre of the innocents" cannot be confirmed as an actual historical event. Moreover, not only did Herod do such things as kill people who threatened his rule, he and his successors as client-rulers of the Roman Empire would have had reason to feel threatened by rival "kings of the Jews" from such villages as Bethlehem. For just at the time of Herod and Jesus, several significant movements emerged among the Judean and Galilean people that were headed by figures acclaimed by their followers as kings or by figures who promised to reenact the deliverance of Israel from foreign rule in Egypt.

The whole story in Matthew 2, including Herod's massacre of the children and the family's flight into Egypt as well as the birth of the child and the visit of the Magi, is one of life-and-death political struggle. In modern terms, the story is about the struggle between the dictator of a third-world people set in place by an imperial government on the one hand, and the birth of the leader of the movement of the people's liberation from that dictator and the imperial order of which he was an integral part on the other. While the story of Herod, the Magi, the newborn Messiah, and the massacre of the children is one of life-and-death political conflict, it does have a certain aura of unreality about it. The Magi appear as the veritable epitome of naïveté. How could they be so naïve or disingenuous as to come to the reigning king of the Jews, Herod, to inquire about the one who had just been born to displace him? The Magi, as advisers to Eastern kings, would surely have known that it was standard practice for a king to designate his successor, presumably the eldest or favorite son. How could they not know that the ascendant star of a new king of the Jews signaled a revolution, an upstart king who would replace the current regime? But the political naïveté of the Magi makes all the more shocking the horrifying events that their question to Herod touches off: the threatened Herod orders the vicious massacre so that the parents and the newborn Messiah must flee for their lives.

The only way we can even begin to appreciate this dramatic story of political conflict is to hear it again in its ancient historical context. Roman imperial armies had conquered and now dominated Israel (the Judeans, Samaritans, and Galileans). But the people of Israel sustained a stubborn resistance to empire and insisted that they should be an independent people under the direct rule of God. This yearning for a life of justice found expression in several popular movements, including that focused on Jesus who came from a Galilean town called Nazareth (Matt. 2:23). Just as the story begins with the Roman imperial order represented by Herod and then moves to the implications for the birth of the leader of the people's liberation, so we will begin from the side of Rome's new world order represented by its model king, Herod, and then move to the side of the third-world people among whom the Messiah is born.[4]

Herod: King of the Jews by the Grace of Rome

Establishing the Roman New World Order in Palestine

The Roman Senate's principal concern in building an empire was to secure control of territory. The Romans particularly wanted to establish and maintain their power in eastern Mediterranean countries, such as Judea, against the rival Parthian empire to the east. In the ancient Roman imperial program, that meant setting up military strongmen as dictators in the areas less "civilized," those areas less agreeable to control by the empire and/or the hegemony of imperial culture. Rather than maintain occupying troops in such areas, the Romans preferred indirect rule through client "kings."

Herod got his start as a military strongman under his father, Antipater, the effective ruler of the Jerusalem temple-state under its high priest Hyrcanus, whom the Romans kept in nominal power after their conquest of greater Judea in 63 B.C.E.[5] From the beginning of his rapid climb to power, Herod attacked and exploited the people and alienated the Jerusalem elite.[6] But it was the impression on the Romans that mattered in the struggle for power in Palestine. Believing that Herod represented their best option for controlling Palestine, despite his unpopularity and utter lack of legitimacy in Judea, the Roman Senate made Herod the king of the Jews, with attendant ceremonial celebration (Josephus, *Jewish War* [*War*] 1.282–85; Jewish *Antiquities* [*Ant.*] 14.381–89; 16.311). When Herod attempted to take control of his kingdom, he met strong and often sustained resistance everywhere. It took him three years of almost constant fighting to subdue the people (*War* 1.291, 299, 303–19, 326, 334; *Ant.* 14.395, 408, 413–36, 450, 457–61)[7] before he was finally able to conquer Jerusalem itself. "When the troops poured in, a scene of wholesale massacre ensued; for the Romans were infuriated by the length of the siege, and the Jews of Herod's army were determined to leave none of their opponents alive. Masses were butchered in the alleys, crowded together in the houses, and flying into the [temple] sanctuary" (*War* 1.351).

Herod now needed to consolidate his power within the areas he ruled. He set about systematically eliminating members of the previous ruling family, the Hasmoneans, but he retained the high priesthood. The Jerusalem temple-state was an imperial institution from its inception, the political-economic-religious center of Judea. The whole city, the high priestly families and the scribes and artisans who served their needs, was supported by the tithes and offerings brought to the temple by the Judean villagers (and later by the Galilean villagers as well). Herod now made the temple and high priesthood instruments of his interests. By the end of his reign, the result of Herod's manipulation of the high priesthood was a completely new high priestly aristocracy of four families that came to dominate the temple-state for the next sixty years, after which it was destroyed by the Romans.[8] Thus "all Jerusalem," that is, the high priests, the scribes who assisted them, and other dependents, would have been "frightened" along with Herod by the news of a new king having been born. And "all Jerusalem," as his own creatures, would have been compliant to Herod's anxious inquiries as to just "where the Messiah was to be born." For they formed an integral part of the apparatus of the Roman imperial order imposed on the Jews.

King of Imperial Revenue and Impoverished People

In the ancient world, more than in the modern world, politics and religion were inseparable from economics. In a capitalist system, possession of great wealth translates, through various means and media, into political power. In the ancient eastern Mediterranean world, political or political-religious power brought with it the control of economic resources. The Roman imperial regime, in placing a military strongman in power in a particular territory, was also granting him the "income" or "take" from that territory. The Jewish historian Josephus indicates matter-of-factly that when the Romans placed Herod and later his sons in charge of certain territories, they were to receive the known income from the taxes or tribute rendered up by the productive peasantry of those areas. Like a contemporary multinational conglomerate that has acquired subsidiary corporations by means of forced buyouts, the CEO and management of the imperial megacorporation ensured that the CEOs of the subsidiary regimes would be handsomely rewarded for their pursuit of the goals of the imperial corporation—from the profits of the subsidiaries. That Herod's yearly "take" simply from the tax revenues of Judea, Samaria, Idumea, Galilee, Perea, Batanea, and Auranitis was nine hundred talents can be deduced from the "revenues" available to his heirs assigned to those territories after he died (Josephus, *Ant.* 17.317–19). Herod's overall income, of course, was considerably larger, since he controlled the "royal lands" in the Great Plain just to the south of Galilee, in the coastal plain, and in the Samarian and Judean hill country, as well as the new territories he "developed" and various royal concessions.[9]

Unlike modern capitalists, however, ancient political rulers did not reinvest their income. Much more than modern multimillionaires, ancient rulers indulged in ostentatious consumption and display of wealth. The latter often took the form of gifts or "bequests" of resources for the construction of public urban buildings and entertainments. In this regard, the Roman Empire-builders must have been pleased with their "king of the Jews." Particularly after his kingship was confirmed by Augustus after the battle of Actium in 31 B.C.E., Herod mounted a most "impressive demonstration of the new order Augustus had introduced into the Roman empire."[10] Adopting for himself titles such as "Admirer of Caesar" and "Admirer of the Romans,"[11] he provided the bulwark the Romans needed on the East by maintaining strict control of his territory and advancing Roman interests in the area. Indeed, Herod became the model Roman client-king, unsurpassed by any other in his "friendship" with the Romans and his massive munificence to the imperial family and to many important cities of the empire.

With the Roman imperial "new world order" solidly secured, Herod turned to what can only be termed massive-scale "development" of his realm, mainly in large-scale building projects. Besides restoring and expanding the Hasmonean fortresses such as Masada and Herodium, he built magnificent palaces in Jerusalem and other cities for the enjoyment and security of his extensive family and elaborate court (*War* 1.419–21; 7.285–91; *Ant.* 16.142–45; etc.). Outside of Judea and Galilee, with their Israelite "sensitivities," Herod built monuments and whole cities in honor of Augustus, such as the seaport city of Caesarea, which was larger than Rome's seaport of Piraeus. Moreover, "on an eminence facing the harbor stood Caesar's temple . . . containing a colossal statue of the emperor, not inferior to the Olympian Zeus, which served for its model, and another of Roma, rivaling that of Hera at Argos" (*War* 1.413–15; *Ant.* 15.331–41). Writes the ancient Judean historian Josephus, "One can mention no suitable spot within [Herod's] realm which he left destitute of some mark of his homage to Caesar" (*War* 1.404, 407; *Ant.* 14.272).

In addition to all this building in his own realm, Herod lavished "benefactions" on many cities in Syria and Greece as well as on the emperor himself and members of his family. Most famous among his many magnanimous gifts were the Pythian temple in Rhodes, paving and colonnade for the long main street in Syrian Antioch, and the endowment of the Olympic games (*Ant.* 12–116, 142, 146; *War* 1.422). "In all things he undertook he was ambitious to surpass what had been done before. . . . Caesar himself and Agrippa often remarked that the extent of Herod's realm was not equal to his magnanimity" (*Ant.* 16.141).

Most famous of Herod's massive building projects was the rebuilding of the temple in Jerusalem: "In the fifteenth year of his reign, he restored the Temple and, by erecting new foundation-walls, enlarged the surrounding area to double its former extent. The expenditure devoted to this work was incalculable, its magnificence never surpassed. . . . The fortress which dominated it on the north . . . he restored at a lavish cost in a style no way inferior to that of a palace, and called it Antonia in honor of Antony" (*War* 1.401). Indeed, Herod's rebuilding of the temple was far more than refurbishing a center of worship. It included Roman features such as the royal basilica and the *stoas*. Pursuant to his own royal propaganda, Herod displayed "the spoils taken from the Gentiles [during his own military campaigns] round about the entire Temple" (*Ant.* 15.402). With this massive reconstruction of the temple as one of the "wonders of the world," Herod made Jerusalem one of the showplaces of the Roman Empire.[12]

Herod's unprecedented building program in his own realm and unmatched munificence abroad had severe implications for his subjects. The "income" available to fund his lavish court and royal lifestyle as well as his huge gifts and massive construction projects consisted almost exclusively of the taxes he extracted from the peasantry under his rule and the produce of the sharecroppers and renters on his royal estates. But Herod's taxes came on top of the tithes and offerings that the Judean and Galilean people owed to the high priesthood and temple. And agricultural producers also must manage to feed themselves, at least at the level of minimum caloric intake, in order to reproduce the labor to raise the crops that provide tax revenues. A recent analysis of the scale of Herod's building projects points up the problem: "After 30 B.C.E. the pace and scale of his projects increased dramatically. Enormous projects were undertaken and several ran concurrently.... In the late 20s his construction activities were staggering"[13]

The already immense burden on the peasant producers of supporting these immense and simultaneous construction projects was further exacerbated by the severe drought, two-year crop failure, and famine that struck in 28–26. Rather than let the peasantry, his own economic base, starve to death, and to counter the continuing hostility of the people, Herod arranged famine relief from Egypt, with welcome further assistance from Queen Helena of Adiabene, who had recently converted to Judaism (*Ant.* 300–316). The economic oppression was so severe by 22–21 that Herod was compelled to grant tax relief (of one-third) so that the peasant producers could regain at least the subsistence level—and so that he could "regain the good will of the disaffected" (*Ant.* 15.365).[14]

The Jewish historian Josephus offers a convincing analysis of the relationship between Herod's massive building program and lavish benefactions to other cities on the one hand, and his oppression and tyrannical rule of his Judean and other subjects on the other:

> Herod loved honors and, being powerfully dominated by this passion, he was led to display generosity whenever there was reason to hope for future remembrance or present reputation. But since he was involved in expenses greater than his means, he was compelled to be harsh toward his subjects, for the great number of things on which he spent money as gifts to some caused him to be the source of harm to those from whom he took this money. And though he was aware of being hated because of the wrongs that he had done his subjects, he decided that it would not be easy to mend his evil ways—that would have been unprofitable in respect of revenue—and, instead, countered their opposition by seizing upon their ill-will as an opportunity for satisfying his wants. (*Ant.* 16.153–56)

As Herod's remarkable munificence to imperial family and foreign cities continued, the severe economic strain on his subjects continued to the end of his reign. When Herod finally died, popular protesters clamored for tax relief. And, according to Josephus, a high-level delegation of Jews who traveled to Rome to lobby against continuation of Herodian rule argued that Herod had "reduced the entire people to helpless poverty" by his heavy taxation and forcible collection of tribute (*Ant.* 17.204–5, 307–9). In "lavishing the lifeblood of Judea on foreign communities, [he had] crippled the towns in his own dominion . . . and had reduced the nation to poverty" (*War* 2.84–85).

Herod's cultural-economic role in the ancient Roman imperial order thus parallels the effects of multinational corporations in the emerging global capitalist order in significant ways. In pursuit of profits, contemporary mega-corporations and banks drain resources from third-world countries that enhance the wealth and lifestyle of the urban elite in the metropolitan centers of the new world order. In the Roman imperial order the motive was different but the effects were the same. In pursuit of honor, Herod drained resources from a subjected people to fund lavish cultural construction projects that enhanced the life of the urban elite in the metropolitan centers.

In addition to bleeding the Judean and Galilean people dry, of course, Herod was also flouting their sacred traditions with his dedications to Caesar, his institution of alien "culture" such as spectacles in the theater and amphitheater, and the style of his building projects. The fact that he did not construct any monuments to Caesar on Jewish territory proper indicates that Herod well knew that his many temples and other dedications to Caesar were anathema to his Jewish subjects. Yet he still had the audacity to erect a huge golden eagle over a gate of the temple, a symbol of Roman domination and a gross violation of the commandment against images (*Ant.* 15.328, 339–40, 364–65; 17.151; *War* 1.650).

Resistance and Repression

It is not surprising that Herod's Jewish subjects never really acquiesced in his rule. Indeed, there was persistent resistance to it. Pharisees and some other scribal circles were never completely reconciled. The Pharisees refused to take a loyalty oath to Herod and some Pharisees at court apparently became engaged in plotting a palace coup (*Ant.* 15.370–71; 17.41–45). Early in Herod's reign a conspiracy to assassinate the king formed, but was discovered through an informer (*Ant.* 15.281–83). The resistance that persisted throughout Herod's reign took a most dramatic symbolic form immediately before his death. Two revered teachers in Jerusalem inspired some of their students to tear down the golden Roman eagle from above the temple gate, in defense "of the law of our fathers!" (*War* 1.648–53; *Ant.* 17.149–59; cf. 17.276; 15.286, 365, etc.).

No effective resistance could take hold, however, because Herod instituted ever more severe repressive measures, replete with informers, secret police, fortresses, and pointedly intimidating brutality. In some of the most ugly incidents, Herod killed his own in-laws or wives, as it suited his purposes or whim at the time. He clearly became increasingly paranoid toward the end of his life. He even had his two eldest sons, who had previously been his intended successors, executed. Augustus is reported to have remarked that it was better to be Herod's pig (*hus*) than his son (*huios*).[15]

Such vicious attacks on his own family members, however, should not divert attention from the brutality with which he treated the people in general and the whole system of exploitation, repression, and fear that Herod instituted in his realm.

"He decided to hem the people in on all sides lest their disaffection should become open rebellion" (*Ant.* 15.291). For his own security "against the whole people," he improved or constructed a network of fortified palaces and fortresses, both in Jerusalem itself and around the countryside (*Ant.* 14.419; 15.242, 323–35; 16.143; *War* 1.265, 419–21). In addition to his own bodyguard, he maintained foreign mercenary troops of Thracians, Germans, and Gauls, and military colonies in Sebaste and Gaba, just south of Galilee, as backup forces (*Ant.* 15.293–94; 17.198). "He placed garrisons throughout the entire nation so as to minimize the chance of [the Jews] taking things into their own hands" (*Ant.* 15.195). We may need to take with a certain grain of salt some of Josephus's portrayals that make Herod's regime sound like a virtual modern police state with its historically unprecedented instruments of torture and techniques of intimidation. Even when we allow for a certain amount of exaggeration, the description is a sobering reminder of the techniques of control used by certain modern third-world regimes that were/are ostensible clients of the United States:

No meeting of people was permitted, nor were walking together or being together permitted, and all their movements were observed. Those who were caught were punished severely, and many were taken, either openly or secretly, to the fortress of Hyrcania and there put to death. Both in the city and on the open roads there were men who spied upon those who met together.... Those who obstinately refused to go along with his [new] practices he persecuted in all kinds of ways. (*Ant.* 15.366–67)

Herod instituted repressive laws in violation of the Jewish law. For example, "that housebreakers should be sold [into slavery]" violated the prohibition in the Torah against selling fellow Jews into slavery to aliens (*Ant.* 16.1–5). He systematically arrested what would be called "political prisoners," as indicated by the crowd's clamor at his death for "the release of the prisoners who had been put in chains by Herod—and there were many of these and they had been in prison for a long time" (*Ant.* 17.204). Others had simply been killed while in prison (17.11).

Herod's retaliation against any serious resistance, finally, was brutal and thorough. The revered teachers of Torah and their students who had pulled down the Roman eagle from the gate of the temple Herod "had burned alive; and the remainder of those arrested [in the incident] he handed over to his executioners" (*War* 1.655). A striking illustration of how Herod's tyranny could touch off a sequence of resistance, violent repression, further frustrated resistance, and brutal retaliation is the conspiracy of assassination early in his reign. When one of Herod's undercover agents discovered the plot, the would-be assassins were caught virtually in the act, tortured, and viciously executed. But sympathizers with the conspiracy caught the informer, chopped him up, and threw him to the dogs. Herod then tortured the witnesses to the latter incident and, having identified the participants, punished them and their whole families as well (*Ant.* 15.281–90). These and two other cases where Herod brutally executed large groups of actual or suspected conspirators (see also *Ant.* 16.393–94; 17.42–44) are particularly important for appreciating the historical verisimilitude of the massacre story in Matthew 2, since they indicate the ruthless retaliation he took against any potential rival or insurrection.

Nor did Herodian tyranny and repression end when Herod "the Great" died, as the story in Matthew 2 indicates in Joseph's fear about relocating in Judea under Herod's son and successor, Archelaus (Matt. 2:22). When, following Herod's death, crowds demonstrated at the Passover festival in the temple for relief from taxes and tyranny, Archelaus sent out the troops: "The soldiers falling unexpectedly upon the various parties busy with their sacrifices slew about three thousand of them and dispersed the remainder among the neighboring hills" (*War* 2.10–13; *Ant.* 17.213–18). After only ten years, the Romans deposed Archelaus as incompetent. But the Roman governors and the high priestly families picked up where Herod and Archelaus left off. The Roman governors such as Pontius Pilate, of course, typically sent out the troops at the first sign of a protest or popular unrest. Continuing through the lifetime of Jesus and the early decades of the Jesus movements, the high priestly families expanded their own wealth by bringing more and more peasants into their control as debtors. With their burgeoning wealth they also continued to build themselves lavish mansions in the New City to the west of the temple. As both Josephus and rabbinic literature attest, the high priestly families became increasingly predatory on the people they supposedly represented. For example, they sent goon squads out to the threshing floors to seize the tithes by force, thus both intimidating the peasants and depriving the ordinary priests of their livelihood. Rabbinic literature recites a lament reminiscent of the exploitative practices of the four high priestly families who monopolized power, whether of scribal violence or of physical violence:

> Woe is me because of the house of Boethus,
>   Woe is me because of their staves. . . .
> Woe is me because of the house of Kathros,
>   Woe is me because of their pens.
> Woe is me because of the house of Ishmael ben Phiabi,
>   Woe is me because of their fists.
> For they are high priests, and their sons are treasurers,
>   and their sons-in-law are temple overseers,
>   and their servants beat the people with clubs.
>   (tractate *Pesahim* 57a in the Babylonian Talmud,
>   tractate *Menahoth* 13.21 in the Tosepta)

Birth of the Messiah:
People's Movements of Rebellion and Renewal

By the time Herod died, the resentment held in check by his repressive regime had built up an explosive pressure. As already noted, shortly after his death and continuing into Passover time, crowds gathered in the temple to protest, crying out for release of political prisoners, tax relief, and the appointment of a high priest more in accord with the Jewish law (*Ant.* 17.204–8). By the festival of Pentecost, the protests escalated into a virtual popular revolt, with groups of villagers from the various districts of Galilee, Idumea, and the trans-Jordan, as well as from Judea, in effect besieging the Roman troops in the city in their eagerness to "recover their country's freedom" (*Ant.* 17.254–68). Within weeks, in every major district of the country, popular movements of rebellion erupted, headed by figures acclaimed by their followers as kings. For the next seventy years, under Herod's successors as Rome-appointed rulers in Jerusalem, many resistance and renewal movements arose among the people. According to the story in Matthew 2, Jesus' birth in Bethlehem and flight into Egypt occurred at the very end of Herod's reign and his return to Nazareth occurred right about the time that Galilean and Judean peasants were joining movements of rebellion headed by these popular "messiahs." An examination of these popular movements makes it clear that the story of Jesus' birth is about the people's persistent rebellion against oppressive rule and burning hopes for liberation from imperial domination.

Messianic Movements: Jesus' Birth as a Paradigm of the Persistence of Popular Resistance

Not surprisingly, given that the Rome-appointed Idumean Herod was utterly illegitimate as "king of the Jews" and a hated tyrant to boot, when the explosions came many took the particular form of *messianic* movements led by popular kings, which were deeply rooted in Israelite tradition. Because biblical scholars deal primarily with texts, they have usually looked to the texts left by the Judean scribal elite, such as the Dead Sea Scrolls, for evidence of "messianic expectation." And there is indeed some evidence for scribal fantasies of a messiah. Josephus reports that in a court intrigue some Pharisees prophesied that the kingdom would be taken from Herod by a new king who would bring the restoration of wholeness (*Ant.* 17.43–45). The visionary Pharisees were executed, of course, but they provide a glimpse of how the people, suffering under an illegitimate and tyrannical king, were yearning for a king who would establish covenantal justice for the people. *Psalms of Solomon* 17 provides a relatively isolated case of scribal hopes for an anointed son of David who, in utter contrast to Herod, would not only liberate the people from the Romans rather than serve as their lackey, but also do so in scribal manner, convincing them by the words of his mouth, rather than by military means. One wonders whether the various references to "anointed" figures in the Dead Sea Scrolls written around this time were also—directly or indirectly—reactions to the reign of an illegitimate and unacceptable king ruling Judea/Israel in ways contrary to the Judean scriptures.

We should not imagine, however, that there existed any standard "messianic expectation" or a widely shared concept of "the Messiah" in Judean and Galilean society. The notion that the Jews at the time of Jesus had a standardized expectation of "the Messiah" who was coming to save the people is a Christian construct to set up the role of Jesus as the fulfillment of that expectation. Except for those scattered references in the *Psalms of Solomon* and the Dead Sea Scrolls, however, extant Judean literature of the Second Temple period makes virtually no reference to a "messiah."[16] Throughout the period, the political-economic-religious head of the Judean temple-community was the high priest. Except for a dissident scribal movement or two in late Second Temple times, there is not much literary evidence for expectations of either an "anointed" (messiah) king or an eschatological prophet. This makes it all the more striking that—beginning at the death of Herod and continuing under the rule of the Roman governors and the Roman client-rulers, the Jerusalem high priests—the Judean and Galilean peasants repeatedly produced movements led either by a popular (anointed) king or a popular prophet. Not the sparse expectations of dissident scribal intellectuals, but the many contemporary movements alive among the Judean and Galilean people provide the background against which we can understand Jesus' ministry in general and the infancy stories like Matthew 2 in particular.[17]

Of great significance for the way Jesus is represented in Matthew and other Gospel materials is the social form assumed by the widespread popular uprisings in Galilee, Judea, and the trans-Jordan area following the death of Herod. Josephus reports that in each of these three areas the insurgent peasants acclaimed one of their own number as "king." If we translate Josephus's Greek-style historiography back into the idiom of Israelite tradition, this suggests that the followers of these "kings" were acclaiming them as their "messiah," just as the Israelites of old had popularly acclaimed David as their "anointed one." It is significant that—besides the stories of Samuel (playing the role of the prophet representing God) pouring oil on the heads of ("anointing") Saul and David—the narrative in 1 Samuel includes accounts of the people themselves (or their representative elders) "anointing" David as king (1 Sam. 2:1–4; 5:1–4). The latter are stories of *popular kingship,* in contrast to the imperial kingship represented in literature that derives from the court life in Jerusalem (e.g., Psalms 2 and 110), where the later Davidic kings underwent elaborate ceremonial coronation. From the biblical portrayals of the young David, and those of Saul and Jehu as well, we can see that popularly anointed kingship involved three key aspects. The young David was popularly elected by the people as their leader. The initial purpose of the popular "messiah-ing" of the king was to lead the people in freeing themselves from oppressive foreign or domestic rule, such as by the Philistines (Saul and David) or by Ahab and Jezebel (Jehu, Kings 9). And such popular kingship was conditional on the "messiah-ed" one maintaining justice. When David established a more imperial monarchy in Jerusalem, the Israelite tribes mounted massive rebellions against him (1 Sam. 15–21).

Thus, when the insurgent peasants in the Israelite areas of Herod's realm acclaimed one of their number as "king," they were acting out an age-old "script" deeply rooted in Israelite biblical tradition. We moderns know of this "script" only because we find evidence of it in biblical literature such as 1 and 2 Samuel and 1 and 2 Kings. But anthropologists and other modern scholars who conduct comparative studies of traditional agrarian societies would recognize what these Judean and Galilean peasants were doing as working out of their own "little" or popular tradition. Peasants may not be able to read, but they know very well their ancestral traditions. They conduct their own village affairs according to time-honored customs, which in the case of Galilean and Judean peasants would have been those of the Mosaic covenant. And in their individual and collective memory they know well the stories of the great heroes of old, in this case Saul, David, and Jehu, who led successful struggles against oppressive foreign rulers. When similar new crises arise, then the people take action informed precisely by those memories. The situation at the death of Herod, the oppressive king imposed by the Romans, the latest empire to bring them into subjection, called for the people again to acclaim their own kings and again retake control of their lives, as had the earlier Israelites under Saul, David, or Jehu.

A number of aspects of these movements have significance for Jesus as a "messiah" of a parallel movement, as represented in Matthew's nativity narrative and the Gospels in general. These were widespread and at least temporarily successful movements of liberation among the Galilean, Judean, and other Israelite people. In Galilee, the movement headed by Judas son of Hezekiah, the popular brigand-chieftain murdered by Herod a generation earlier, successfully attacked the royal fortress-palace in the district capital of Sepphoris and took back the goods that had been seized from the people and stored there (agricultural produce seized as taxes? *Ant.* 17.271). In Perea and the Jordan valley, the people (in their "madness"=divine inspiration?), proclaiming Simon, a former slave of Herod, as their king, burned the royal palace at Jericho after reclaiming the goods that had been seized there, and attacked the mansions of the wealthy elite (*War* 2.57–59; *Ant.* 17.273–77). In Judea, the most successful of these movements acclaimed a "mere shepherd" named Athronges as their messiah, who held councils for democratic discussion of major decisions. This movement in Judea, by conducting guerrilla warfare against the Herodian mercenary troops and the Roman troops sent in to reconquer the country, was able to maintain the people's independence for two or three years before the Romans could finally "pacify" the countryside again.

The sustained success of the messianic movements in Judea indicates just how serious these messiah-led peasant revolts were for the Romans. They had to commit a huge army of three legions, four troops of cavalry, and auxiliary forces from Syria for their reconquest of Palestine. The Roman army conducted a "scorched earth" campaign, with "search and destroy" missions throughout the countryside (*War* 2.66–75; *Ant.* 17.286–95). For example, they burned Sepphoris (or the area around it, including the village of Nazareth) and enslaved the inhabitants. They burned to the ground the town of Emmaus (known also as the scene of one of Jesus' resurrection appearances in Luke 24). After the "search and destroy" missions, the Romans crucified the "rebels" they caught as a combination of retaliation for the revolt and as a terrorizing warning to the people of the consequences of disrupting the "Roman peace."

The Gospel representations of Jesus as well as Jesus himself and his ministry must be understood in connection with these popular messianic movements—in several interrelated ways. The social form taken by these widespread revolts, that of popular messianic movements, was one of the principal forms also evident in the Gospel portrayals of Jesus' preaching and practice. Most obvious perhaps is that Jesus was crucified as "the king of the Jews/Israel." The memory of these movements and the Roman reconquest would have been vivid in the minds of people involved in or acquainted with the Jesus movement in such places as Nazareth and Emmaus, where whole villages of people had been slaughtered, enslaved, or crucified. As we know from modern experience of warfare and its effects, in areas where a "whole district became a scene of fire and blood," the collective memory, not to say trauma, would have left deep scars in the social fabric. Such effects would have influenced the Jesus movement itself and the formation of Gospel materials. The additional messianic movements that emerged during the great Jewish revolt in 66–70 C.E. would have further influenced the shaping of the Gospel materials and Matthew's Gospel, which was written well after 70. Particularly significant would have been the movement headed by Simon bar Giora in Judea and Idumea that emerged as the largest rebel force fighting against the Roman reconquest from 68–70. Simon himself was the captured enemy "general" taken to Rome and ceremonially executed as "the King of the Judeans" in the formal Triumph of the *Imperator Vespasian* and his son Titus. To be telling yet another story about a child "who has been born king of the Jews" (Matt. 2:2) in the aftermath of the great revolt of 66–70 would have required firm resolve in resistance against the Roman imperial order.

Prophetic Movements: Jesus' Birth as a New Exodus from Imperial Domination

Other popular initiatives toward independence and renewal of Israel, in opposition to Herodian and Jerusalem high priestly and Roman imperial order, took the social form of *prophetic* movements. In Judea, two in particular were memorable, the first coming almost immediately following the reign of another "Herod," Agrippa I, as king of the Jews in 41–44, another Herod with a flair for costly massive building projects, lavish gifts to Greek cities, and festivals in honor of Caesar that would have been highly objectionable to those faithful to the Law (*Ant.* 19.299–311, 327, 331–52):

> When Fadus was governor of Judea (4–46 C.E.) a charlatan named Theudas persuaded most of the common people to take their possessions and follow him to the Jordan river. He said he was a prophet, and that at his command the river would be divided and allow them an easy crossing. (*Ant.* 20.97)[18]

The other most memorable movement in Judea proper came a decade later under the governor Felix:

> At this time, a certain man from Egypt arrived at Jerusalem, saying he was a prophet and advising the mass of common people to go with him to the Mount of Olives, which is just opposite the city.... He said that from there he wanted to show them that at his command the walls of Jerusalem would fall down and they could then make an entry into the city. (*Ant.* 20.169–70; cf. *War* 2.261–62)

Through Josephus's hostile portrayal of these and other such movements, we can discern that, like the popular messianic movements, these also were informed by and patterned after important events in Israelite tradition. Josephus reports that such prophets led their followers out into the wilderness to show them "wonders and signs" that would happen "in accordance with God's design" as "tokens of their freedom" (*Ant.* 20.168; *War* 2.259). With such terms he indicates that they were promising new events like those of the exodus from foreign rule in Egypt, the formative event in Israel's history, and the further events, once the people had taken possession of the land, when God the divine warrior fought on behalf of his people against outside forces who threatened to reestablish foreign domination (e.g., Deut. 26:7–8; and many examples in the books of Joshua and Judges). The movement led by the "Egyptian" Jewish prophet was clearly expecting God to effect a new action of liberation of the land similar to the "battle of Jericho" led by Joshua (Josh. 6), with the result that the Judean people would again be free of foreign rule once the Romans were eliminated from Jerusalem (clearer in the account in *War* 2.261–62). In expectation of parting the waters of the Jordan river, Theudas was leading a movement of new exodus and/or new occupation of the land, as the new Moses and/or Joshua. A similar movement had sprung up in Samaria a decade before the one led by Theudas, in which a prophet led his followers to the top of the sacred mountain Gerizim, where he promised to find the sacred vessels buried there by Moses (*Ant.* 18.85). All of the prophetic movements that occurred in mid–first century were clearly anticipating new acts of deliverance patterned after the great formative events of Israel's liberation from Egypt and establishment in the land, led by Moses and Joshua.

Like the messianic movements, moreover, these movements involved a large number of followers from the peasantry and appeared as a serious threat to the Roman governors charged with maintaining the Roman imperial order. Josephus may well be exaggerating when he says that the "Egyptian" Jewish prophet had gathered about thirty thousand to his cause, but he consistently writes that the prophets had rallied the "mass" or "majority" of the common people. Josephus also gives clear indications that these movements were fired by the Spirit, the people responding to divine inspiration and revelation, and that the "freedom" they anticipated would have meant "revolutionary changes" in the established imperial order (*War* 2.259). It seems fairly clear that these prophetic movements, far from being revolts like the popular messianic movements, were nonviolent actions in anticipation of miraculous divine intervention. Nevertheless, the Roman governors sent out the troops and/or cavalry who simply killed those they captured. "Having captured Theudas himself, they cut off his head and carried it off to Jerusalem" (*Ant.* 20.98, 171).

These prophetic movements that occurred shortly after the ministry of Jesus and during the time that Gospel materials were taking shape are even more significant than the messianic movements for our understanding of the story in Matthew 2 and for the Gospels in general. The prophetic movements provide windows onto the popular pattern or "script" that informs not only the story in Matthew 2, but the Gospel materials generally, and indicates how deeply rooted it was in Israelite popular tradition and in village life at the time. In their attempts to resist Herodian, high priestly, and Roman domination, and to renew their society according to Israelite traditions, the Judean people did not necessarily mount revolts led by popularly acclaimed kings. The continuing memory of Moses and Joshua, of the exodus and the claiming of the land, were still very much alive among the people as a model they could follow in generating a renewal movement.

The clear presence of this pattern of memory and action among the people in the historical context in which Jesus and the Gospel materials emerged makes it all the clearer that the story in Matthew 2 is drawing heavily on exodus tradition. Comparison with these other Moses- or Joshua-like prophets and their movements, however, enables us to discern more precisely the way Jesus is presented in the infancy story and how this prologue prepares the way for the rest of the Gospel of Matthew. The features of Jesus' infancy in Matthew 2 that repeat or allude to similar motifs in Moses' infancy, such as the threat from a hostile king, should not lead us to conclude that the story presents Jesus as a new Moses. Rather those motifs are parts of a larger scheme that presents the events surrounding Jesus' birth and infancy as recapitulating the events of the origin of Israel as a people.[19] The sequence of events in Matthew 2—that Herod sought to kill Jesus so that he had to go down into Egypt, whence God called the "son" to return to the land of Israel—re-presents the origins of Israel in the origins of Jesus. The story in Matthew 2 in effect juxtaposes two scripts, that of the popular messiah like

David who is (to be) "a ruler ... to shepherd my people Israel" with that of
the new exodus pursued by the popular prophetic movements. But Jesus in
Matthew 2 is not a new Moses—yet.

In the infancy story that provides the prologue to the rest of the Gospel, Jesus represents (the child) Israel about to undergo deliverance. When
Matthew then presents Jesus in his ministry, he does place him in the role
of a new Moses, delivering the renewed covenant on the mountain (Matt.
5–7), performing miraculous sea crossings and wilderness feedings, appoint-
ing twelve representative heads of the people, and sending out envoys for
the mission in renewal of the house of Israel. In the infancy story, however,
Jesus is not a new Moses. He is the one born "the king of the Jews," but
is also representative of the people in desperate need of renewal, oppressed
under the Roman-imposed imperial client-rulers. His very origin consists of
a recapitulation of the exodus origins of Israel, their deliverance from foreign rule. And that deliverance is comprehensive, inclusive of the political
dimension. There is no warrant in the story for reducing it to an event in
the history of (religious/spiritual) salvation. The child born in Bethlehem is
"the king of the Jews" who, as "a ruler who is to shepherd my people Israel," will displace Herod as "the king of the Jews"—and by implication the
Roman imperial order that maintains Herod in oppressive power over the
people. Even if modern Western interpreters, with their separation of church
and state, religion and politics, do not "get it," Herod certainly does, and
orders out the death squads. But Israel has been through repression before,
beginning with its origins. And Joseph, trusting in the Lord who has brought
Israel through other crises, receives the needed message from the Lord and
takes action to lead Jesus through the recapitulation of the exodus that prepares him for his role in the renewal of Israel that the rest of the Gospel is
about to present.

The Magi's Visit:
International Political Implications of Jesus' Birth

The Magi appear politically naïve in going to the reigning "king of the Jews"
to inquire where they can find the newborn child who will displace him. But
they have a political significance in the story that raises the struggle between
Roman imperial client-king and subjected people to a level of global conflict between empires, Eastern versus Western and, ultimately, God's versus
Rome's. To appreciate their fuller function in the story as a whole, it is necessary to understand some of the dynamics of inter-imperial politics around
the time of Jesus.

Although the Greek term *magos* was used for a magician, astrologer,
or dream interpreter, it had a more distinctive meaning in Greco-Roman
culture, as indicated in many Greek and Latin sources. The Greeks and
Romans were intrigued by the *magoi*, who had originally been high-ranking

political-religious advisers in the imperial court of the Medes and then the Persians. Early Christian art portrays the Magi in the same typical Persian or Parthian dress of trousers, belted tunics with full sleeves, and Phrygian caps as they appear in Roman imperial art.[20] In the Persian empire, the Magi had been the royal priestly assistants of the Great King or King of Kings who specialized in communication with the gods in order to ensure the welfare and productivity of the empire (Herodotus 1.132, 140; 7.191, 133–34; Strabo 15.3.13–14, 18; Xenophon, *Cyropaedia* 7.5.35, 57; 8.1.23–24). "The Magi attend the Persian kings...guiding them in their relations with the gods," says the geographer Strabo (15.1.68). Xenophon specifies further that "the Magi interpret the will of the gods.... The college of Magi was instituted [by Cyrus] and he never failed to sing hymns to the gods at daybreak and to sacrifice daily to whatsoever deities the Magi directed. Thus the institutions he established at that time have continued in force with each successive king even to this day" (*Cyropaedia* 4.5.51; 8.1.23–24).

In the legend of Cyrus's own infancy, the Magi interpreted the Median king Astyages's dream and advised him on the appropriate course of action (Herodotus 1.107–8, 120, 128, 204; Cicero, *De divinatione* 1.23.46). Their interpretation of heavenly bodies could affect international politics. When an eclipse of the sun occurred at the beginning of Xerxes' expedition against the Greeks, the Magi advised him that the god was indicating to the Greeks the desolation of their cities (Herodotus 7.37). It is thus not surprising that they were associated in Greco-Roman circles with astrology. The book of Daniel (1:20; 3:3; 4:7; 5:7) portrays them pejoratively as "magicians and enchanters" at the Babylonian court, retrojected from Jewish scribal familiarity with the Persian regime. Generally the Magi were indeed "wise and learned men" (Cicero, *De divinatione* 1.23.46), cultivating knowledge of the heavens as part of their role of interpreting the will of the gods. During the Hellenistic empires, the Magi were settled in a wide variety of places, from Babylon and Cappadocia to western Anatolia and even Arabia and Egypt (Strabo 15.3.14–15; Pliny, *Natural History* 25.13). They attended the goddess Anahita, who had been fused with Artemis at Ephesus (Thucydides 8.109; Cicero, *De divinatione* 1.23.47; Plutarch, *Alexander* 3.4). With the Magi operating in such close proximity, the Greeks' and Romans' knowledge of their roles was more than a dim but exotic memory.

What goes unnoticed among interpreters of the Gospels, because they tend to ignore ancient political affairs, is that the Magi apparently played a significant role in ancient Near Eastern opposition to Hellenistic (Western) imperial rule.[21] The Greeks had long looked down upon "barbarians" as inferior peoples, an attitude that carried over into Hellenistic imperial rule of Eastern peoples such as the Persians, who were regarded as decadent and weak. The dream in Daniel 7 represents the Hellenistic empire as far more brutal and ferocious than the earlier, Eastern empires. We should not imagine, however, that the Judeans were the only people to resent Hellenistic rule. Prior to the book of Daniel (early second century B.C.E.), the standard scheme of an increasingly decadent or oppressive series of empires had developed and may even go back to a Persian source.[22] In addition, various prophecies articulated a yearning among Near Eastern peoples for a restoration of Persian or other indigenous kingship.[23] Because of their previous attachment to the Persian regime as the divinely ordained imperial order and their wide dispersion in the Near East under Hellenistic imperial rule, the Magi appear to be prime candidates for the authors and/or carriers of such resistance to Western imperial rule.[24] Cicero passed on a story very revealing in this connection: "Everybody knows that on the same night in which Olympias was delivered of Alexander [the Great] the temple of Diana at Ephesus was burned, and that the Magi began to cry out as the day was breaking: 'Asia's deadly curse was born last night'" (*De divinatione* 1.23.47). As already noted, during the first century B.C.E. and continuing into the first century C.E., the Roman and Parthian empires were in continual confrontation and often warfare. Would not the Magi have identified—and been identified—with the Parthians in opposition to the Roman Empire?

In connection with this East-West struggle between empires for control of the eastern Mediterranean peoples, we should take another look at a famous, spectacularly staged political event in 66 C.E. that may provide a revealing comparison and contrast with the story in Matthew 2. Facing the impossibility of maintaining its own puppet ruler in Armenia against Parthian power, Rome agreed to accept the Parthian candidate as king if he would receive his crown from the Roman emperor. Thus, with an entourage of other Parthian client-kings, servants, three thousand horsemen, and Magi, the Armenian king Tiridates launched on a triumphal procession, greeted with great pomp and circumstance along the way, to Naples, where he did obeisance to Nero, the Roman emperor. Then in a triumphal procession in Rome itself, "as the king approached . . . the emperor at first let him fall at his feet, but then raised him . . . and kissed him. Then, while the king made supplication, Nero took the turban from his head and replaced it with a diadem" (Suetonius, *Nero* 13; and more elaborately, Dio Cassius, *Roman History* 67.1–7). Pliny even calls Tiridates himself a magus, and claims that he initiated Nero into the sacred banquets of the Magi who were accompanying him (*Natural History* 30.6.17). The many accounts of this event indicate clearly the international political context of such a "journey of the Magi" and its political as well as religious implications. The East-West imperial conflict was still a burning issue and the Magi were known as ranking political-religious advisers to Eastern kings in the Roman Empire just at the time the story in Matthew was taking form and being told.

In light of this well-known international political event, by including the visit of the Magi the story in Matthew 2 situates the birth of "the king of the Jews" squarely in the context of the sustained struggle between Rome (and Hellenism) and the East. That is, it is not enough simply to acknowledge that the birth of Jesus has political significance. That should be clear enough from the star that the Magi are following. Common among ancient peoples, including the intellectuals who wrote literature, was the belief that heavenly signs marked the births or deaths of great political leaders and rulers.[25] The visit of the Magi signals that something of far more ominous historical significance is happening with the birth of Jesus. Here are figures famous in the West as the ranking advisers to the Persian King of Kings, seeking out and doing obeisance to the newborn king of a small, insignificant people supposedly subject to Rome. For the people telling the story, moreover, who are not the Romans but those people subjected to Roman imperial rule, the Magi also represent the longing among Near Eastern people generally, including but not only the Jews, for liberation from alien Western imperial rule and restoration of their own independence and/or indigenous rule. Here at last the indigenous king of the Jews has been born. And here are the Magi (*the* Eastern figures who would possess the requisite wisdom and divine revelation to know about this) come to do obeisance to the king—or to the new "king of kings." The obeisance they render is not worship of a divinity, but an act of homage and submission to a political ruler, expressing the international political import of the child's birth. This raises the level of importance of the child's anticipated displacement of the tyrannical Herod as king of the Jews to worldwide political significance. The story is not about the displacement of an old religion by a new one, "Judaism" by "Christianity," but about the displacement of the Roman imperial order, represented by Herod, by the newborn "king of the Jews," who brings a liberation from imperial rule that has international implications.

Along with the international political aspect of the Magis' visit, finally, we must appreciate the wide gulf of class division that is being bridged in their action. The Magi, high-ranking royal priests and advisers to the Persian kings, are proclaiming in their obeisance that an ordinary peasant child has been born as the new king. Matthew has already indicated that Jesus is in the lineage of Abraham and David. But insofar as he is born in Bethlehem, a peasant village, he is hardly born into a position of power and privilege. That is what Herod in the capital city of Jerusalem represents in the story and that is what the birth of Jesus is challenging. There was a distinct difference between the Israelite tradition of *popular* resistance to foreign imperial rule and yearning for liberation of the people, on the one hand, and *aristocratic* resistance to Western imperial rule elsewhere in the ancient Near East, on the other. The Magi represent the latter, doing homage to a newborn leader of a popular movement of liberation and renewal.

The story of Herod, the Magi, the birth of Jesus, and Herod's massacre of the children of Bethlehem reminds the hearers that Jesus, the movement he spearheaded, and the communities that focused on him as the martyred and vindicated Messiah began in recapitulating the exodus origins of Israel from foreign rule in Egypt. The story reminds its hearers that the client-rulers of the Roman Empire took the most violent measures to stamp out movements by subject peoples to reclaim and renew their common life. And yet, under the providential care of God, Jesus survived to launch a movement of renewal, as the Messiah and the new Moses. By the time Matthew was composed, the movement had expanded through the people of Israel and beyond, among other peoples subject to Rome. The Judean and Galilean people had sustained a revolt against Herodian rulers and the high priestly aristocracy in Jerusalem, along with their Roman imperial sponsors. And the Roman armies had devastated the countryside and destroyed Jerusalem and its Temple. The movement that finds expression in the Gospel of Matthew, however, persisted in its attempt to structure life in communities that stood up against and provided an alternative to the Roman imperial order.[26] The story of the life-and-death struggle between Herod and the newborn "king of the Jews" grounds the continuing struggle of people to form and maintain an alternative to the kind of power relationships that Herod represented.

Notes

1. David R. Bauer, "The Kingship of Jesus in the Matthean Infancy Narrative: A Literary Analysis," *Catholic Biblical Quarterly* 57 (1995): 306–23, recognizes that "the kingship of Jesus challenges the rule of Herod" (314), yet still holds that Matthew does not understand Jesus' kingship in political terms, perpetuating the anachronistic imposition of modern separation of religion and politics onto biblical texts.

2. Krister Stendahl, "*Quis et Unde*—Who and Whence? Matthew's Christmas Gospel," (1961), repr. in Stendahl, *Meanings* (Philadelphia: Fortress, 1984), 71–83; G. M. Soares Prabhu, *The Formula Quotations in the Infancy Narrative of Matthew,* Analecta Biblica 63 (Rome: Pontifical Biblical Institute, 1976).

3. Concisely summarized and briefly evaluated by Arland Hultgren, "Matthew's Infancy Narrative and the Nativity of an Emerging Community," *Horizons in Biblical Theology* 19 (1997): 91–108.

4. For fuller development and documentation, see Richard A. Horsley, *The Liberation of Christmas: The Infancy Narratives in Social Context* (New York: Crossroad, 1989), chapter 3, on which the following arguments depend.

5. On Herod's rise to power, see the more detailed treatment in Peter Richardson, *Herod: King of the Jews and Friend of the Romans* (Columbia: University of South Carolina Press, 1996), 103–30.

6. For an example, see Richard A. Horsley, "Josephus and the Bandits," *Journal for the Study of Judaism in the Persian, Hellenistic, and Roman Periods* 10 (1979): 37–63.

7. For more detailed analysis of Herod's conquest of and rule in Galilee in particular, see Richard A. Horsley, *Galilee: History, Politics, People* (Valley Forge, Pa.: Trinity Press International, 1995), 52–61.

8. Critical analyses of the role of the high priestly families in the Roman imperial order in Richard A. Horsley, "High Priests and the Politics of Roman Palestine," *Journal for the Study of Judaism in the Persian, Hellenistic, and Roman Periods* 17 (1986): 23–55; and Martin Goodman, *The Ruling Class of Judea* (Cambridge: Cambridge University Press, 1987).

9. Concise general sketches of the political economy of Palestine under Roman rule in Richard A. Horsley, *Sociology and the Jesus Movement* (New York: Crossroad, 1989), chapter 4, and K. C. Hanson and Douglas Oakman, *Palestine in the Time of Jesus* (Minneapolis: Fortress, 1998), 101–25. More detailed analysis of various aspects, such as the Herodian royal lands, in Horsley, *Galilee*, chapter 9.

10. Menahem Stern, "The Reign of Herod," *World History of the Jewish People,* 7.79.

11. Presentation and interpretation of Herod's inscriptions on monuments and coins in Richardson, *Herod,* 203–15.

12. "The grandeur of the design, far from being incidental, was aimed at altering the image of Jews in the Roman world....It was the greatest religious precinct in the Roman world and...Herod was redefining the arrangements for Israel's temple worship." In Richardson, *Herod,* 247, 249.

13. "Sebaste was still under construction (27–12), Caesarea (22–10), the Temple in Jerusalem (23–15 for the main parts), Herodium (23–15), Panias (ca 20), Nicopolis (sometime after 27)." In Richardson, *Herod,* 193–94, who applies modern economic assumptions to interpret Herod's agenda.

14. Recent assessments of the Judean economy under Herod are Magen Broshi, "The Role of the Temple in the Herodian Economy," *Journal of Jewish Studies* 38 (1987): 31–37; and E. Gabba, "The Finances of King Herod," in *Greece and Rome in Eretz-Israel,* ed. A. Kasher, U. Rappaport, and G. Fuks (Jerusalem: Jerusalem Exploration Society, 1990), 160–68.

15. Macrobius, *Saturnalia* 2.4.2. That this late (around 400 C.E.) non-Christian writer links this quip with Herod's massacre of the children from Matthew 2 suggests that the two separate incidents had already come together in popular or literary tradition.

16. See, e.g., the many essays in Jacob Neusner, W. S. Green, and E. S. Frerichs, eds., *Judaisms and Their Messiahs at the Turn of the Christian Era* (Cambridge: Cambridge University Press, 1988); and James H. Charlesworth, ed., *The Messiah: Developments in Earliest Judaism and Christianity* (Minneapolis: Fortress, 1992).

17. On the preceding points and the ensuing presentation, see the fuller treatment in Richard A. Horsley with John S. Hanson, *Bandits, Prophets, and Messiahs* (San Francisco: Harper & Row, 1985; new edition, Harrisburg, Pa.: Trinity Press International, 1998), chapters 3 and 4; with closer analysis and documentation in Horsley, "Popular Messianic Movements around the Time of Jesus," *Catholic Biblical Quarterly* 46 (1984): 471–93; and " 'Like One of the Prophets of Old': Two Types of Popular Prophets at the Time of Jesus," *Catholic Biblical Quarterly* 47 (1985): 435–63.

18. This and the following passage in the translation by John S. Hanson, in Horsley with Hanson, *Bandits, Prophets, and Messiahs,* 164.

19. The parallels in Matthew 2 with the Moses story in Exodus 1–2, 4 are primarily in particular terms, thus probably allusions, but do not amount to parallel overall patterns of story. On why Matthew 2 cannot be understood as a midrash on a particular Exodus text, see Brown, *Birth of the Messiah,* appendix 8, 557–63. For potential parallels between Matthew 2 and accounts of Moses' infancy or the exodus story more generally, see recently Hultgren, "Matthew's Infancy Narrative," and Allison, *New Moses,* 140–64. The latter's suggestions about parallel patterns are intriguing but not convincing. I am suggesting that the discussion of Jewish accounts of Moses and/or the exodus be deepened and complicated, from the usual

focus on written texts and "intertexuality" of the literate circles ("great tradition") to include the popular ("little") tradition in a predominantly oral communications environment. The popular prophetic movements, known through Josephus's written accounts, give us one means of access.

20. See Richard C. Trexler, *The Journey of the Magi: Meanings in History of a Christian Story* (Princeton, N.J.: Princeton University Press, 1997), 22.

21. On this issue see the discussion in S. K. Eddy, *The King Is Dead* (Lincoln: University of Nebraska Press, 1961), chapter 3.

22. J. W. Swain, "The Theory of the Four Monarchies: Opposition History under the Roman Empire," *Classical Philology* 35 (1940): 1–21.

23. Eddy, *The King Is Dead,* 23–36.

24. Ibid., chapters 1–3.

25. Presumably the tellers and hearers of the story in Matthew 2 would have known that the Romans were uneasy about the appearance of heavenly bodies/signs. Nero, for example, was anxious about the appearance of a comet, "because it is commonly believed to portend the death of great rulers" (Suetonius, *Nero* 36). Seneca comments that "on even the slightest motion of heavenly bodies hang the fortune of nations" (*To Marcian on Consolation* 18.30). Several first-century emperors expelled astrologers from Rome: Tiberius (Tacitus, *Ann.* 2.32; Suetonius, *Tiberius* 36; Dio Cassius 57.15.8–9), Claudius (Tacitus, *Ann.* 12.52; Dio Cassius 61.33.3), Vespasian (Dio Cassius 65.9.2, 13.2), etc.

26. For a concise examination of how the Gospel of Matthew stands against the Roman imperial order, see Warren Carter, "Contested Claims: Roman Imperial Theology and Matthew's Gospel," *Biblical Theology Bulletin* 29 (1999): 56–67.

Part 4

Theoretical and Theological Reflections

Chapter Eight

Christmas

The Religion of Consumer Capitalism

Richard Horsley

A gigantic spruce tree erected on Boston Common near the State House was lavishly decorated in preparation for the annual Christmas tree lighting ceremony. In the hours preceding the ceremony in the city's center, the mayor moved from one neighborhood to another giving the signal to start the buses moving, all of them designed like old-fashioned trolleys and decorated for the season. People from every neighborhood then rode the trolleys downtown to the joyous ceremony on the Common, where they were joined by throngs from the suburbs. Gathering in a congregation of thousands around the multicolored holiday shrine there on the Common, and led by a chorus of hundreds, the people raised their collective voices in such favorite carols as "White Christmas" and "Rudolf the Red-Nosed Reindeer." The mayor, flanked by an entourage of city and state officials, spoke about the wonders of the holiday season and how the whole of greater Boston was ready to celebrate as never before. Finally, the mayor threw the switch that brought the lights alive, dazzling the whole congregation, who oohed and awed and cheered. Then, right on cue, Santa Claus made his epiphany. Another holiday season had "officially" begun... although the downtown, the malls, and the neighborhood centers had been elaborately decorated for weeks.

All of this was sponsored by Macy's, one of the big department stores, both downtown and in the malls around greater Boston, as announced in a full-page spread in the front section of both major Boston newspapers—the same gigantic retailing firm that has sponsored the nationally televised Macy's Thanksgiving Day parade in New York City every year since 1924. After the people from the city's neighborhoods and suburbs had participated in the lighting of the city Christmas tree, they made many more trips downtown or to the malls for their holiday shopping. To get further into the "holiday spirit," they could also experience the Enchanted Village, an extensive panorama of life-sized dioramas of Christmas in an early New England village, designed to induce intense nostalgia for an old-fashioned Christmas. Originally built and still sponsored by one of the big department stores, the

Enchanted Village has in recent years become more publicly installed on City Hall Plaza.

The American Holiday Festival as Religion

Although the extensive festival of Christmas or "the holidays" in America displays remarkable similarities to what we would call religious ceremonies in ancient Roman or Egyptian society, it is viewed as secular rather than sacred.[1] This is surely because of the separation of church and state, and the supposed broader separation of religion and politics and economics assumed in the United States. In America most people think of religion as what goes on in churches, synagogues, and mosques. If we ask students in an "Introduction to Religion" class what religion is, their first response is that it is personal faith. But this understanding of religion is peculiarly Western, indeed peculiarly American. It is heavily determined by the individualism that is so extreme in America, compared to other societies. When we then, in the course materials, come to societies that have no churches and no state, nothing discernible as individual faith, and/or no gods, we obviously need to broaden our understanding of religion.

In most societies, religion has been inseparable from politics and economics. In ancient Judea at the time of Jesus, for example, the temple was the political capital and the center of the economy, the high priests were the governing aristocracy, and sacrifices were offered daily for the Roman emperor. Tithes and offerings brought to the temple priests were, in effect, the taxes that supported the ruling institutions. Even in the 1780s a newly independent people in the United States understood the Bible to contain political history and teachings. The newly written United States Constitution was patterned after the covenant that God gave to Israel on Mount Sinai, which New England preachers viewed as a model of civil government. Reflective ancient Roman intellectuals such as Varro saw three interrelated kinds of religion operating in their society: "natural religion," which we might call metaphysics, ontology, or simply worldview; "mythic religion," which we would similarly call "mythology" or stories about the gods; and "civil religion," the religion of a city-state such as Rome. There was no such reality as *a* religion, let alone a world religion such as Christianity, the emergence of which as a separate religious institution was historically unprecedented in Western antiquity. Religion was simply one aspect of society that in turn had various aspects, such as the accepted view of the world/cosmos (natural religion), the stories of the gods of a society (mythic religion), and the temples, celebrations, shrines, and so on of the society (civil religion).[2]

Religion serves several interrelated functions in most societies. Among the most important are the establishment of personal and group identity, the embodiment of community, and the articulation of an overall meaning of life. All of these are expressed in systems of symbols, stories (myths, legends), and rituals. In ancient Athens, for example, the citizens' identity was constituted by being an Athenian, Athens being the corporate city-state community of which they were members. Both their community and their identity were expressed in the regular sacrifices and other rituals performed in the temples and shrines of the city. In the far more complex society of the Roman Empire, however, religion also was complex and took multiple forms. An elaborate ceremony of initiation into the mysteries of the (originally Egyptian) goddess Isis, for example, might establish a new transcendent identity for a "lost soul" in one of the great faceless cities of the Roman Empire, but not provide much of a supportive community.[3] A Diaspora Jewish "assembly" in that same city, however, provided Jewish residents both membership in the wider community of Israel and a meaning of life connected with the historical destiny of the Jewish people. In that same Roman Empire, however, the religion of a semi-separate people such as the Judean temple-community combined all aspects, identity, community, and meaning, in a way that distinguished them from the larger Roman Empire. The celebration of the Passover in Jerusalem by Judean villagers would have united the Judean people in reenactment of their formative history of liberation from slavery in Egypt and reinforced their longings for God's new act of deliverance from Roman rule.

From these examples it is clear that in a complex society divided into different classes and/or varied ethnic communities, religion usually operates at multiple levels, from those of the individual, the family, and the local community to those of the whole nation or even the international community. Buddhist meditation and "saying the Rosary" operate at the individual level. Cereal offerings and libations set on ancestral graves in an ancient Roman or a traditional Chinese family established solidarity and continuity with the ancestors and conveyed a sense that the family would continue into future generations. The gathering of the village assembly (=synagogue) at the time of Jesus or services in a small town Methodist church or Mass in an Irish Catholic parish in Boston would reinforce the solidarity and cooperative spirit of the (relatively homogeneous) local community. The annual celebration of the New Year's festival in ancient Mesopotamia established the order of the whole society settled in the Tigris and Euphrates River valley, including their worldview focused on the order of their universe. The modern family-based celebration of Passover unites all Jewish families around the world as a people, Israel, and confirms their distinctive Jewish worldview.

As is becoming clear in a number of recent investigations and in the preceding chapters, the traditional and current celebration of Christmas in America has little to do with the birth of Christ. In fact, Christmas was only very partially and superficially "christianized" in the late nineteenth and early twentieth centuries. As delineated in these studies, Christmas has grown exponentially into more than a month-long season of *holydays* stretching from before the previously most important holy day of the American civil religion, Thanksgiving, to New Year's (or even to the Super Bowl on Super Sunday). These holidays are arguably the most sustained and elaborate

society-wide festival in history. More important, this historically unprecedented festival incorporates every aspect of religion (meaning, community,
identity, symbol system) at every social level of society (individual, family,
community, national). Moreover, the holiday festival includes every major
function of religion in ways that blur or collapse the supposed separation
between religion, politics, and economics. Not only are religion and civil society conflated; more to the point, religion and the economy are fused into
an inseparable whole in which "natural religion" (the order of the world),
"civil religion," and "mythic religion" (the stories and symbols we live by)
also become inseparable.

The great festival of Christmas occurs not only at the end and beginning
of the annual calendrical cycle of life, but at the end (and beginning) of the
natural cycle in the Northern Hemisphere. It began as a combination of harvest festival, celebrating the bounty by indulging in plentiful food and newly
brewed ale, and the winter solstice, with celebrations to ward off anxiety
about the renewal of light and life. Christmas—metaphysically based and
solidly rooted in nature—is culturally constructed. With the abundance of
goods produced by the industrial revolution and the need for expansion of
markets for corporations seeking profits, Christmas was transformed into a
virtual orgy of consumption of goods, increasingly far beyond the necessities
of life. With the advent of the electronic age, the holidays were also transformed from local village bonfires (to hasten the end of winter's darkness) to
the brilliant and ostentatious decoration of both private and public space:
from family Christmas trees and illumination of house fronts to downtown
shopping areas, malls, and city halls. The annual festival of light even transcends the usual separation of private and public space with the spread of
elaborate house and lawn displays. Newspapers print special articles on the
best holiday light displays, both the best of the town displays and the most
elaborate displays by private households. Insofar as the massive Christmas
festival takes place after harvest time at winter solstice and New Year's, it
incorporates all of these annual markers that structure the lives of individuals and of the whole society. The festival celebrates the order of the cosmos
and its meaning—more or less equivalent to what the ancient Romans called
"natural religion."

In traditional agrarian society, the combination of winter solstice, Christmas, and New Year's had been a relatively limited public festival of
carousing. In the first half of the nineteenth century, however, the nascent
American middle class transformed it into a domestic festival focused on the
home and family, especially on children.[4] Hand in hand with the escalation
of consumption via holiday gift giving—and as an antidote to the impersonal features of urbanization and industrialization in the late nineteenth
century—the Christmas festival became ever more domestic as a time of
togetherness for family, with heightened expectations and nostalgia for the
lost era of the old-time Christmas, as constructed in the Victorian era and
cultivated ever since. Within the festival now running from late November

through New Year's Day, the two most important sacred times for family in American society are now Thanksgiving Day and Christmas Eve and Day. Not coincidentally, those holy days for the family are also by far some of the biggest travel times of the year by all modes of transportation.

Once the principal mode of expression of family affection and togetherness became gift giving, along with a surfeit of food and drink, the elaborate holiday festival effectively combined the expression of family solidarity with the profitable functioning of the economy. The holiday festival is now the most crucial "season" for the economy and the economy is now dependent on the holidays. Such a high percentage of goods are retailed during the four weeks between Thanksgiving and Christmas Day that the economy of the United States would collapse without them. Holiday gift giving is essential to the "community" of the American economy, ensuring that sales and profits are high and, to illustrate the interdependence, that people have jobs and salaries in order to afford to purchase the gifts necessary to "grow" the now consumer-oriented economy.

There is yet another community-establishing and community-sustaining aspect of the holiday festival: the Christmas season is generally the only time during the year that companies hold company parties. In these affairs, as the lore goes, employees join across ranks in festive excess, with liberal latitude for behavior that crosses the boundaries of corporate propriety maintained in the workplace at all other times throughout the year. Some of the carnival atmosphere and conviviality expressed in the old wassailing of a simpler society, which respectable middle-class families tried to replace with the domestic celebration of Christmas, continues in somewhat different form in the company Christmas party.

Often missed in analyses of Christmas are the ways in which the grand American holiday festival expresses and embodies community in civic affairs, whether in small towns, large cities, or the nation as a whole. In this connection, the holidays as a whole have become a prolonged expression of the "civil religion" in the United States. As the holidays, driven by the escalation of retailing, expanded in length from the two weeks around the winter solstice, Christmas Day, and New Year's, Thanksgiving became the beginning of the prolonged festival. Thanksgiving had previously been the most important holy day in American civil religion, when families celebrated the foundational legend of the nation, as well as the abundant harvest, with a festive meal.[5] With the expanding importance of holiday retailing for the economy, the previously variable date of Thanksgiving was standardized to allow at least four weeks of retailing before Christmas Day. As the inaugural celebration of the holidays, Thanksgiving became articulated with the national economy as the shopping season was "officially" inaugurated with holiday parades sponsored by Macy's and other commercial giants. The Friday after Thanksgiving became the biggest shopping/retailing day of the year.

The holiday festival has also come to include many other "customary" or "traditional" rituals of American civil religion as well, at both the local and national level. Mayors preside at ceremonies lighting the city/town Christmas tree, celebrating at the local level what the President presides over in the lighting of the national Christmas tree in front of the White House, the residence of the "First Family." City and state buildings and at least the White House among federal buildings are decorated with lights and displays. Cities and towns have parades, usually sponsored by local stores and national corporations. And the Macy's Christmas parade in New York City has become a national event since it has been televised live. Such holiday parades also illustrate the degree to which the local and national "business community" is an integral and driving force in the expression of the civic community. In some areas, the concluding celebration of the holidays, New Year's Eve, is also becoming an expression of the civil religion, a celebration of civic community. Recently developed "First Night" festivities include parades that bring together various neighborhood and/or ethnic groups, with bands, costumes, and floats, followed by indoor and outdoor performances, displays, and exhibits, climaxing in a bombastic display of fireworks.

The extensive holiday festival has also come to include expressions of and participation by the communities of organized religion. The burgeoning festival proved so alluring by the twentieth century that the major religions and ethnic groups in the United States could not resist joining in. Having dropped their earlier opposition to the celebration of Christmas, Protestant churches joined with Catholic and Episcopal churches (which had traditionally observed Christ's Nativity with Christmas Eve services) to make Christmas an increasingly important festival in church services and Sunday school. In a closely related development, merchants (often pious Christian lay leaders), with their increasingly sophisticated modes of advertising and spectacular displays, "christianized" the holidays with window displays of manger scenes and the gift-bearing Magi. American Jews, in contrast to Jews living in other countries, developed Hanukkah into a major festival of lights that includes gift giving. More recently, African Americans developed Kwanzaa to provide a distinctively African content to the holidays. The Muslim festival of Ramadan also happens to coincide with the American holidays (although the emphasis of Ramadan is on daytime fasting). Thus by developing major celebrations in churches and synagogues during the holidays, American Christian denominations and Jewish congregations have contributed to the ways in which those whose religious loyalty is primarily Christian or Jewish become involved in the distinctively American Christmas, which now involves and unites virtually the whole society in the festivities.

In all of these overlapping communities and at all of these levels, the rituals and celebrations of Christmas establish individual and group identity. Most important, central, and effective is individual and family identity, which is the focus of much of the festivity. The festival of light, holiday gifts, and the many special rituals in which families participate during the holiday season are surely crucial in solidifying the sense of family for children. During the crucial years of transition out of the family of origin, young adults often go "home" for Thanksgiving and/or Christmas, even if not at other times of year. The holidays provide the occasions when extended families gather across three generations and collateral branches. At all stages in personal life, festive family meals and gift exchanges during the holidays secure family identity as well as family solidarity. At the level of individual identity within families, the interplay of a person's communicating those special items that "I want for Christmas" and the follow-through by family members is an important expression and validation of personal identity, insofar as clothes, jewelry, and other possessions "make" the person feel special.

It is more difficult to pinpoint the ways and the degree to which holiday rituals are instrumental in establishing and expressing people's civic or national or class identity. This probably varies considerably from person to person, and works far more in terms of participation in a larger whole than ideological articulation. For those who maintain some continuity in expressions of family ethnic identity, participation in civic holiday festivities serves to integrate them into the dominant American culture and identity while allowing them the freedom to follow their "traditional" ethnic customs in family celebrations. Insofar as ceremonies such as the lighting of the city Christmas tree and festivities such as First Night have replaced the old wassailing, class identities have been suppressed and replaced by civic and national identities.

All of these functions of religion served by the holidays—the articulation of the order of things, the constitution of community, and the establishment of identity—are expressed in a rich range of symbols, stories, music, visual displays, and a variety of performances. Culturally the holidays are by far the richest time of year, with as many performances in many different media as in the rest of the year put together. Santa Claus, particularly in "A Visit from St. Nicholas" and the pictures of Thomas Nast, became the central symbol. The Christmas tree became the domestic shrine. Its bright colored lights and other lively decorations, with the lavish display of brightly wrapped presents underneath, made it the symbol of abundance and gift giving. This domestic shrine, of course, expanded its functions to the civic and national levels, becoming central in the festival of lights and standing tall as a symbol of civic festival.

A rich variety of stories, mostly in various media of performance, articulate the "meaning" of Christmas. Dickens's *A Christmas Carol* quickly became a standard fixture of the holidays and is now performed in theaters in most towns and cities around the country. Consumer Christmas fostered considerable creativity, with "Rudolf the Red-Nosed Reindeer," written for the holidays in 1939, quickly becoming a major and influential contribution to American "folklore," as well as a favorite carol sung by everyone. Beloved children's author Dr. Seuss wrote the widely read and then performed *The Grinch Who Stole Christmas*. Hollywood did its part in creating standard national patterns through movies such as *White Christmas, Miracle on Thirty-Fourth Street,* and *It's a Wonderful Life,* some of which are shown on television many times during the holidays. "Christmas specials" on television have long since become standard fare, with multiple versions of most of the classics such as *A Christmas Carol* and *The Grinch,* along with newly created shows. And, for those who can afford it, "The Nutcracker" is performed in every city with a ballet company, often in forty or fifty performances during the season. With the ballet as with other cultural institutions, economics is inseparable from the cultural dimension of the holidays as the great festival of the society, for the revenues from performances of "The Nutcracker" support the rest of the season of every ballet company in the country.

Of special importance in articulating meaning, community, and identity, again at every social level, is music, because virtually everyone participates in the singing of the favorite songs and carols like "Jingle Bells," "White Christmas" (from a holiday movie), and "Rudolf." Most musical performing groups, including school choruses, offer an annual Christmas concert as one of their (usually only two) yearly offerings.

In the development of Christmas in the twentieth century, stories and symbols derived from Christianity and, more recently Hanukkah and Kwanzaa, have been integrated into the holiday cultural mix. As recent historical investigations have indicated, the story and symbols of Christ's birth were not a factor in the formative development of the American Christmas. Beginning with the incorporation of Santa Claus into Sunday school programs and the display of manger scenes in store windows early in the twentieth century, the birth of Christ has for many, perhaps for most Americans, been "put (back) into Christmas," has even become "the reason for the season." While the story and symbols of Christ's birth are becoming gradually less important to Christmas in public displays and in the marketing of goods, the star of Bethlehem has been assimilated into the festival of lights, the three kings bearing gifts are important in connection with gift giving, and the Christmas crèche focused on the Holy Family is a paradigm for the domestic family scene for many—although a humble picture that might seem to be at odds with the domestic Christmas with its abundance, even opulence, under the tree. More recently Jewish families and communities have contributed their Hanukkah candles to the festival of lights in a way that enables them to participate in the American holidays while following a distinctively Jewish tradition of commemoration of the unquenchable supply of oil in the ancient Temple.[6]

By far the most important factor in the twentieth century expansion of the American Christmas into a festival of historically unprecedented scope is its role in the consumer economy—appropriately symbolized by the nationally televised Macy's Christmas parade which begins the festival of retailing in the financial capital of the world. The extended retailing season commences ceremonially with the Macy's parade in New York City, now paralleled by corresponding commercial Christmas parades in other major cities. The intense flurry of purchasing is kicked off by the largest shopping day of the year, the day after Thanksgiving. What drives this orgy (the Greek word *orgia* meant ritual) of consumption is the historically unprecedented extent of holiday gift giving as induced and channeled by intense, subtle, and pervasive marketing, which has also reached historically unprecedented levels of subtlety and sophistication. Christmas now entails a dazzling and pervasive display of abundance and subliminal as well as blatant ways of cultivating and channeling people's desire for every imaginable object of pleasure and enjoyment. The spectacle of display now pervades not only public space but also the electronic media that attack our senses of sight and sound, whether in public or in private, and even the aroma of the air we breathe, inducing us into consumption of luxurious goods and overindulgence of every kind. For a period of four weeks and longer, we live in this rarified atmosphere of pervasive, ubiquitous, high-powered marketing. All of this is absolutely integral to and necessary for the economy, for the holidays have become the climax of the society's annual economic cycle without which the economy would quickly and catastrophically collapse.

But this spectacle of marketing and consumption is inseparable from the lavish festival of the holidays. In holiday retailing, economics is inseparable from religion. One of the now standard definitions of religion, from the great anthropologist Clifford Geertz, is: "a system of symbols which acts to establish powerful, pervasive and long-lasting moods and motivations" in people.[7] This is precisely what is done during the holidays, effectively inducing people to purchase goods for gifts and other aspects of the extraordinary level of consumption during the prolonged festival. Major retailers such as Macy's present massive displays of old-time Christmas scenes that induce moods of nostalgia and other emotions inspiring holiday spirit. These elaborate displays are not designed to sell particular products, but to induce a broad general motivation to purchase gifts as the principal expression of the holiday spirit. Companies with products to offer sponsor Christmas specials on television, contributing to the holiday spirit by tapping the reservoir of holiday cultural tradition, while also advertising their products. Not just radio stations, but stores and malls play holiday music, further inducing the spirit, the mood, and motivation conducive to consumption. The material world of the gifts marketed and purchased is inseparable from the holiday spirit; the consumer economy inseparable from religious mood and motivation.

This survey of the multiple dimensions of the American Christmas, the most sustained, massive, and pervasive religious festival in history, indicates that we are fooling ourselves if we believe that there is a separation of religion and economics along with a separation of religion and politics i American society. Of course the separation of synagogue and church se vices on Saturday and Sunday from the economic activities of the workpl during the weekdays continues—although retailing is now done seven ¢ a week and advertising for goods, services, and the multinational cong erate corporations that produce them extends into virtually all home into the minds of their inhabitants. During the prolonged Christmas season, however, there is no longer any separation between religion and retailing, between the spirit and consumption. Christmas has developed into the religion of consumer capitalism. It would be safe to say, moreover, that Christmas has become not only the major religious festival in America, but in its pervasion of public space, the air waves, and electronic media, and even its manipulation of our olfactory sense, it plays a dominant role in the functions of religion—in determining the values, identity, community, and meaning of members of this society!

The Analogy between Modern America and Ancient Mesopotamia

Since American society, despite its considerable complexity, is becoming so monolithic—at least in its determinative festival of Christmas—it may be helpful to examine another relatively monolithic society in order to make comparisons that may illuminate what has developed in the fusion of religion and economics—developments that go largely unnoticed because we still assume the separation of church and state, religion and economics.

The civilization of ancient Mesopotamia was a truly astounding achievement.[8] In what is modern-day Iraq, the ancient Mesopotamians built many large cities along the banks of the Tigris and Euphrates Rivers. The burgeoning population was supported by a massive irrigation system. The construction both of the cities, with their massive monuments (ziggurats), and of the extensive irrigation system required a sophisticated organization of the labor of the masses of people. What motivated the people to toil in the fields under the hot sun (110 degrees Fahrenheit) day after day and to cooperate in the huge labor gangs necessary to construct irrigation systems and palaces for their rulers and their gods was an intense fear of the superhuman forces that determined their lives. They lived in persistent fear that the great force River would overflow his banks in a fit of rage, or that the even greater force King Storm would arbitrarily swoop down upon the cities so laboriously built along the banks of River and topple buildings and fill the irrigation canals with sand from the desert.

In ancient Mesopotamia, as in almost any traditional agrarian society, religion was utterly inseparable from other aspects of life, such as politics, economics, and even the natural cycle. There was no such thing as the separation of church and state, or between religion and economic production. The yearly cycle of religious festivals celebrated the yearly cycle of nature, particularly the planting and harvesting of crops. Planting and harvesting were particularly religious activities, surrounded with special prayers, sacrifices, and other rituals. Those who dominated society combined the functions of managers, political rulers, and high priests. In Mesopotamia, the climax of the annual natural-economic-political-religious cycle was the

New Year's Festival (Akitu) that celebrated both the end and the beginning, the completion and the renewal of the cyclical political-economic-natural-divine order. The renewal of order against the threat of chaos was focused in a great ritual drama acted out in the grand temple-palace of Marduk, principal god of Babylon, who as King Storm stood at the head of the divine Forces of Order. This ritual drama, the enactment of which at the climax of the New Year's festival reconstituted the established divine order, provides fascinating glimpses both of the relationships among the divine Forces and of the people's relationships to the forces that determined their lives.

River and Sea, intermingling their waters, generated Silt and Sediment, who in turn gave birth to Horizon of Sky and Horizon of Earth. The latter generated Sky=Authority, who generated Irrigation=Wisdom and other offspring. Annoyed at the noise that his offspring were making, old Father River threatened to destroy them all. But the enterprising Irrigation=Wisdom, drawing up a map of the (Mesopotamian) universe and casting a magical spell, put River to sleep (or "killed" him). In the drama so far, it is not difficult to discern the Mesopotamians' sense of the origins of their irrigation civilization, that initially took the form of communities centered on the "house" of one of the divine Forces, presided over by high-ranking specialists (priests-managers) in communicating with those divine Forces. At that relatively simple stage of the evolution of irrigation civilization, the temple communities were held together by "authority" (Sky) and "wisdom" (Irrigation), with no coercion by violent, military force yet being necessary to establish and maintain order. As the nascent civilization became more complex, however, with the evolution of larger cities up and down the rivers, the system experienced chronic political conflict.

As the ritual drama enacted at New Year's continued, Sea went on a violent rampage to avenge her consort's defeat. She and her violent Forces of Chaos were too much for Irrigation=Wisdom and Sky=Authority, the older Forces of coherence/cohesion, to handle. To cope with the desperate situation of the world in chaos, Irrigation generated a new Force, Storm=Kingship, who was acclaimed King by the Forces struggling to assert order over chaos. In a scene remarkable for the extremity of its violence—and juxtaposing domestic relations with the order of the universe—Marduk (god of Babylon) as Storm=King slaughtered his (great-great-grand) Mother Sea, then butchered her body, making the heavenly order symbolized by the zodiac out of the upper half and the corresponding earthly order from the bottom half of her carcass. After the cosmic victory of the Forces of Order over the Forces of Chaos, of course, palaces had to be built for Marduk=Storm King and the other victors. But it would not do for the vanquished Forces, who were also divine, to be subjected to physical labor. So Marduk created people as slaves of the gods, to build the palaces for the divine Forces as well as to raise the crops necessary for the banqueting of the Forces in the style to which they had become accustomed. In the concluding ceremony, Marduk=Storm was celebrated as eternal King of the universe.

This climax of the cosmic drama reflects the establishment of empire by military violence in Mesopotamian civilization. After several generations of chronic warfare among the city-states that developed along the Tigris and Euphrates Rivers, one city-state was finally able to impose its rule by military conquest of the others. The earthly order thus achieved by military conquest was understood as the earthly counterpart of the cosmic order achieved by the Forces of Order headed by Marduk=Storm=Kingship over the Forces of Chaos, led by Sea, who was such a threat to the order of civilization that she had to be subdued by extreme violence and literally dismembered and reordered. Once the empire was established, of course, the military state headed by the high priest of Marduk, chief Force of the imperial city of Babylon, would use military force to quash any challenge to the divine Cosmos=political-economic order established by the victory of the Forces of Order.

When my university students study ancient Mesopotamia they are struck by how its monolithic political-economic system resembles the one in which we live and work. The giant corporations that employ most workers in our society resemble the temple-communities or city-states in ancient Mesopotamia or other ancient civilizations in significant ways. The principal productive forces, the agricultural lands, belonged to the gods, were the estates of the gods. The gods demanded tithes and offerings in return for the people's use of the land, a certain percentage of the value of the crops raised on the land. Similarly, in modern corporations, the productive resources—the automobile factories of General Motors or the lands of United Fruit Company or the franchises of MacDonald's—are the property of the owners or stockholders of the corporations. All employees of a given corporation work for, serve, the owners of capital, who demand a certain profit/ return on their investment of capital; the managers of the corporations control the deployment of labor so that the owners receive their profit. A brief examination of the New Year's festival in the context of the relations between the people, the managerial class of "great ones," and the Forces they all served in the monolithic system of ancient Mesopotamia may help elucidate the significance of the American holiday festival in the context of the relationships between the people, the corporations, and what forces they are all serving in American society.

The Festivals

Festivals were held in the ancient Mesopotamian cities at key points corresponding to the annual natural and productive order. The most elaborate of all Mesopotamian festivals was the twelve-day New Year's festival (Akitu) celebrated every spring for the first twelve days of the first month of the year (*Nisan*); it was an extended celebration of the end of the previous cycle of nature and productivity and the beginning of the new cycle.[9] This prolonged New Year's festival, while centered in Babylon, was an empire-wide celebration. The statues of the Forces who were the chief gods of other cities were brought by boat with great ceremony to the capital city of Babylon where they greeted Marduk=Storm-King, the chief god of Babylon, hence of the empire. Then the statues of all the Forces/gods accompanied Marduk=Storm, leading the procession on his ceremonial float, out of the huge palace-temple complex of Marduk in a magnificent procession that progressed down the wide avenue from Marduk's palace through the Ishtar gate (the divine Force of love-fertility) to the Akitu hall outside Babylon's walls. Most important in the series of elaborate rites was the ritual performance of the ritual drama *Enuma Elish,* the Mesopotamian "myth of origins," which climaxed with Marduk=Storm's great victory over Sea (and her Forces of Chaos) and his coronation as eternal King of the Universe. With the order of the universe thus ceremonially (re-)established, Marduk was escorted back to his palace-temple and the other great Forces=Gods returned to their own cities and palaces-temples. In another ritual of the Akitu festival, the king of Babylon and the chief priestess acted out the sacred marriage between the king of Babylon and the chief goddess Zarpanitu, further ensuring the newly renewed cycle of fertility and productivity.

Modern Westerners are accustomed to thinking of power relations in a given society in terms of politics, whether in democratic societies where the voters elect the government or in authoritarian regimes established and maintained by military violence. But the rulers of traditional large-scale societies seldom maintain power relationships strictly by violent coercion. They depend instead on what we think of as religious belief and ritual to establish and maintain the power relations in which the ordinary people dutifully obey and supply produce and labor for the ruling class. Indeed, the classical civilizations such as ancient Egypt and China and the great American civilizations of the Aztecs, Incas, and Mayas maintained order in their complex systems as much or more by elaborate and awesome religious pomp and circumstance than by military coercion.

As in other classical civilizations, so the ancient Mesopotamian political-economic order under Babylonian imperial rule was maintained (not simply by military force but) by awesome festivals in honor of the Forces that determined the people's lives in the civilizational order. The annual ritual performance of this drama was thus not simply an impressive religious ceremony that Mesopotamians attended for mere entertainment. Performance of the ritual effected the renewal of the cosmic order. In the yearly performance of this drama the world-constituting metaphysical aspect, the economic cycle of productivity, and the political order of Mesopotamia were utterly inseparable from the ceremonial aspect. The very performance of the drama was instrumental in reestablishing the cosmic order of Mesopotamian civilization, the order of the political-economic-religious system, for another annual cycle, just as it had constituted the order of things for the previous annual cycle and would do so again for the following annual cycle. The spectacles of the twelve-day New Year's festival performed in the massive building complexes of the great cities such as Babylon regularly re-instilled in the people a deep sense of awe and fear of the overwhelming power of the Forces that determined their existence. The performances and the sense of fear they induced thus effected the political-economic order that was articulated with the natural order by motivating the people to continue in the productive labor that constituted their faithful service of the gods.

The Christmas festival is the modern American equivalent of the ancient Mesopotamian New Year's festival, except that it lasts three times as long and is far more pervasive and dominant in the overall system. Like the Mesopotamian festival, the American Christmas is rooted in and articulates the climax and renewal of the annual natural cycle, as culturally construed. As noted previously, Christmas has also become an increasingly important expression of civic order and identity, locally and nationally, particularly in such ceremonies as the opening parades on Thanksgiving Day, civic and national Christmas tree lighting ceremonies, festive decoration of cities, and First Night festivities. Most important has been the steady expansion of the holidays into the climax of the annual economic cycle. Just as the Mesopotamian New Year's festival generated the faithful rendering of tithes and offerings that supported the construction and management of the cities, so the American holidays now generate 40 percent of the retailing that drives the consumer capitalist economy. Just as ancient Mesopotamian festivals such as Akitu instilled awe in the people in their pomp and ceremony, Christmas with its multiple media of light, entertainment, and festive excess induces a pervasive heightening of expectations of abundance and stimulation of desire. Just as the ancient Mesopotamian New Year's festival heightened the awesome mystery of the Forces, so Christmas creates a fantastic magical wonderland the surrounds the crass business of retailing and shopping with an aura of the holiday spirit. And just as the ancient Mesopotamian New Year's festival cultivated a sense of fear in the people that induced them to fulfill their obligation of service to the Forces, so the modern American Christmas induces a sense of obligation, even eagerness, to purchase gifts for relatives and friends, which in turn provide sales and profits for corporations.

The People

In Mesopotamian civilization the people were the "servants" of the divine Forces, created specifically as slaves to perform the labor necessary to build the huge palace-temple complexes for the Forces and to supply them with the produce necessary for their banqueting. The lands of a city were understood as the estates of the Forces, the palaces-temples as the houses in which they dwelled. The motivation was supplied by the people's fear of the divine Forces who not only determined their lives but also were unpredictable in their temper and behavior. After all, if River became angry he might overflow his banks, or if Marduk=Storm became angry he might become destructive in his violence, just as he had done to Sea in the battle preceding the final creation of the heavens and earth out of her slaughtered carcass. So the people were prepared to appease the awesome Forces on whose good will the cosmic order and their own livelihood depended.

The people's service (=worship) of the Forces did indeed involve rituals. They were expected to bring their offerings and sacrifices, along with prayers of thanksgiving and petitions for divine grace before the great Forces. Moreover, one of the principal duties of the chief servants, the priestly managerial elite, was serving at the tables=altars in the palaces=temples of the Forces, offering burnt offerings, sacrifices, and libations, providing the care and feeding of the great high gods.

Such symbolic offerings, however, required what is called *hard service* in the Hebrew Bible (which was recoiling against such concrete service of the Forces in the ancient Near East). Service of the Forces required hard labor of two broad categories. The people had to labor in the fields to produce, over and above crops for their own subsistence, crops owed to the Forces as "tithes" and "offerings" (taxes), used to support the ruling class and their extensive apparatus of military and scribal retainers, artisans, and palace servants in the lifestyle to which they had become accustomed. The people had also to perform labor services, *corvee,* on "public works" such as the irrigation system and the massive building complexes that comprised the palace-temples of the Forces.[10]

The peasant "servants" of the Forces were always marginal producers, living at the subsistence level. They were in perpetual danger of not being able to make it through to the next harvest after rendering up a high percentage of the products of their labor, their crops. Most peasants found it necessary to borrow, at steep rates of interest, to feed their families after paying their tithes and offerings to the priestly managerial elite. And of course, since the latter had the keys to the temple storehouses, the peasants fell into debt to the managerial elite who, as officers of the priestly state, were the tithe/tax collectors. The interest the peasants paid on their debts thus provided an additional side income to the elite creditors and placed yet another burden on the producers from which they ordinarily never recovered. They often became sharecroppers on what had once been their own land (as leased to them by the Forces-owners), now yielded to the control of the wealthy creditors.

The industrial and service workers in modern corporations correspond to the ancient Mesopotamian peasants or agricultural workers, who were created by the gods as their servants. Modern workers are required to relinquish a certain percentage of the value of their labor to the owners of the corporation as profit on the owners' investment, just as ancient Mesopotamian peasants were required to render up tithes and offerings to the priestly managerial elite who received and controlled them on behalf of the gods who owned the lands. When students first learn of the lives of people in ancient Near Eastern civilizations, they recoil at the utter lack of freedom that the people enjoyed, the people who were created by the gods as "slaves" of gods to do the labor that would have been unfitting even for the vanquished gods.

Ironically, despite the belief that modern people enjoy more freedoms than their ancient counterparts, the ancient workers had certain rights, leverage, and security that modern workers do not have. Ancient peasants were socially embedded in their families and village communities, in contrast to the freedom and rights of the individual citizen of modern civil society. But those ancient peasants also had rights over the land on which they worked, whereas modern workers have no rights with regard to the forces of production, except under some collective bargaining agreements negotiated by labor unions. Ancient peasants, moreover, had job security and a supportive and mutually cooperative village community, whereas modern industrial and especially service workers have no job security and are relatively atomized, with no supportive community—other than the state, with its limited unemployment payments.

The modern worker, however, is also a consumer. Besides rendering up a high percentage of their crops as tithes and offerings to the priestly managerial rulers, ancient peasants also provided their own necessities of food, clothing, and shelter, along with their own "ceremonial fund" for family and village celebrations, by their own labor on the land. Modern workers, however, since they do not produce their own food and other necessities, must purchase these as commodities in the market. The consumer capitalist system thus has the modern workers both coming and going. First, the surplus value of the products of the producers—whether industrial commodities or services—are taken as profits for the owners of the corporation for which they work. But then the producers who are now consumers as well must also use their wages to buy necessities such as food and clothing and shelter, and thus pay prices set to provide profits for the corporations that produce, transport, and retail the commodities.

The great Christmas festival of American society has also become the principal factor in marginal workers' families regularly falling heavily into debt, which keeps them beholden to the system with little or no hope of gaining any economic maneuverability within it. Advertising and the attendant social pressure keep economically marginal parents feeling obligated to provide their families with an appropriately abundant Christmas, including the latest in expensive toys. In the old Christmas clubs, families used to save ahead for the huge expenditure incurred at Christmastime. With the advent of credit cards, however, people are induced to buy now and not worry about the 18 percent interest charges. Enabled by credit cards to partake in the Christmas abundance, people quickly pile up large debts at 18 percent interest, debts that a large percentage of families take six or more months to pay off, only to repeat the cycle every year.

The Managers (Rulers)

Modern scholars sometimes have difficulty understanding just how monolithic Mesopotamian society was. This difficulty stems from the modern Western assumption of the separation between church and state and business, between religion, politics, and economic enterprise. Scholars habitually label the huge storage-administrative-ceremonial buildings of ancient Mesopotamian cities as "temples" and the people who ruled the society from a base in these building complexes as "priests." But to thus categorize them as religious obscures the political-economic functions of these huge buildings and the managerial elite (rulers) of Mesopotamian society. To understand how such a society worked, however, we must recognize that economics, politics, and religion were inseparable in ancient Mesopotamia. Those huge building complexes must thus be recognized for what they were: storehouses for food and political-economic-administrative centers as well as ceremonial centers.

Mesopotamians themselves referred to them as the "houses" ("palaces") of the Forces. The principal houses of the principal Forces of a city, in fact, consisted of large complexes of buildings with vast storage rooms, workrooms, dormitories, and kitchens, as well as shrines, sanctuaries, and a tower or ziggurat. The palace-complex of Marduk=Storm at Babylon was an enormously large and wealthy institution, nearly a hundred meters square and fifty meters high, with perhaps hundreds of people on its immediate staff. These building-complexes, built by *corvee* (forced) labor and managed by their large staffs of administrators and service personnel, were supported by the agricultural produce of the people's labor, the revenues owed to the Forces. The actual recipients and custodians of these revenues, of course, were the "great ones," the managerial elite (the ruling class) in charge of these palace-storehouse-administrative complexes and of the city and its political economy. The elite deployed the resources as needed and, not surprisingly, in their own interests. These "great ones" were thus the managerial class, the political-economic rulers as well as the chief priests who ministered to the Forces (as their chief servants) and directed the Mesopotamian political economy based on its vast irrigation systems. Most of the managerial elite inherited their positions, although some gained positions by conquest. At the most advanced stage of Mesopotamian civilization, the imperial structure was built up by one urban corporation (city) taking over (conquering) others.[11]

Once we recognize that what used to be called "high priests" were the political-economic managers of the city-states and empire, then we can also recognize that the modern American equivalents of the ancient Mesopotamian "great ones" are the managerial elite of the great corporations. Corporations are ruled and managed by their boards and officers who hold their positions of power either by having inherited wealth and/or by "leveraged" buyout in a "hostile takeover," as corporations have built up imperial structures through corporate "mergers." The managerial elites make all the key decisions that affect the productivity and profits of the corporations, such as how much will be produced, how and what percentage of the value of the produce of the corporations will be given to the owners/ stockholders, and what is left for the support of the workers who actually produce the products and/or services generated by the corporation. The executive officers of corporations then have huge staffs of administrators and service personnel deployed to actually run the business they conduct or the production in which they are engaged. It may also be significant to note that the equivalent of the huge palace-administrative complexes in the Mesopotamian cities with their ziggurats are the huge high-rise buildings that house the "corporate headquarters" and administrative offices of the large corporations. Such high-rise headquarters of large corporations have long since come to dwarf the churches and cathedrals in the landscape of modern urban society. It would not be surprising if we began to recognize, through critical analysis, the ways in which these modern "great ones" have been taking over traditionally "religious" roles in the formation and perpetuation of symbols of meaning and the order of life, the establishment and cultivation of individual and collective identity, and the generation and cultivation of moods and motivations.

The Forces (Gods)

In the grand ritual drama performed at the climax of the New Year's festival in Babylon, people were created to serve the Forces that constituted and determined the Mesopotamian universe. The ancient Mesopotamians knew no such reality as a transcendent god in the Jewish, Christian, or Muslim sense. It is not even clear whether they had a generic term or concept of "gods," analogous to the determinative forces of other ancient Near Eastern peoples. They do not appear to have called the Forces they served "gods." Coming to grips with the inseparability of religion and political economy in ancient Mesopotamian society forces us to abandon some of our favorite concepts that often do not fit historical realities, such as the concept of gods and God. To say that the ancient Mesopotamians were "polytheists" while Jews, Christians, and Muslims are "monotheists" would simply repeat a pious platitude. It may be suggestive when we come back to modern American society to have looked closely at what those Forces were that the Mesopotamians served with their labor and produce.

As can be seen in the ritual drama performed at the climax of the New Year's festival, the principal Forces in their universe had names such as Sea (Tiamat), River (Apsu), Sky (Anu)=Authority, Irrigation (Ea)=Wisdom, and Marduk=Storm=Kingship. Similarly, other ancient Near Eastern peoples served Forces such as Lord Storm, Sky, and Earth, and some of the principal gods of the Greeks were Sky (Ouranos), Earth (Gaia), and Time (Kronos). It would be misleading to think that these Forces were somehow "supernatural." Sea, River, Sky, and Storm are not supernatural forces but natural forces. But to stop there is also misleading. What about Irrigation (Ea/Nudimmud) and the clear indications in the ritual drama *Enuma Elish* that "Sky" also means "Authority" and that Marduk carries out precisely the actions of "Storm" in other Mesopotamian literature and that he is both born and acclaimed "King"? In the ritual drama of origins ceremonially performed at New Year's and apparently generally in Mesopotamian religious practice, these political-economic forces are disguised as natural forces, Forces that are simply givens in the nature of the universe, such as Sky, Irrigation, and Storm. But we can discern that these Forces are also economic and/or political and are even human-made, the products of the Mesopotamians' own *corvee* and the Mesopotamian political-economic system. Correspondingly, what the Forces demanded and received from the people was not simply service in the sense of spiritual worship, but concrete material service in the form of labor on building projects and agricultural produce brought to the palace-storehouses.

The result of this probe bears repeating. The "gods" that the Mesopotamians served with their labor and agricultural produce, while appearing to be personified and divinized *natural* forces, were actually personified and divinized political-economic forces that they themselves had generated by their labor and supported by their produce. The late-Israelite critique of the rival ancient Near Eastern gods was almost modern in its perception that people were serving the creation of their own labor as gods (idols). The great French sociologist Durkheim was only slightly less critical in his theory of religion, that what people worshiped as their gods were the representative symbols of their own values and social order. Were we to state this relationship in terms of a theory of religion, which in Mesopotamia as in most societies was inseparable from the political economy, religion is people's service of the forces that determine their lives in significant and formative ways.[12]

The modern American equivalent of the Forces who owned the lands and expected service in produce and labor from the Mesopotamian people would have to be the owners of the corporations that correspond to the Mesopotamian cities. However, whereas the Mesopotamians had what appears to be a personal relationship with the Forces they served, such as the personified Storm=Kingship or Irrigation, modern Americans by and large have an impersonal relationship. It would thus be more appropriate to say the Force that Americans serve in their work and shopping is investments generally, or *capital,* that demands a return or profit. In terms of the theory of religion as the service of the forces that determine our lives, this fits. For the lives of nearly all people in America are dependent on and determined by investment of capital in multiple ways: jobs, sustenance, insurance, medical care, retirement, recreation, and so on. The extent to which our lives are determined by and dependent on investments/capital in advanced industrialized and capitalistic society is unprecedented historically. It has steadily expanded during the twentieth century. According to the "logic" of capitalism, corporations must continually produce not only profits for the owners but also some growth in the wealth of the corporation and the portfolios of the stockholders. They are thus continually driven to find new markets for their goods and services, new ways of inducing workers who are also consumers to desire and purchase more and more goods and services, in order to produce return on the investment of capital. It is precisely in the expansion of industrial capitalism into consumption capitalism during the twentieth century that the holiday festival of Christmas developed into the religion of the system. The Force that now determines our lives is capital, and the holidays constitute the religious festival of historically unprecedented scope in which we serve that Force with the value of our labor in fantastic rituals of abundance and consumption.

This aspect of the analogy we are pursuing may not be immediately apparent because in American culture the people's service of capital is not revealed or open but is veiled by all sorts of religious activities and illusory appearances. Interestingly enough, these are best exemplified by aspects of the holiday festivities. Most important and central to the consumer economy of course is gift giving, all hedged about with smoke and mirrors. Ostensibly we are giving gifts to relatives and friends. And as part of Christmas, our gift giving is encouraged in every imaginable way by stories (the three kings), symbols (the tree), performances (*A Christmas Carol*), the decorations, the music, and of course all the festive advertising. By giving gifts to loved ones, however, we are also giving profits to investments/capital via our payments to the corporations that produce and retail the products we purchase as gifts. Other forms of excess, such as festive meals and parties, focus attention on the ceremonial bonding of family, friendship, and community, while also channeling resources through the supplying companies into profits for investments. Santa Claus, the old-time Christmas, and other displays also veil the service of capital during the holidays. Santa enables us to pretend that the gifts are not mass-produced for profit by industrial firms but handmade by elves or the kindly avuncular Santa himself and personally delivered on Christmas Eve. The "old-timey" displays transport us into a magic time and place that never existed except in our wish-fulfillment, where life is down-to-earth, homey, and secure around the family hearth.

Other ways in which the relationship of worker-consumer to capital is veiled involves the churches and synagogues, organized religions, which are ostensibly separate from the business as well as the state. "Worship service" due to God is understood in mainly or only nonmaterial spiritual terms, and most economic matters are not considered to come under the jurisdiction of God and the scope of serving God. Virtually by definition, therefore, the expenditure of resources on holiday abundance and excess is secular, supposedly with no religious implications. But that opens the field for the cultivation and motivation of desire by means of ostensibly secular festivity and holiday advertising to extract people's resources in material service of capital. It only seems contradictory that once Christian symbols and stories and Jewish customs have been incorporated into the holidays, it then seems like a genuine Christian activity to participate fully in the rest of the holidays or a genuinely Jewish custom to celebrate Hanukkah in ways inseparable from other aspects of the holidays. In both the concrete economic service of capital is veiled.

Another way in which the religious aspect of the American religious-political-economic system that climaxes in the holidays differs from the ancient Mesopotamian is with regard to faith or belief. The performance of the ritual drama of the Forces in cosmic battle inculcated in the Mesopotamians not only continuing belief in but fear of the Forces that determined their lives, Forces that might become destructive in their anger if not appropriately appeased with service. The wonderland and magic of the American holidays cultivate make-believe. This is best exemplified by Santa Claus. Ever since Clement Clark Moore's "A Visit from St. Nicholas," there has been "nothing to fear." The religion of the American Christmas also ostensibly makes no demands of service—except for gift giving. The holiday lights, decorations, displays, music, and general festivities simply invite everyone into a fantasyland of wonder and abundance.

Yet all the while this religious festival is inducing us into service of the Force that determines our lives. This service, generally veiled during Christmas itself, usually becomes evident only afterwards, when "the presents are all scattered and broken, I fear," and the 18 percent interest on the huge credit card debt now due to Capital makes many Americans wonder how they can possibly make it. Ancient Mesopotamian religion cultivated fear of the divine Forces that determined people's lives in the hearts and motivation of the people. The people were always obligated to the system, fearful of what the Forces might do if they did not serve them. Modern religion stimulates and channels desire for abundance and/or a sense of obligation for one's kids to have what others have, which must then be purchased by credit card, through which one is then obligated to pay the high interest as well as the base cost of the conspicuous consumption during the preceding holidays. While high-income people may not be fazed by this cycle, low-income people annually become locked into debt which they must pay off. They can thus never climb out of their "debt service" to capital (via the banks sponsoring the credit cards). In both cases, people are serving—with the produce or value of their labor—the forces that determine their lives (gods). The ancient Mesopotamians rendered produce and labor to the Forces that constituted the very conditions of their lives, the forces of nature and production. Modern Americas render the value of their labor to the Force that determines the conditions of their lives, the Force of industrial production and consumption, capital.

After examining the parallels between the historically unprecedented American Christmas festival, the great annual *holydays,* and the New Year's festival of ancient Mesopotamia, it is difficult to avoid the conclusion that Christmas has become the great religious festival of consumer capitalism. Having previously domesticated and commercialized the old pagan winter solstice celebrations of lights and abundance in the face of winter darkness, cold, and deprivation, commercial forces relentlessly cultivated and expanded the orgy of gift giving at Christmas, with the help of the distinctively American Santa Claus and the imported domestic shrine of the Christmas tree. Finally incorporating the key civil religious festival of Thanksgiving, turning it into the opening of the shopping season, and fusing civil religious ceremonies with corporately sponsored civic celebrations and domestic togetherness, consumer capitalism created its own grand *holydays*. Hidden in the mystery and magic of all the lights, glitter, gifts, and glorious performances of the season, is the god that the great festival serves.

Notes

1. See further chapter 6 above and chapter 10 below.
2. Just as an ancient city-state such as Athens or Rome had its own distinctive civil religion, the celebrations of which constituted the coherence of the society, so the Roman Empire virtually required and indeed developed its own imperial "civil religion" embodied in newly built temples to the emperor, statues of the emperor in all other temples, and shrines at every turn in the city centers, along with annual or semi-annual games dedicated to the emperor, so that in every major city of the empire the presence of the emperor pervaded public space and determined the annual calendar. See chapter 6 for a detailed explanation.
3. On the Isis mysteries, see Sharon Kelly Heyob, *The Cult of Women in the Graeco-Roman World* (Leiden: Brill, 1975); and Reginald E. Witt, *Isis in the Greco-Roman World* (Ithaca, N.Y.: Cornell University Press, 1971).
4. As delineated by Stephen Nissenbaum, *The Battle for Christmas* (New York: Alfred A. Knopf, 1996).
5. The classic analysis of civil religion in the United States is Robert N. Bellah, "Civil Religion in America," in Bellah, *Beyond Belief* (New York: Harper & Row, 1970), 165–84.
6. For (a critique of the implications of) the Supreme Court's acceptance of the nativity scene in public Christmas displays, see Paula Cooey's article, chapter 10 below.
7. Clifford Geertz, "Religion as a Cultural System," in *Reader in Comparative Religion*, 2d edition, ed. William A. Lessa and Evon Z. Vogt (New York: Harper & Row, 1965), 206.
8. Survey histories and reviews: A. Kirk Grayson, "Mesopotamia, History of" (including "History and Culture of Assyria" and "History and Culture of Babylonia," with bibliographies), *Anchor Bible Dictionary* 4:732–77; Muhammed Dandamaev, "Neo-Babylonian Society and Economy," in *The Cambridge Ancient History: The Assyrian and Babylonian Empires and Other States of the Near East, from the Eighth to the Sixth Centuries, B.C.*, ed. John Boardman et al., vol. 3, part 2 (Cambridge: Cambridge University Press, 1991), 261–75; Norman Yoffee, "Political Economy in Early Mesopotamian States," *Annual Review of Anthropology* 24 (1995): 281–311. Classic treatments: Thorkild Jacobsen, *The Treasures of Darkness* (New Haven: Yale University Press, 1976); and H. W. F. Saggs, *The Greatness That Was Babylon* (New York: Praeger, 1962). Although often admitting that it is inseparable from political-economic aspects of Babylonian and Assyrian imperial orders, scholars nevertheless attempt to abstract the "religion" of ancient Mesopotamia: e.g., W. H. Ph. Roemer, "Religion of Ancient Mesopotamia," in *Historia Religionum: Handbook for the History of Religions*, ed. C. Jouco Bleeker and Geo Widengren, vol. 1 (Leiden: E. J. Brill, 1969), 115–93. On how the overall imperial civilization operated, see also P. Michalowski, "Charisma and Control: On Conti-

nuity and Change in Early Mesopotamian Bureaucratic Systems," in McG. Gibson and R. D. Biggs, *The Organization of Power: Aspects of Bureaucracy in the Ancient Near East* (Chicago: University of Chicago Press, 1987), 55–68; and A. Westenholz, "The Old Akkadian Empire in Contemporary Opinion," in *Power and Propaganda: A Symposium on the Ancient Empires,* ed. M. T. Larsen (Copenhagen: Akademisk Forlag, 1979), 107–24.

9. The sources are fragmentary and reconstructions vary. Brief treatments in Saggs, *Babylon,* 384–89; Grayson, "Mesopotamia," 774–75; Roemer, "Religion," 145–46; and Tikva Frymer-Kensky, "Akitu," in *The Encyclopedia of Religion,* ed. Mircea Eliade (New York: Macmillan, 1987), 1:170–72.

10. The Hebrew Bible complains about such service, which was routinely expected in Mesopotamia and other ancient Near Eastern civilizations: "[the king] will appoint for himself commanders of thousands and commanders of fifties, and some to plow his ground and to reap his harvest, and to make his implements of war and the equipment of his chariots.... He will take one-tenth [or two- or three-tenths] of your grain and of your vineyards and give it to his officers and his courtiers. He will take the best of your cattle and donkeys, and put them to his work. He will take one-tenth of your flocks, and you shall be his slaves" (1 Sam. 8:11–18).

11. In transition from the ancient Mesopotamian "great ones" to the managers (and "God") of modern corporations, a comment by Saggs (*Babylon,* 369) is pertinent: "The king was not only the representative of humankind to the god, and so responsible for the due maintenance of the god's abode: he was also the god's steward, and as such responsible to the god for the welfare of his land." (Note that he is not responsible to the people!) The parallel to the CEO of the modern capitalist corporation is obvious from the corporate rhetoric: CEOs and the boards of corporations have responsibility to the stockholders, to capital.

12. This theory of religion as people's service of the forces that determine their lives in significant ways is confirmed by the emperor cult in the far more complex society of the Roman Empire (as explored in chapter 6 of this volume). Thus the Greek subjects of Caesar Augustus, who in his great military victory over the opposing forces of Anthony and Cleopatra at Actium brought peace and order to the world after decades of the chaos of empire-wide civil war, began to honor him as a god, the savior of the world, whose advent marked not only the beginning of the New Year, but the beginning of a New Era. Caesar Augustus was the most immediately effective, empirical as well as imperial, force determining their life. Thus the Greek elite redesigned the centers of their cities, with newly built temples to Caesar as well as Rome, Mistress of the World; placed statues of Caesar in the temples of all the other gods and shrines all around the perimeter of the city squares, the center of outdoor urban life; and dedicated new and renamed old festivals such as the Olympic Games to Caesar. The presence of the emperor quickly came to pervade public space, just as the presence of the Forces such as Storm-Kingship, Irrigation-Wisdom, and Sky-Authority had dominated public space and public festivals in ancient Babylon. See further chapter 6 above.

Chapter Nine

Santa Claus as an Icon of Grace

Max A. Myers

The contemporary American Christmas is not directly related to Christianity; it has actually become the holiday of a rival religion, the religion of global consumer capitalism.[1] The chief icon of the American Christmas, Santa Claus, is a symbol of a very different kind of grace than is preached by Christianity. The grace preached by Christianity is connected with the execution of a leader whose message threatened those who held political and social power. The grace represented by Santa Claus legitimates the institutions of political, economic, and social power. Thus, there are two radically different icons associated with these two understandings of grace: the icon of Santa Claus and the icon of the crucified Christ.

The basic understanding of life promoted by the American Christmas is quite compatible with capitalism's quest for the sale and consumption of commodities. Because American Christmas presumes ultimate reality to be one of resource scarcity, primary value is placed on meeting the needs of the self. Self-interest is the primary virtue of this religion. The only grace recognized by this understanding of reality is the favor shown to those who can consume more and better products. Their consumption shows that they are divinely favored, and Santa Claus as the symbolic gift bearer of commodities becomes a channel of this divine grace.

For Christianity, on the other hand, the understanding of ultimate reality is that life is a gift given in abundance. Imitation of this in the life of the individual and of the group leads to a life of sharing. The icon of the crucified Christ, in fact, extols a lifestyle of self-sacrifice to meet the needs of the other as the highest virtue. In this understanding, self-interest becomes a vice if it takes priority over helping to meet the needs of others, or if it leads to inordinate consumption. More and better consumption actually indicates the need for divine grace and a transformation, rather than its presence.

The American Christmas is part of the ideology of contemporary American society. Accordingly, we can say that its purpose is to mediate or reconcile contradiction(s) in human social relations through symbolic means—the function of all ideology. In this way, it brings about more satisfaction or more intense satisfaction for the participants in that society than would otherwise be the case. In this sense, human satisfaction is the condition signified by the images and rituals (the signifiers) of Christmas, although the route through which the signification travels is often circuitous and indirect. With respect to Christmas, one of the first questions we must put is, "Does this increase or enhance human satisfaction?" Then, once we have an answer to this question, we must go on to ask about the place of ideological images and rituals within the total cultural world of the society. Further, we have to ask whether and how these images and rituals contribute to more general satisfaction by an analysis of their ecological impact.

However, it is difficult to ask these questions in any straightforward way. Insofar as cultural formations do reconcile contradictions in social life, individuals who participate in them sense both the reconciliation and the contradictions beneath it. Even though they may not be able to thematize or articulate any of these aspects, participants have a kind of inchoate, semi-conscious knowledge that they are deriving satisfaction from the symbols themselves or from their place in their society's unique culture or way of life. The first case is illustrated, for example, by the adult who experiences a vague sense of satisfaction, insofar as this can be distinguished from nostalgia or aesthetic enjoyment, while sitting and staring at electric, colored lights on a tree bought in a parking lot and brought home. The second is illustrated by an incident which recurs in many movies of the Second World War in which soldiers or sailors having Christmas on the battlefield or at sea stifle a tear as if to say, "This is what we're fighting for." The point here is certainly not to deprecate any genuine human experience but to understand it in relationship with ideological cultural formations such as the American Christmas.

Santa Claus is central to the American Christmas complex. He serves as a general icon for the series of activities and images grouped together as the Christmas holidays. Santa Claus signifies a range of phenomena, both sensuous and conceptual, associated with Christmas. In fact, for the general consciousness of our culture the image of Santa Claus would be iconic for Christmas in a way that the Nativity of Christ would not. At any rate, there are certainly more visible and credible images of Santa Claus in our malls and in the mass media than there are of the Nativity or any other single image.

Why Santa Claus is able to function in this way is best answered by uncovering the contradictions that the image of Santa Claus reconciles. Santa Claus is indeed, as many have pointed out, a commercial icon. But his special appeal lies in the fact that he goes beyond that status to become what Stephen Nissenbaum calls an "anti-commercial commercial icon."[2] Santa Claus, in essence, can function at two levels simultaneously. He is a successful commercial icon whose image helps to induce people to buy commodities as Christmas gifts. However, Santa Claus transcends that function, which after all is shared by many other images, since he has built into his icon a narrative that has nothing to do with the world of commerce and capitalism. In fact, he is able to evoke the home, handmade gifts, and spontaneous giving—the opposite of modern commercial activity. He is a figure whose function is at once out in the open, so to speak, since he is featured like any other advertising icon, but at the same time is totally invisible. His is an image that can persuade people to buy commodities, but allow them to forget that the exchange is a commercial exchange. It is this quality of an image—to hide or mask its real function—which makes for a highly successful ideological icon. To perform one operation and to appear to negate it at the same time defines an ideological mediation of a contradiction. In the case of Santa Claus, the fit is almost perfect. Santa Claus is, according to the ideological narrative, the gift bringer who brings gifts to all without charge or any other material exchange, just as in the narrative of Christ's Nativity it is God who brings favor to all without charge. In reality, of course, what is hidden is the opposite of the Santa Claus narrative, since whatever gifts are actually given are given by particular people who had to purchase them in the marketplace according to their means.

Moore's poem "A Visit from St. Nicholas" was published in the 1820s, the same decade that factory-produced commodities began to appear in American stores and shops. One of the many ideological problems facing contemporary storeowners was how to persuade Americans to buy mass-produced commodities. These merchants had somehow to overcome a barely conscious reluctance to buy any mass-produced goods, especially commodities that were perceived as luxuries. Both giving gifts at Christmas and buying mass-produced goods went against the republican ideology of self-reliance and frugality regnant in the late eighteenth and early nineteenth centuries in the newly independent nation. The figure of Santa Claus, as imagined in Moore's poem, and the ritual of gift giving that he legitimated, became a solution to both problems at once. It had the additional advantage of providing an alternative to the rowdy "wassailing" of the lower classes, which was threatening the physical safety and comfort of the urban upper classes. The adoption of Moore's version of Christmas could move Christmas celebrations off the streets and into the parlor, where it became a domestic holiday of the hearth and children.[3]

For both children and adults, this symbolic function of Santa Claus in the American Christmas was truly a "mystification." It displaced conscious attention away from actual material exchanges onto a fictive character. Adults, under the aegis of Santa Claus, were encouraged to buy mass-produced, industrial commodities and to give them to those within their domestic circle as personal, unique tokens of their individual affection. Children, and by associative extension, women, could receive these gifts as the outpourings of the generosity of the figure of a kindly old man, not as the result of capitalist exchange based purely on the cash-nexus. In somewhat later elaborations of the Santa Claus narrative, moreover, the gifts were the product of a preindustrial workshop, not the real factories of nineteenth-century America where less fortunate children labored long hours in the cold and dark with little to eat.

Even the fact that these commodities were usually luxury goods was finessed in a very telling way through this process of mystification. In the first place, the introduction of luxury goods relied heavily on their legitimation by religious and cultural values. The most popular early luxury gifts were Bibles and "annuals," gift books produced each fall by collecting short stories, poems, and other "genteel" forms of art. Thus, the purchasing public was habituated to buying luxury goods as gifts, made easier by the fact that they were of indisputable cultural value and were purchased for an ostensibly Christian holiday. The fact that these items could be "personalized" by handwritten completion of elaborately engraved dedicatory pages only increased the illusion of their genesis in spontaneous individual affection. Of course, the gift books were mass-produced for profit like any commodity and the very personal dedicatory pages were stereotyped, but under the mystification of Christmas gift giving that inconvenient detail could be overlooked and forgotten. Thus, Christmas with Santa Claus as an icon helped to overcome old-fashioned inhibitions against the purchase of mass-produced luxury goods and abetted the pretense that commodities could be personalized by minor modifications. These steps were important in helping the American economy shift from an agricultural model based on self-reliance and small-scale production for use at home to an industrial model based on purchase of commodities mass-produced in factories for profitable sale.

We can discern here an interesting inversion. Whereas in a pre-industrial society, the gift giver in the Christmas celebration was the landlord and the recipients were the workers, in the burgeoning industrial society of nineteenth-century America, the gift giver became an idealized father figure and the recipients were children. These transformations are reflected in the changing role and character of the Santa Claus figure. In Moore's poem, Santa Claus is an idealized and domesticated worker who brings gifts to the family as projected from the point of view of a member of the gentry. However, this was an unstable mediation as social and economic conditions changed in the early nineteenth century. The rise of industrial capitalism meant that the landed gentry diminished in numbers and in influence, to be replaced by owners of the industrial means of production. At the same time, the working class grew in numbers, swelled by the influx of immigrants of different ethnicities, connected with the new owners of the means of production only by the cash-nexus. In such a situation, the old contradictions between the workers and the gentry expressed in the wassail made little sense, and the cultural connection that made the wassail significant to both groups was disappearing. The new contradiction expressed at Christmas was between the purchasers of commodities and the producers and suppliers of those commodities. The point of contradiction was the exchange process itself, particularly the price charged for the commodities.

At the same time, a new contradiction was making its appearance in modern industrial society. As many writers have pointed out, the modern social notion of childhood had started to appear in tandem with the domestication of Christmas, at first among the families of the older gentry and then in the rising middle class. Unlike agricultural societies, in which children were expected to share the work of the farm and the home as soon as they were able, or, the children of the industrial working class who were expected to share the work of the factory or mine as soon as they could, the children of the industrial upper and middle class came to occupy a unique position. Not only were they educated, but also they were increasingly sheltered and idealized by their parents. For the first time in history, childhood itself became a time sentimentalized as innocent and wondrous; children became part of the solace that the home offered to the hardworking father. Gradually, children became the focus of Christmas and gift giving; the newly fashionable Christmas tree, symbolically near the hearth, became the center of the holiday and the locus of gifts. Santa Claus's special role was to give the children gifts, while they pretended not to expect them, and the presents to the adults became a kind of afterthought. The whole ritual process that grew up in nineteenth-century America, as Nissenbaum recounts in detail, was reinforced by the borrowing of the Christmas tree from Germany and the fiction of "surprising" the children anew each year. The logic of the new symbolic development was turning from the elfin, working-class St. Nicholas of Moore's poem in favor of an idealized, almost larger-than-life father figure. Concurrent with this change in the form and function of Santa Claus, there was a change in the recipients. Whereas in the wassail of preindustrial society the recipients were adult workers, in the Christmas of nineteenth-century American industrial society they were children, usually the children of the upper and middle classes. What these two groups have in common, vis-à-vis the actual gift bringer, is that they are inferiors. And, it might be added, at least in the idealized version of events, both groups received their gifts with gratitude and good will.

During the Christmas seasons of the mid–nineteenth century, the workers were not entirely forgotten, despite their virtual disappearance from the middle-class Christmas and the neglect of the wassail tradition in the urban centers. Indeed, one of the functions of Charles Dickens's novella *A Christmas Carol* was to remind well-to-do capitalists both large and (like Scrooge) small that part of their obligation at Christmas was to provide for their own workers and for the larger group of the "deserving" poor. Actually, *A Christmas Carol* was only one of a series of very popular Christmas books that Dickens turned out each year during the politically and socially explosive 1840s which he used to voice his own slightly socialist views, views expressed more directly in his novel *Hard Times*. But *A Christmas Carol* was following in the well-established middle-class tradition of presenting systemic social and economic problems in terms of individual personal relations. *A Christmas Carol*, like other middle-class reformist fiction of the nineteenth century, suggests that changing the hearts of individuals can solve problems such as poverty and class conflict, as Scrooge's heart was changed by his ghostly visitors. In this context, an emphasis on Christmas as an essentially domestic holiday in which the good will generated in the family circle spills out into the larger world in the form of charity fits quite neatly.[4]

In fact, in the later nineteenth century charities became systematically institutionalized in the United States, at a time when even some committed capitalists had to admit that the disparity between the few fabulously wealthy and the many poor was becoming obscene. Many of these charities found that Christmas proved to be a propitious time for appeals to the well-off. So the Christmas tradition that the rich had an obligation to give to the relief of the less well-off continued, with the difference that the recipients of this beneficence, while working-class, were often immigrants, out of work and extremely impoverished, not the wassailing workers of the early nineteenth century. Perhaps the most important and attractive feature of this new arrangement for the wealthy was that they no longer had to open their homes to the poor or even meet them face-to-face. The rise of institutional charities meant that the wealthy, like Scrooge, could simply give a contribution to a sometimes equally well-off representative of the charity and stay home with a good conscience. Interestingly enough, the mystification of Santa Claus penetrated even this realm of charity, when organizations such as the Salvation Army began to use men dressed as Santa Claus to solicit contributions on the street. Indirectly, this fed into and reinforced the image of Santa Claus as the gift giver mediating between superior and inferior groups.

Santa Claus is described as an elf, a figure situated at the intersection of the categories of the natural, the human, and the divine, and having features taken from each category. His numinous character is further limned by having him carried through the air by "eight tiny reindeer." Of perhaps even greater import, however, is his mode of entry into the house. He comes down through the chimney. This is significant because in the traditional symbolism of the house, there are two features vulnerable to the spirit world: the threshold (*limina*) and the chimney. Perhaps because of the obvious analogy with the smoke drifting out of the home and the contrary motion of the wind blowing into the home through it, the chimney was considered a point of entry and exit for spirits and ghosts. Historian of religion Mircea Eliade recounts how shamans in Mongolia and among Native Americans make their spiritual journeys when in a trance by leaving and returning through the chimney.[5] And the cultural historian Clement Miles noted that the pre-Christian winter festivals in Europe centered on the hearth as the place where the ghosts of the ancestors would come back to visit their descendants.[6] Hence, these descendants would leave offerings of food on the hearth for the hungry ghosts to feast on, just as children in modern America leave cookies and milk for Santa Claus to eat. Connecting St. Nicholas to the spirit world in this way would appear to have been a wholly original contribution of Clement Moore. The original model for Santa Claus, St. Nicholas of Myra—although he was associated with gift giving and, since he was a saint, with the supernatural—entirely lacked the mythic associations that Moore gave his St. Nicholas. After all, according to legend, St. Nicholas was associated with the sea and sailors, not the air and flying animals, and the money he gave was either thrown over a wall or through a window, not down a chimney. The detail of Santa coming down the chimney is highly significant in deciphering his symbolic character. Santa's liminal character is rounded off by the blessing he pronounces on all as he leaves the house. Since Santa Claus's role as a mediating figure has already been clearly established, and since one of the major functions of good spirits was the blessing of homes and their inhabitants, especially at the winter solstice and other seasonal occasions, this action is wholly congruent with his mythic status.

This mediating, complex, and overdetermined character of Santa Claus was just what allowed him to change functions and images in response to changing contradictions. Of course, Santa Claus is a spirit, and a spirit, even a good spirit, is a "shape-shifter."

Santa Claus is a complex mediating figure. He mediates the world of commerce and production with the world of the home and the family, the two major worlds of modern society, which have been to a considerable extent the carriers of that society. In fact, those two worlds need mediation since each has traits that can make them contradictory to one another, in spite of their ideological concord. The cash-nexus always tends to destroy the family and any other group built on traditional relationships and loyalties, since the function of cash is to replace relationships based solely on the realization of expectations and the satisfaction of inherited ties with relationships built on mutual profit and self-interest. In turn, the cash-nexus is opposed by family and ethnic loyalties and bonds that interpret cash-based relationships as cold and unnatural, as artificial and meaningless, as calculated rather than spontaneous. This contradiction is concealed by the image of Santa Claus who brings the products of industry and commerce into the domestic circle not as commodities, but as freely exchanged gifts. Of course, these commodities are not gotten freely, there has been an entirely normal exchange that led to their appearance in the home, but the idealized image is contrary to that fact. We call this operation "mystification," since it renders silent any analytic discourse by its subterfuge—a characteristic shared by many successful commercial icons.

But Santa Claus's symbolic function as the idealized gift bringer stands in opposition to the real genesis of Christmas gifts. As a powerful father figure, Santa Claus can magically produce these gifts from his limitless resources. In reality, though, the gifts given at Christmas are produced in a world of scarcity by human labor using tools and machines. It is noteworthy that Santa Claus is a generative father figure who seems to have adopted a maternal function by giving birth to these gifts "from a sack." This ambiguity teeters on the brink of androgyny if we recall Santa Claus's original description as an elf and the fact that any liminal figure that occupies a place at the edge of ordinary categories, like a Herme, is often sexually ambiguous. Despite the fact that some later extensions of the Santa Claus narrative do provide Santa with a wife, he is still a father figure who opens a sack and gives birth to gifts on a holiday ostensibly devoted to the birth of a child who lacks a human father according to part of his narrative. This may be related to the complementarity of the Virgin Mary and Santa Claus in the popular imagery of Christmas scenes.

The American Santa Claus, although a remote descendant of a Christian bishop, has become a dispenser of a grace that is incompatible with the Christian notion of grace. The gifts that Santa Claus brings are signs of ultimate favor, but they are merited, as are the gifts of coal or switches for the bad. Moreover, the system that produces the gifts that Santa Claus brings is the market system of global capitalism. Proximately, the gifts are, of course, commodities that are the product of natural resources, human labor, and capital. If one questions where these factors of production come from or why certain people should be favored by them and others not so favored, there is no answer other than luck or chance and no interest in providing an answer to be had in the Santa Claus narrative.

In Christianity, on the other hand, even if some of the gifts that one receives are also proximately the product of human labor applied to natural resources, there is recognition of a further dimension and an encouragement to seek after it. Even though it is acknowledged that this ultimate dimension cannot be fully grasped by intellectual means, there is still the assertion in Christianity and in other traditional religions that all of existence comes from and is dependent on this other dimension, that there is in it something like an intentionality, a drive or nisus, for the harmony of all beings. Moreover, there are several points in life where existence is open to this dimension, which offers the possibility of a better, more just life in the future, as well as a striving within all beings to realize this future. Dissatisfaction with consumer capitalism as a system closed to other dimensions of life is common to many critiques, religious or not. Ultimately, for Christianity all of existence has the character of a gift and tends toward the most harmonious and just good for all. This characteristic of existence makes thanksgiving the most appropriate response, and makes sacrificial love—as demonstrated in the life and teachings of Jesus of Nazareth—a fitting paradigm for the direction of the cosmos.

The system in which Santa Claus is the mediator also differs from the Christian notion of grace with respect to its effect on individuals. It would be better to say here "desired effect" on individuals, in order to avoid the invidious habit of comparing two religious positions by speaking realistically of one and idealistically of the other. For consumer capitalism, the effect is a dual and a dynamic one. On the one hand, the individual is taught to measure her or his worth by the value of her or his possessions and consumption. On the other hand, and as a consequence of the previous point, individuals are taught to want more and better commodities. These two features are an intrinsic part of the institutions of consumer capitalism and, in fact, are necessary for its continual growth, since its growth depends on the restless desire of consumers for more and better commodities. This is the structural reason for the well-known acquisitive character of the capitalist consumer. It is also the nearest to the notion of infinity that the religion of the market comes. Its approximation, however, is merely additive and quantitative, what Hegel called "the bad, false, infinite." This notion is entirely characteristic of capitalist culture and society for good and for ill. It works for good insofar as it acts as a spur to innovation and an increase in productivity, highly positive traits of consumer capitalism. On the other hand, this continual search for more and better and the willingness to destroy and re-assemble anything and everything in that quest have had devastating consequences for the environment and for the personalities shaped in its image.

In the Christian notion of grace, by contrast, the individual experiences her or his own life as a gift whose value comes from simply existing as a part of the cosmos. The infinite here is experienced as a creative mystery that supports an increase of value and an increase in the intensity for all of life. The future is experienced as an invitation to an adventure to make life better and to ensure that whatever values are realized in concrete goods must be distributed fairly, while at the same time sustaining a complementary notion that the ultimate value of life is secure whatever the future holds. This is the somewhat paradoxical notion of peace in Christianity and in other traditional religions such as Buddhism. Peace is the serenity that comes from being able to live in change, pursuing a more harmonious and intense life while at the same time not basing the value of the present on future achievement. In Paul's phrase, it is the ability "to have and have not," or as T. S. Eliot articulates the same paradoxical orientation, to sit still and "to care and not to care." In such a conception, the individual is released to experience the universe in a contemplative mode at the same time that he or she works to innovate or produce for the good of all, knowing that success is important but is not the basis for self-worth. This is all made possible because there is a sense that there is a center of valuing in the cosmos which is not human but which does value humans. As a result of being valued, each individual is stimulated and empowered to cooperate with others, even at the cost of some of her or his self-interest.

The differences between the grace that is mediated by the icon of Santa Claus and the grace that Christians claim to be revealed through the life and teaching of Jesus of Nazareth appear at their starkest, perhaps, at the point of self-transformation. The self that is formed by the gifts of Santa Claus is a self that may be affirmed, but is led by that affirmation to search for possible new experiences only among the goods produced by the capitalist system of production and available only at the exchange value assigned to them by the market mechanism. There is a choice for the transformed individual in consumer capitalism, but it is a choice where options are conditioned by their availability in the market and by the purchasing power of the individual. Both advertising and the background reality of media programming, including news programs, cooperate to make the rather limited and stylized options of experience seem everyday, unquestionable, familiar, and inevitable. Indeed, the transformation desired here would better be described as cheerful resignation to a "normal" life, or finding joy in conformity. The "transformation" wrought by participation in the American Christmas is one of giving in to the course of life engineered and made to seem inevitable by our socially constructed reality.

A further symbolic function of the icon of Santa Claus as a dispenser of grace is that it allows groups other than Christians to participate in the American Christmas celebration, to participate fully in consumer capitalism and its culture. As many historians have noted, until the nineteenth century Christmas was not widely celebrated or observed in America. Many of the dominant religious groups in colonial America were Christian churches that did not, as a matter of principle, celebrate holy days such as Christmas. This makes all the more remarkable the feat of Santa Claus not only in largely causing Christmas to be established on the American cultural calendar in a few short decades, but in creating the illusion that its celebration had always been observed. But Santa Claus's cultural work did not stop there. As Christmas became increasingly associated with him and with his narrative, it ceased to be identified with the specific religion of Christianity and came to be simply part of the American cultural tradition. One had the right to celebrate Christmas merely by virtue of being an American, and one could exercise that right simply by participating in consumer capitalism. The purchase of a tree, decorations, cards, food, and gifts was all that was needed in the way of religious activity in order to celebrate Christmas as an American.

The grace of Santa Claus is neither free nor universal, however. It harks back, in fact, to an ancient religious sentiment, one of the most ancient and one that is still keenly alive: the notion that the divinity shows its favor by material blessing. This allows the obverse reading of experience, namely, that material blessing, wealth and health, is a sign, the only reliable sign, of divine favor. This can take various forms: military success attends those who are right in the sight of the divinity, abundance is a sign of divine satisfaction, good health is a special gift from God, living to old age is a token that God is pleased with one's life. There is a negative side to all these judgments, of course, that must be part of this religious view: military defeat is a consequence of divine wrath, poverty is a punishment from God, illness is a curse from God, and dying young is a result of sin. There is a strong current in American society that finds this religious worldview natural and self-evident. Those who believe that AIDS, for example, is a punishment for sin or that the reason for poverty has to do with the moral vice of the poor are expressing the theological conclusions of this religion, as are those who believe that "greed is good." The American Christmas, while not directly articulating this religious conclusion, is nonetheless logically involved with it.

In Christian theology, grace means that God loves all beings in the universe, not because they do or accomplish anything, but just because they are. There is nothing that anyone can do to deserve or earn this grace; it is objectively there as part of God's being. Because of this grace, God is forever forgiving us at every new moment, so that we are constantly being reborn and renewed in God's sight.

In the Christian view of grace, other values have a higher priority than self-interest. Illness, poverty, loss, and even death are not signs that one is not worthy or acceptable, but that there are large parts of the world where God's will is not done and where the values that make for the future peace and harmony of the cosmos are not given the highest priority. It is part of the traditional Christian theory of action that humans do better when they are first valued and then shown tasks to perform for the common good. Naked self-interest is for traditional Christian ethics a vice, while suffering for a good cause from which one will garner no personal gain is a virtue. The Christian claim is that becoming like God, loving all creatures with an equal love and working for their just good, will lead to the kind of peace that stands in stark contrast to the satiated state of an idealized American Christmas. This all begins with acceptance of God's unconditional acceptance of each person, moral logic quite different from that of consumer capitalism and the values associated with its icon, Santa Claus.

Notes

1. The notion that contemporary consumer capitalism could be regarded as a religion is probably a strange one for many readers. However, the use of the category "religion" to describe phenomena not usually so understood has a long history among theologians and scholars of religion. The approach generally followed in this essay is represented by the project on "New Theology on Population, Consumption and Ecology," directed by Harold Coward and Daniel Macquire; compare the five articles by members of this project published in the *Journal of the American Academy of Religion* 65, no. 2 (Summer 1997): 257–353.

2. Stephen Nissenbaum, *The Battle for Christmas* (New York: Alfred A. Knopf, 1996), 169–75.

3. Ibid., 90–131.

4. Ibid., 222–26.

5. Mircea Eliade, *The Sacred and the Profane* (New York: Harper and Brothers, 1961), 172–79.

6. Clement A. Miles, *Christmas Customs and Traditions* (New York: Dover, 1976), 180–92.

Chapter Ten

What Child *Is* This?

Lynch v. Donnelly and the Celebration of
Christmas in the United States

Paula M. Cooey

The United States Constitution states, "Congress shall make no law respecting an establishment of religion, or prohibiting the free exercise thereof."[1] There are necessary limits to free exercise of religion, usually relative to a stated public good or to individual welfare. So, for example, human sacrifice on religious grounds would be prohibited. In some situations, however, the limits are not so obvious. Religiously authorized polygyny, the use of spiritual healers for children who are ill, parental refusal on religious grounds to allow their children to have blood transfusions, the use of animals for public sacrifice, and the rights of prisoners to practice religiously authorized dietary codes number among these.[2]

As with free exercise of religion, so with the establishment clause. The religious history of the country is complicated regarding what constitutes the establishment of a state religion. Is establishment defined exclusively by proclaiming a particular religion the religion of state? Or does establishment more subtly extend to the appropriation of distinctively religious practices into the practices and the work of the state? Attempts by those who would strictly separate all religious practices from the official life of the state have obviously been unsuccessful. At the same time, attempts by those who would have officially and exclusively Christianized political institutions have likewise failed. Nevertheless, it is difficult at best to negotiate with consistency what defines a constitutionally acceptable accommodation to religious practices and beliefs and what, in intention or in effect, marks an entanglement of government and religion that violates the establishment clause. Prayer in the public schools and its most recent manifestation as a moment of silence provide two of the most controversial examples of the twentieth century.

The Supreme Court is the court of last resort to determine what establishment and free exercise mean in any given situation, and its record is anything but consistent. Indeed, the opinions in the case of *Lynch v. Donnelly* exemplify a history of inconsistency as majority and minority alike cite precedents to support their mutually exclusive claims.[3] This inconsistency arises over how, where, and on what grounds to separate religion or church and state from one another. The intention would seem to be to determine how to accommodate religious and nonreligious plurality, and the chief discursive strategy would be to create a secular (nonreligious) space within which free religious exercise, within certain limits and irrespective of differences, might occur.

Intentions notwithstanding, sociologist of religion Robert Bellah argued decades ago that the United States government practices in effect a civil religion, rooted in Protestant Christianity.[4] More recently, sociologist of religion Ronald Flowers has argued that the history of Supreme Court decisions on establishment (as well as free expression), while not consistent, is also hardly neutral, and in fact, tends to favor religion.[5] The question repeatedly arises whether such a religiously neutral space called secularity actually exists. As a major turning point in an already muddled history of Court decision making, *Lynch v. Donnelly* suggests the contrary. As I shall argue, the Supreme Court, in its very efforts to uphold religious freedom as guaranteed by the First Amendment, played a particularly ironic role in establishing a religion of state. If this is so, what then are the effects and implications of distinguishing between religion and secularity? Does this conceptual pairing become a discursive strategy for sanctifying the power of the state?

In *Lynch v. Donnelly* the Supreme Court determined that it was not a violation of the establishment clause of the First Amendment to erect a Nativity scene, paid for by local government, in a public space. The vote was narrow, five to four, with Justice Sandra Day O'Connor the swing vote. The case exemplifies many of the tensions that necessarily arise in a secular, religiously plural democracy in which White Christianity nevertheless serves as the culturally dominant religious tradition.[6] Rather than argue for or against the final decision, I propose to explore the tensions themselves as reflected in the opinions of the majority and the minority. As I hope to clarify, both majority and minority opinions assume a concept of religion that is problematic both in theory and in practice, especially when defining religion in relation to secularity and the state. Both opinions also intervene as representations of the state in the construction of the concept of religion itself in ways that are troubling with respect to the power wielded by the state. Moreover, the theological implications of both majority and minority opinions are disturbing.

Lynch v. Donnelly

For some four decades the city of Pawtucket, Rhode Island, in cooperation with a local retail merchants' association, annually erected a Christmas display in Hodgson Park, a park owned by a nonprofit organization, located in the heart of the shopping district. The display included a number of Christmas figures and decorations, among them a Santa Claus house, reindeer pulling Santa's sleigh, candy-cane poles, a Christmas tree, carolers, cutouts of a clown, an elephant, and a teddy bear, a banner heralding SEASONS GREETINGS, and a Nativity scene. The Nativity scene included life-size figures of the infant Jesus, Mary, Joseph, angels, shepherds, the three kings, and associated animals. The local government purchased the display, including the Nativity scene, at taxpayers' expense.[7]

Pawtucket residents, individual members of the Rhode Island affiliate of the American Civil Liberties Union, and the affiliate as a whole originally sued the city in the United States District Court for the district of Rhode Island.[8] The litigants claimed that the inclusion of the Nativity scene violated the establishment clause of the First Amendment of the Constitution. The city appealed the decision, first unsuccessfully at the appellate court level, then successfully before the United States Supreme Court.

On appeal the Supreme Court overturned the lower courts' rulings on several grounds. The majority, including Chief Justice Warren Burger with Justices O'Connor, Powell, Rehnquist, and White, determined that the city's involvement with the Nativity scene did not violate the establishment clause. The majority based its decision on a three-point test, established as criteria by a previous Court decision: the Nativity scene had a secular purpose; the city had not advanced religion; and the Nativity scene did not create excessive entanglement between religion and government or excessive political division along religious lines.[9] Justice O'Connor, while concurring with the majority, advanced a separate opinion, distinguishing at length between intention and effect, that the Nativity scene at issue was not intended to endorse and did not have the effect of endorsing Christianity. Justice Brennan, along with Justices Blackmun, Marshall, and Stevens, dissented, claiming that the city's display was an unconstitutional endorsement of a particular faith. Brennan argued that the majority had not in fact applied the three criteria earlier established with sufficient rigor. Blackmun, joined by Stevens, added a separate dissent on the grounds that precedent itself *required* that the presence of the Nativity scene in a government sponsored display violated the First Amendment. The decision came to be known as the "plastic reindeer rule."

The majority opinion argued that the Nativity scene did not violate the Constitution on several grounds. In the first place, the majority argued, the Constitution does not require complete separation of church and state; rather, it "affirmatively mandates accommodation, not merely tolerance, of all religions, and forbids hostility toward any" (at 670). So, for example, children may wear religious garb such as yamulkes for Jewish males or head coverings for Muslim females to public school to accommodate the requirements of their respective traditions. Accommodation in itself does not advance a particular religion and has historically occurred and continues to occur in a number of governmental practices. For example, the majority reasoned that had the founders intended complete separation, they would not have employed congressional chaplains to offer daily prayers, nor would they have established Thanksgiving and Christmas as official holidays, in effect financially subsidizing them by giving government employees time off. There are additional economic connections as well, opined the majority, for example, the national motto, "In God We Trust," inscribed on money. Furthermore, according to the majority, including a Nativity scene in a Christmas display does not differ from hanging religious art in the National Gallery or the Smithsonian and, like such exhibitions, simply bears witness to our religious history. The majority noted other accommodations including: the incorporation of "under God" into the pledge of allegiance; the presidential proclamation, at the behest of Congress, of a national day of prayer; and the representation of Moses with the Ten Commandments decorating the very chamber in which the oral arguments in the case were heard. From the majority point of view, displaying the Nativity scene did not advance a particular religion.

In addition to the arguments for accommodation rather than strict separation, the majority argued that the Nativity scene had a secular purpose; it accepted the city's claim that its reasons for including the Nativity scene were the same as its reasons for exhibiting the display as a whole. The city argued that it displayed the Nativity scene for the purposes of portraying the historical origins of the holiday and to establish good will. The city further stressed the economic purposes of connecting good will to gift giving. The majority concurred that, given the wider context in which the Nativity scene was placed, namely, the Santa village, the intent was indeed purely secular.

Finally, the majority opinion rejected the plaintiffs' arguments that displaying the Nativity scene evidenced excessive entanglement of government with religion by creating political divisiveness among people of different religions or no religion. Other than the suit itself, there was no evidence of such divisiveness. From the majority perspective, "[a] litigant cannot, by the very act of commencing a lawsuit…create the appearance of divisiveness and then exploit it as evidence of entanglement" (at 685).

In a separate concurring opinion, Justice O'Connor distinguished further between intent and effect. She, in short, went beyond the three criteria the majority presumed to apply. She argued that not only must the government not intend to advance or prohibit religion, its acts must not inadvertently have the affect on a perceiver of advancing or prohibiting religion. She made this distinction by stressing the context in which the Nativity scene appeared. The context clarified that the city's purpose and effect "was not promotion of religious content of the crèche but celebration of the public holiday through its traditional symbols. Celebration of public holidays, which have cultural significance even if they also have religious aspects, is a legitimate secular purpose" (at 691). She concluded:

> [G]overnment acknowledgments of religion [e.g. congressional prayers, references to God on money and in the pledge, public holidays, etc.]

serve, in the only ways reasonably possible in our culture, the legitimate secular purposes of solemnizing public occasions, expressing confidence in the future, and encouraging the recognition of what is worthy of appreciation in society. For that reason, and because of their history and ubiquity, those practices are not understood as conveying government approval of particular religious beliefs. The display of the crèche likewise serves a secular purpose—celebration of a public holiday with traditional symbols (at 693).

The minority opinion, written by Brennan, argued that the majority had not rigorously applied the three criteria, established by precedent, to determine violation. In a separate opinion that supplemented the minority opinion, Blackmun, with Stevens, argued that by not rigorously applying the three criteria the majority was, in fact, overturning its own previous decisions. Blackmun further argued that displaying the Nativity scene, given its theological meaning, was offensive not only to non-Christians, *but also to serious Christians alike*. In short, the government had advanced Christianity by including the crèche or Nativity scene in the display while simultaneously defiling one of its central symbols.

In laying out the minority opinion, Brennan began by attacking the majority claim that the inclusion of the Nativity scene had only a secular purpose. First, he noted that the display itself did not require the presence of a crèche to accomplish its intentions of promoting good will that would manifest itself through increased economic consumption. Second, he pointed to the contradictions in the testimony of Mayor Lynch who, having asserted that the crèche was displayed solely for secular purposes, also claimed that the people of the town supported the mayor's efforts to put Christ back into Christmas by including the crèche in the display. Brennan further argued that, the majority opinion notwithstanding, the government in effect, if not intention, advanced a particular religion because no effort was made by city officials to include symbols from other religious traditions celebrated during the season. Finally and very importantly, the minority opinion claimed that the crèche promoted excessive entanglement on the grounds that in light of the Court's present ruling, the local government would foreseeably become excessively entangled as it negotiated the inclusion or exclusion of other icons from other traditions, for example, a menorah.

The dissenting opinion refutes the majority opinion at three points, each of which is crucial to the topic of Christmas as an issue of ongoing conflict between religion and state. These include the significance of context, where to draw the line on accommodation, and the majority's claim for support for its decision from American historical experience. Brennan argued that the wider context provided by the other, secular elements of the display, rather than secularizing the crèche, trivialized it. Noting that the Nativity scene was a prominently displayed, life-size scene without accompanying cautionary messages, Brennan wrote, rather testily:

I refuse to accept the notion implicit in today's decision that non-Christians would find that the religious content of the crèche is eliminated by the fact that it appears as part of the city's otherwise secular celebration of the Christmas holiday. The nativity scene is clearly distinct in its purpose and effect from the rest of the Hodgson Park display for the simple reason that it is the only one rooted in a biblical account of Christ's birth. It is the chief symbol of the characteristically Christian belief that a divine Savior was brought into the world and that the purpose of this miraculous birth was to illuminate a path toward salvation and redemption. For Christians this path is exclusive, precious, and holy. But for those who do not share these beliefs, the symbolic reenactment of the birth of a divine being who has miraculously incarnated as a man stands as a dramatic reminder of their differences with Christian faith (at 708).

Brennan went on to point out that, when government appears to sponsor such views by putting up such a display, the practice could not possibly reflect a neutral posture toward religious institutions. On the contrary, the effect for the non-Christian is necessarily to be excluded by an elected government, an effect that cannot be countenanced by the establishment clause.

Brennan then proceeded to address the majority claim that the practice of displaying a crèche should be accommodated on the same grounds that other governmental practices of religious origin are accommodated (for example, the establishment of religious holidays as national holidays, religious inscriptions on money, and so forth). Brennan argued that the secular elements and practices of Christmas, which he located in folk traditions and patriotic practices, could be distinguished from the religious elements, which he identified with the supernatural as manifested in particular symbols and beliefs. Though secular elements could clearly be accommodated with respect to any public holiday, it did not follow that all governmental associations with a public holiday were likewise constitutional.

The majority had located the authority for the accommodation of religious expression in governmental practices in American historical experience. Brennan challenged the majority's view of history. He charged that they never did a serious historical analysis, precisely because the facts would have substantiated the ambiguity of traditional practices. He noted that among the Christian denominations, serious conflict erupted over both whether and how to celebrate Christmas. Brennan distinguished eighteenth-century differences between Catholics, Anglicans, and Lutherans, on the one hand, all of whom celebrated Christmas as a religious holiday, and Presbyterians, Congregationalists, Baptists, and Methodists, on the other hand, who opposed the celebration, regarding it with suspicion at best, even into the nineteenth century. He surmised, "For those who authored the Bill of Rights, it seems reasonable to suppose that publicly celebrating Christmas would have been regarded as at least a sensitive matter, if not deeply controversial. As we have repeatedly observed, the Religion Clauses were intended to ensure a benign regime of competitive disorder among all denominations, so that each was free to vie against the others for the allegiance of its followers without state interference" (at 723).[10] The text goes on to trace the history of the declaration of Christmas as a federal holiday (1870) and concludes that there is no evidence whatsoever that "the Framers would have expressly approved a federal celebration of the Christmas holiday including public displays of a nativity scene.... Nor is there any suggestion that publicly financed and supported displays of Christmas crèche are supported by a record of widespread, undeviating acceptance that extends through our history" (at 724). In short, the American historical experience could not be evoked as authoritative because historical analysis contradicts the majority's claim. Brennan concluded, "the role of safeguarding 'our religious heritage' and of promoting religious beliefs is reserved as the exclusive prerogative of our Nation's churches, religious institutions, and spiritual leaders.... [T]he [establishment] Clause demands that government play no role in this effort" (at 725).

Blackmun's additional dissenting opinion, joined by Stevens, remarks:

> Not only does the Court's resolution of this controversy make light of our precedents, the majority does an injustice to the crèche and the message it manifests.... [T]he mayor of Pawtucket undertook a crusade to "keep 'Christ' in Christmas"... [but] Pawtucket's display invites people to "participate in the Christmas spirit, brotherhood, peace, and let loose with their money." The crèche has been relegated to the role of a neutral harbinger of the holiday season, useful for commercial and other purposes, but devoid of any inherent meaning.... The import of the Court's decision is to encourage use of the crèche in a municipally sponsored display, a setting where Christians feel constrained in acknowledging its symbolic meaning and non-Christians feel alienated by its presence. Surely this is a misuse of a sacred symbol (at 726–727).

Theorizing Religion and the State

The differences between the majority and the minority in the ruling on *Lynch v. Donnelly* are extremely important and, for the most part, obvious; however, the commonalities are not so readily apparent. As I shall shortly argue, the commonalities indicate that this is an in-fight over where to draw the line between secularity and religion. This in-fight bears significant witness to the role of the state in the actual production of both religion and secularity. To grasp the full implications of this claim requires some background on how scholars theorize religion and on the roles they themselves play in the social construction of both the various particular traditions and the general concept, *religion.*

The understanding of religion as a generic concept for categorizing certain kinds of beliefs and practices that are "spiritual" and thus distinguishable from other beliefs and practices designated as political, economic, scientific, and artistic is modern. The restricting of the spiritual to realities designated as "supernatural" in contrast to the "natural" order is likewise a relatively recent development of Western history. Until the European Renaissance and the Protestant Reformation, what we now call human identity or subjectivity was neither as individualized nor as compartmentalized as we take for granted today; nor were the lines between nature and supernature strictly drawn. By the time of the European Enlightenment, philosophers assumed the distinction; furthermore, with the later emergence of the social sciences, social scientists and Anglo-European Christian theologians alike began to show interest, though for different reasons, in studying spiritual beliefs and practices across the different traditions that framed their contexts.

I do not intend to rehearse the full history of the concept or to trace the development of the discipline that studies religion.[11] I propose instead to point briefly to the reciprocal role played by particular beliefs and practices in the making of culture and society, as well as the social production of the general concept of religion itself. This will provide the background for focusing more narrowly and at length on the state's current involvement in various processes of the social construction of reality to preserve its own interests. In agreement with most scholars of religion and many social theorists, I, as a White feminist Reformed Protestant theologian, assume that what we now call religious traditions are themselves human artifacts that reciprocate in the making of human society and culture. In other words, human beings, however unconsciously and unintentionally, make up what we now call the various religions they practice as a way of ordering human life. The religions in turn effectively make up human individual and social identity to the extent that they effectively authorize and order human socio-cultural thinking, habits, and practices.[12] Thus, the general concept *religion,* itself also a human artifact, plays a far from innocent role in the social production of the state and its maintenance.[13]

Because of the dominating historical role played by White Protestant Christianity in the formation of the United States, theological debate and discussion during the Reformation of the sixteenth century bear especially telling witness to the reciprocal role of religious practices and beliefs in the actual making of United States culture.[14] To be more precise, the middle of the sixteenth century in Europe, commonly known as the Protestant Reformation, was an age of several reformations within Anglo-European Christian traditions. In addition to the Protestant Reformation, these included the radical reformation movements of Anabaptists and Unitarians, among others, and the reform efforts within the Roman Catholic Church marked especially by the Council of Trent and the founding of the Jesuit order. Without question, the upheaval of the times resulted from a variety of material conditions including new technologies, colonial expansion, and disrupted patterns of labor due to rising capitalism. At the same time, this period of about four decades also saw great public theological debates over human salvation in relation to human freedom. Are humans free to choose between good and evil, a freedom that makes sin inevitable and requires a human role in salvation? Or is the inevitable sinfulness of such choices the very antithesis of freedom? Does salvation lie instead in release from the bondage of bad choices, a release that depends on God's grace alone? What are the origin, status, and role of ethical action or works within the religious life? What are the significance of ritual and spiritual formation in the economy of salvation? In posing and addressing such questions, a major shift took place in how humans came to understand their ethical, political, and spiritual agency. This shift redefined their relations to their immediate communities, to ecclesial and governmental authority, to the cosmos, and to God. We live today with the legacy of this redefinition. Furthermore, the process of redefinition continues into the present, as witnessed by the recent signing of the Augsburg Accords by the Roman Catholic and Lutheran Churches.

Such debates exemplify how theological ideas and clerical institutions, practices, and identities are both products and coproducers of human culture and society. Studying the primary texts in their historical context allows a glimpse of the growth, if not the birth, of both capitalism and socialism, of democracy, of individualism, and of literacy among laity in the midst of colonial expansion, institutional deterioration and corruption, fanatical apocalypticism, and religious and political torture and massacre.

One witnesses at this time the emergence of religion as a separate category defining human existence, as well as the ascendance of belief over practice as the defining characteristic of religion. The works of the early Reform theologians exhibit a characteristic tendency to distinguish a something called "religion," defined in terms of right belief. Accordingly, right belief, although it stands at the heart of identity or one's soul, exists in a meaningful way separately from one's worldly obligations and activities. Moreover, this something called "religion" can be judged true or false, largely based on the orthodoxy of one's belief and practices.[15] Orthodoxy, in turn, depends ultimately upon subordinating practice and observance to sacred text, as according to specific but often implicit standards. In short, study of this historical period teaches something about the history of the concept of religion itself. The theological debates illuminate a moment in the birth of the distinction between a religious realm and a secular realm. This distinction comes to play a central role in a later tendency, problematic to modern scholars of religion, to define religion by reducing religious life to a worldview or "a system of belief." As we shall shortly see, this tendency becomes a strategy employed by the United States Supreme Court to delineate religious practices, detached from belief and deemed secular, that the state may exercise to enforce its own hegemony.

As recent scholarship has emphasized, the concept *religion* as a general category is not epistemologically, morally, or politically neutral, nor does it possess a single essential meaning.[16] The concept itself has intervened in human communal life to alter the very practices and beliefs that the concept designates. Two examples from different traditions will suffice.

In the case of Christian traditions, relegating biblical texts, creedal formulations, liturgy, and theology to the spiritual realm as religious artifacts has rendered the sociopolitical and economic milieu and activism of Hebrew and Christian origins, as well as later practices, invisible. Insofar as religion, so defined, becomes naturalized, the origins of what becomes Christianity are obscure, the teachings are mystified, and the power of the actual texts and practices to challenge oppressive, reigning political structures diminishes. Spiritualizing Christian traditions to the exclusion of all other facets of human life has further played a role in the emergence of White Christian fundamentalist insistence on literal interpretation of the Christian Bible, as well as claims by biblical historical critics to be "objective" and value neutral in attempts to reconstruct elements of a Christian past.[17] In this case, the concept religion intervenes at the hands of philosophers, theologians, biblical scholars, and clerics to spiritualize ethnically and culturally diverse Christian beliefs and practices.

As another case in point, in an effort to order indigenous subcontinental Indian traditions, British colonial census-taking practices created the religious category "Hinduism" and its cognates, which in turn became assimilated as a self-designation by Indian practitioners.[18] The same census-taking practices further led to the appropriation of so-called religious conversion across traditions on political grounds in order to attain rights accorded to some religions in preference to others.[19] In this case, the concept religion intervenes at the hands of governmental officials and bureaucrats of the British Empire. This last example particularly demonstrates how the state, in this case the British Empire, can use the concept religion to create a religion.

To return to the relative present, the employment of the category religion to secure political hegemony likewise continues today in this country, as exemplified by both the majority and the minority opinions in *Lynch v. Donnelly.* While the majority and the minority disagree sharply over the place of the crèche in the Christmas display, they appear to share a surprising number of assumptions about what religion is and its relation to secularity. For example, both sides agree that the Nativity scene is a "religious" symbol. Both tend to reduce religion as a whole and the particular symbol itself primarily to belief, centered on the supernatural. For the majority, the wider context of the display shifts the meaning of the crèche, relieving it of theological and spiritual content. The minority, by contrast, sees the symbolic meaning as trivialized and a constraint on Christian belief, nevertheless, present and effectively excluding those who do not share more specifically White Christian beliefs (though racial discrimination goes unrecognized).

The most astonishing set of shared assumptions to my mind, however, has to do with the Court's implicit distinction between belief and practice, an effect of its Protestant legacy. Both Burger and Brennan have to confront the history of United States public governmental practices as these are centered on God. For the majority, the practice of displaying a crèche in Pawtucket does not differ fundamentally from the already existing and historically enduring incorporation of theological language and prayer into the daily business and ceremonial occasions of government. For the minority, the crèche is a highly particular, distinctively Christian symbol that by definition cannot be assimilated to existing historical practices. Nevertheless, both sides acknowledge and assent to practices such as prayer and the swearing of oaths and to theological language inscribed on money and incorporated into the pledge of allegiance as recited daily in educational institutions throughout the land. O'Connor justifies these practices as necessary to solemnize public occasions. Brennan portrays them as a "ceremonial deism," not in violation of the First Amendment because they are relatively irrelevant due to a lack of serious theological content or belief. It would appear that for Brennan, God can be sufficiently emptied of meaning by means of the shifting of the context for what were otherwise (and continue to be) Christian practices. Furthermore, the governmental declaration of Christmas as a public holiday can be justified by reducing all non-Christian historical symbols like the Christmas tree to mere "folk traditions," not "religious" because they are merely practices without connection to a belief. The crèche, however, qualifies, apart from any context, as a genuinely religious symbol because its belief content, characterized by its focus on the supernatural, renders it permanently "sacred," thus overwhelming any attempts to de-sacralize by shifting context.

These shared assumptions have both practical and theoretical consequences. Practically speaking, while admittedly the concept God is shared across the monotheistic traditions, as well as across various philosophical traditions, the kind of praying and oath taking practiced, by virtue of their association with the Christian Bible, is distinctively Christian (though not inclusive of all Christian sects and denominations). These practices are neither Muslim nor Jewish, nor are they generically philosophical. Even if one could argue persuasively for a generic monotheism, many traditions practiced in this country are not monotheistic, and many citizens have no identifiably religious affiliation. Such practices exclude them. Speaking theoretically, regardless of the form of theism or lack thereof, most scholars know better than to subordinate either practice or belief to the other in some generic sense. Furthermore, generic definitions of "religion," however disputed they may be, have not for some time defined the category either exclusively or even centrally in terms of belief or the supernatural.

From the standpoint of a theorist of religion, the attempted stripping of symbolic meaning associated with a particular practice such as praying or taking an oath, and its assimilation into a supposedly nonreligious context, perform simultaneously a masking of particular theological content and the production of a religious tradition. What poses as a merely ceremonial practice in a religiously neutral space becomes in effect a masked and expanded form of predominantly White Christianity—a dilution and nationalization of the tradition, if you will. The Court, through its various rulings, authorizes and participates in the creation of a religion. Thus, the Court ironically establishes a state religion of its own making.

Lynch v. Donnelly may redraw the line between religious and secular, but this redrawing does not challenge an already well-established practice of making religion up and making it real by transferring practices, supposedly stripped of belief, into a supposedly neutral ("not religious") context under the aegis of "accommodation." Hypothetically speaking, Brennan's dissenting opinion does not go nearly far enough. Had the dissenters carried the day, "ceremonial deism" would have nevertheless remained intact. In the end, it is an ironic dialectic at work. Christian symbolism and practice, which rely for their meaning in part upon previous Hebrew traditions and in part upon the practices and framing concepts of the Roman Empire, become the central resource to authorize yet another empire. This is certainly not the first time in history that a state recreates Christian symbolism, teaching, and practice in its own image to serve its own ends. Nor is it the first time a state authorizes its power by appealing to religious authority. The history of the inconsistencies of Supreme Court decision making on the religion clauses of the First Amendment, particularly as exemplified by *Lynch v. Donnelly,* appears, however, to be the first time that such fabrication flows from conscious intentions *not* to establish a religion of state.[20]

To understand more fully the implications of this irony, one needs to revisit the Court opinions, this time with a view to clarifying the discursive practices surrounding the category *secular.* Again the commonalities between the majority and the minority are telling. As already noted, secularity and religion depend on each other for their meaning. Burger, Brennan, and, in her separate opinion, O'Connor associate secularity further with national interests and patriotic loyalty. All three note that Christmas is designated a national holiday in conjunction with other national holidays that foster patriotism. Both the majority and the minority concur that it is appropriate to incorporate religious practices into public occasions and public holidays, citing specifically the National Day of Prayer as an example. O'Connor, in approving the display of the Nativity scene, cites in support specifically the need to solemnize public occasions through religious symbols and practices (provided, of course, they neither advance nor prohibit a particular religion). Both the majority and the minority associate with approval the further identification of nation and patriotism with capitalism. Burger, in the majority opinion, accepts without challenge the defendants' argument that the purpose of the Nativity scene is ultimately to create a gift-giving spirit among shoppers in the heart of the business district. While the minority opinion allows that the Nativity scene is not necessary to producing this end, it likewise assumes the conflation of politics, national loyalty, and economics as ingredients of a national identity that Brennan, like Burger, associates with Christmas, insofar as it is celebrated as a secular holiday. While Brennan notes that connecting such an identity to what he calls "ceremonial deism" is not without its problems, he nevertheless continues to distinguish the incorporation of the crèche from ceremonial deism as an integration of select Christian practices with patriotism and *with capitalism,* relatively untroubled by the identification of a specific economic ideology with a loyalty to the state. In contrast to Burger and Brennan, Blackmun's separate opinion, supplementing the minority opinion and citing the testimony of one of the witnesses, notes that, "Pawtucket's display invites people 'to participate in the Christmas spirit, brotherhood, peace, and let loose with their money.'" He further observes with appropriate horror that "[t]he crèche has been relegated to the role of a neutral harbinger of the holiday season, useful for commercial and other purposes, but devoid of any inherent meaning and incapable of enhancing the religious tenor of a display of which it is an integral part" (at 727). Like Brennan, Blackmun finds the commercializing of the crèche offensive; on the related subject of a national identity and its commercialization, he remains silent beyond his concurrence with the general minority opinion.

In short, secularity in this context designates an ostensible, religiously neutral space that may nevertheless employ religious practices, under certain conditions, in the service of building a national identity that preserves national political interests, as they are associated with a capitalist economy. Such celebrations publicly validate national economic and political interests and authority. They further provide the vehicle by which citizens internalize both. Why else solemnize public occasions? At the same time, for those who recognize the particular traditions from which the practices are imported, the symbolic content remains; indeed, even for those who do not recognize the practices as imports, unconscious evocation may occur. Thus the traditions, in this case, predominantly White Christian traditions, become nationalized for commercial as well as political ends. Christian faith conflates with patriotism, which conflates in turn with capitalism in a global economy. Those who are not Christian, along with those Christians for whom such conflations constitute at the very least trivialization and idolatry, are excluded by such practices. White, conservative, evangelical Christians are correct when they claim that the government practices a religion, but ultimately wrong to designate it as "secular humanism." The government-sanctioned religion of the United States restructures elements of Christian traditions, selected for imperial ends. This nationalized Christianity is as troubling for its entanglement with economic ideology as it is for its political ideology. It is neither secular with respect to religious neutrality nor is it humane.

Thinking Theologically

In a world where religion is understood as a "something spiritual," separable from politics, theology constitutes reflection on the spiritual and is restricted to representing particular religious institutions. Disconnected from material life, religion becomes sentimental, nostalgic, and otherworldly, and the role of the theologian as social and cultural critic, including critic of religious institutions, becomes muted and even lost. Meanwhile power, as exercised daily, appears to locate exclusively in the world of commerce, law, and self-governance. Yet *Lynch v. Donnelly* illuminates just how impossible it is to imagine a spiritual realm totally without reference to a material order. Likewise, a secular order, where "secular" is understood as a realm in which the life of the spirit is absent, a religion-free zone if you will, simply does not exist. To construe the world in such a manner results in self-deception, both individual and collective. Christian teaching has historically taken its Hebrew heritage seriously, as one in which God engages humans within history, and has claimed that God has further entered human history in the life, death, and resurrection of Jesus as Christ. From this perspective, life, as it is lived daily, exemplifies instead a wonderfully messy intercourse of the life of the spirit with the material order. In my opinion, part of a theologian's task is to illuminate this messiness.

I use "life of the spirit" provisionally here, in ways that I hope escape or at least minimize reification. We cannot know such a life outside history and nature precisely because we are historical, material beings. We also know that at any given time we do not know all there is to know, nor can we ever know it, because of novelty and human finitude. We do know with certainty that we suffer and that we do damage to other life. We also know that life can be and often is extraordinarily beautiful and good. Within this context of not knowing and knowing, the life of the spirit, fully enmeshed in material conditions, de-centers human self-interest and energizes us to the possibility of transforming conditions of suffering and damage for a provisionally better life with and for others. Such a spirit and such a life are simultaneously both present and other to us; as realities they transcend us because they have not yet been made materially real, even as they reveal themselves partially and tentatively to us in the ethical and political ambiguities of the here and now. Thus, even though "life of the spirit" is itself obviously a conceptual construction, reflecting what are obviously Christian traditions of thought and practice, it is an attempt to confront human tragedy and the limitations of being human from a necessarily agnostic, yet hopeful and joyful perspective.

This seems so paltry. Or is it? The Gospel narratives surrounding Jesus' birth themselves exemplify the life of the spirit at work in and with material conditions, the very messiness of which I speak. Note, however, that part of the messiness lies in this, that while the narratives may reveal the life of the spirit, they do not lend themselves merely accidentally to later imperial and capitalist appropriations.

The birth narratives have received extensive treatment elsewhere.[21] I wish to focus simply on one central feature as it is particularly exemplified in the Gospel according to Matthew, namely, the element of political conflict surrounding kingship. The conflict takes place essentially around kingship and is filtered through the lens of Israel's history of exile and exodus. In the beginning of the narrative, the Gospel writer identifies the infant Jesus with the Davidic line as a king of the Judeans. This line is divided into three sets of fourteen generations each—from Abraham to David, from David to the deportation to Babylon, and from the deportation to Joseph, Jesus' stepfather. According to this account, three Magi (often translated *kings* or *wise men*) visit the newly born child in a house in Bethlehem where they bestow gifts upon him. These Magi have sought Jesus first in Jerusalem at the palace of Herod, king of Judea. Herod is secretly frightened by the news that a new king has been born. He nevertheless feigns positive interest in the child, admonishing the three sojourners to find Jesus and then let him know of Jesus' whereabouts so that Herod might pay him homage. The three travelers, having found Jesus, do not reveal his location to Herod, but instead return surreptitiously to their homeland. An angel warns Joseph in a dream to take his family and flee to Egypt, which he does. Herod, unable to find Jesus, becomes infuriated and has all children under the age of two killed. The Gospel writer identifies this slaughter with Rachel's lament found in Jeremiah (Jer. 31:15). Jesus' family remains in Egypt until the death of Herod. The family, at an angel's behest, thereupon returns, though not without fear of the new ruler Archelaus.

This saga is far richer in meaning than I can do justice here, and the theme of kingship is further taken up in a different way in the Gospel according to Luke. I shall simply restrict myself to a brief gloss on the Matthean account. The birth of Jesus marks a conflict between the imperial power of Rome as represented by Herod, Augustus Caesar's appointee, and a resisting power attributed to God as the representative of the Palestinian Jews and residing in the infant Jesus as a new, popular king. Jesus' kingship presents a clear challenge to the reigning powers of the time. Moreover, Jesus' kingship can be recognized by the association of his birth history with the history of the Israelites, particularly the exodus from Egypt and the Babylonian captivity. Not only does Jesus belong to the Davidic line through his stepfather, Joseph, but his life recapitulates the exodus of Israel, led by Moses, who escapes death at the hands of the king of Egypt in his infancy and grows up in the royal household, only to confront the king and ultimately lead his people from bondage. Herod's genocide also parallels that of the king of Egypt by putting to death the children under two, though in this case the text curiously refers to "all the children," not just the males (Matt. 2:16).

The Gospel writer further associates Jesus' birth with exile. The Babylonian captivity is clearly flagged as significant to the genealogy. The slaughter of innocent children not only evokes the memory of the slaughter of the Israelite male babies in Egypt, but also is explicitly identified with Rachel's lamentation and supplication in behalf of the captive Hebrews in transit through Ramah to Babylon. Biblical scholars have often reduced this wealth of detail to a contrivance by the Gospel writer to fulfill the ancient prophecy, "Out of Egypt I will call my son . . . " (Hos. 11:1), largely because the Gospel writer makes this connection explicit. The introduction of the Babylonian captivity, however, would seem superfluous to this end. And even assuming that the flight into Egypt and the slaughter of the innocents constitute a contrivance, why would it be important to the Gospel writer to fulfill this particular prophecy unless the exodus story, along with the exile, has special significance?

The preoccupation with exodus and exile marks the context as political, and highlights that the issue is the liberation of a people from foreign conquest to a new order, centered by God's authority rather than that of imperial Rome.[22] While the text lends itself to a number of possible interpretations, I concur with New Testament scholar Richard Horsley that it is supremely a story of resistance to imperial power. A new king, God's child, has been born, before whom other, earthly kings will bow. Imperialism is to be displaced by God's rule, to which all else is subordinated. In this sense the Gospel writer deconstructs monarchy by subordinating its authority to a different power. God's rule, described elsewhere in the Gospel euphemistically as the kingdom of Heaven, challenges and transforms political and economic oppression, as well as religious institutions that explicitly or tacitly support the status quo of that era. These latter would include not only the religious institutions and practices of Palestinian Judaism, challenged from the inside by an insider, Jesus himself, but also the religion of state, one that deified its emperors and proclaimed peace on the backs of the conquered. This claim to kingship constitutes treason, and this birth is a disruptive event, fraught with violence, tragedy, and lamentation, qualities altogether lacking in most contemporary Christian celebrations of Christmas in the United States.

A child, conceived out of wedlock, is born to a woman whose fiancé is not the father. Trusting divine authority, her fiancé nevertheless stands by her, marrying her, only to find the new family at risk at the hands of the imperial state. Royal strangers show up out of the East, distribute gifts, then leave as abruptly as they appeared. Warned by a messenger from God, the family goes into exile so that the baby might live. Their return under a different human ruler is not entirely secure. No one in the family belongs to the dominant culture (Greco-Roman) or to the dominant ethnic group (Roman) or to the dominant religious tradition (the cult of the emperor). The family does not appear to be particularly affluent. What a strange but telling context for the birth of the King of kings!

Just as God responds to Rachel's supplication according to the prophet Jeremiah, so, according to the Gospel writer, God, through God's messengers and through Joseph's efforts, upholds Jesus and Jesus' family—in transit, displaced, and at home. In this particular instance, life triumphs over death. The baby lives. This upholding does not, however, compensate for the hideous slaughter of the other children. Furthermore, Jesus himself goes on to die the ignominious death of a political traitor. The life of the spirit is messy, immersed in material existence rather than aloof from it, resistant to imperialism but vulnerable to it as well.

Nagging Questions

Lynch v. Donnelly as one "moment" in the history of the creation of a religion of state, placed alongside the Matthean narrative of Jesus' birth, viewed with attention to the Gospel's political concerns, poses very troubling questions surrounding the celebration of Christmas as presently practiced in the United States and now extended to "the holidays." Within the context of those communities that celebrate Christmas on theological grounds, what might Advent and Christmas liturgies look like that take seriously both the politics of Jesus' birth and the tragedy, as well as the joy, that surround it? For those who practice faith in Jesus' name, would giving gifts be modified?[23] Would affluent White Christians come to recognize the affinities of their social location with that of the beneficiaries of the Roman state? Would they further recognize how their culture has racialized their celebrations? (Jesus was not, after all, of European extraction.) Would visual representations of the Holy Family be de-racialized? ("White" is, after all, a color.) How might the multiple implications of the conditions of Jesus' birth, according to the birth narratives, be incorporated into daily life throughout the year? At present, Christmas practices tend to exemplify by default, if not by intention, loyalty to a national religion that authorizes an empire, rather than loyalty to the one whose birth and death challenge the building of empires.

Equally as important, the Court narrative and the birth narrative challenge us to rethink what it means to live in a religiously plural democracy that purportedly relishes differences by preserving the right to dissent. Can there be a secular space that is not simply a faded form of White Reformed Protestantism, a public space that welcomes a full range of traditions now called religious, with nonreligious traditions, without privileging any particular tradition? For Christians across the spectrum of Christian traditions, what would it mean to live and work as a citizen in such a space, as just one among many rather than as the beneficiary of the dominant group? For all of us, whether religious or not, can there be the cultivation of a critical, penultimate, yet deep loyalty to one's country that acknowledges the authority of prior and different loyalties to transcendent realities? A loyalty that is not tied to an oppressive economic ideology and its practices? A loyalty that seriously confronts the Whiteness, sexism, classism, and homophobia of these practices? In short, one that challenges empire building at every level? Could the state itself honor such a loyalty that would subordinate loyalty to its own interests? How would such a state solemnize its occasions in light of such a loyalty? The ambiguities of our historical origins notwithstanding, the present religious, political, and economic practices of the United States align far more clearly with those of imperial Rome than with its resisters.

The road from the narrative of competing kings and political resistance to the placing of a Nativity scene, peopled by White mannequins, in a Christmas display with Santa, reindeer, clown, and teddy bear, so that "people might let loose with their money" and so that the United States might "solemnize" its public occasions, is politically and theologically treacherous. In its very vulnerability the life of the spirit happens to be ironically appropriated along the way. The birth narrative lends itself to multiple interpretations because the language of kingship and gift giving is ambiguous and because no people, most especially not God's people, whoever they may be, are immune to the temptations of imperialism and the corruption of power. The kings who, bearing gifts, bowed down before the infant Jesus and the king who sought to kill him recognized him or feared him as the King of kings, a title that carries with it a triumphalism that has plagued Christianity throughout its dubious history. Furthermore, the traditions of Christian resistance that have also existed side by side with Christian triumphalism have ironically depended to some extent upon the success of the triumphalists for continued transmission of the traditions themselves. That triumphalist interpretations would wed happily with imperialism is simply logical; that resistance would nevertheless survive at all is an utterly amazing gift. So the baby lives on.

Notes

1. The Constitution of the United States, Article 1.

2. These are only some of the examples of issues brought before the Supreme Court. The first case ever tried was *Reynolds v. United States,* 98 U.S. 145, 164 (1879). The Court determined that the Mormon practice of multiple wives was not a protected exercise of free expression because it violated a wider public good.

3. 465 U.S. 668 (1984). All future references to this case cited by page number in parentheses in text.

4. Robert N. Bellah, *The Broken Covenant: American Civil Religion in Time of Trial* (New York: Seabury, 1975) and the collection of essays Bellah edited as *Varieties of Civil Religion* (San Francisco: Harper and Row, 1980). For more recent discussions, see the transcript "In God We Trust and Uncivil Religion in America," from the series *Encounter,* produced by the Australian Broadcasting Company and aired on Radio National, Sunday, October 17, 1999.

5. Ronald B. Flowers, *That Godless Court? Supreme Court Decisions in Church-State Relations* (Louisville: Westminster John Knox, 1994).

6. It is important to flag "White" here. One need only look at the racial marking of most Nativity scenes displayed in the United States—the whiteness of the "Holy Family" and attending figures, with the exception of one of the Magi on rare occasions—against the backdrop of Nativity scenes produced around the world, to grasp the racism of Christmas as it is currently celebrated in this country. The influence of idealizations of Victorian practices assimilated into current celebrations highlights

the classism and sexism of our practices as well. Last but not least, gender difference plays a central role in strategies promoting consumerism at work in the marketing of Christmas. Addressing the full scope of these interactive forces, as they pervade not only Christmas but also the holidays taken as a whole, is unfortunately beyond the scope of a single essay.

7. For historical overview and, in some cases, critique of Christmas traditions in this country, see J. M. Golby and A. W. Purdue, *The Making of the Modern Christmas* (Athens: University of Georgia Press, 1986); Stephen Nissenbaum, *The Battle for Christmas* (New York: Alfred A. Knopf, 1996); Penne L. Restad, *Christmas in America: A History* (New York: Oxford University Press, 1995); and Lee Eric Schmidt, *Consumer Rites: The Buying and Selling of American Holidays* (Princeton, N.J.: Princeton University Press, 1995), 105–91.

8. 691 F.2d 1029.

9. The Supreme Court established these criteria, known as the "Lemon test," in *Lemon v. Kurtzman,* 403 U.S. 602, 614 (1971).

10. A free market model for the religious consumer should not escape the careful reader's notice here.

11. Several scholars are at work putting together different pieces of this history. For one of the best examples, see Samuel J. Preus, *Explaining Religion: Criticism and Theory from Bodin to Freud* (Atlanta: Scholars Press, 1996).

12. See Emile Durkheim, *The Elementary Forms of the Religious Life* (New York: Free Press/Macmillan, 1965); Peter L. Berger and Thomas Luckmann, *The Social Construction of Reality: A Treatise on the Sociology of Knowledge* (New York: Doubleday and Company, 1966); and Clifford Geertz, "Religion as Cultural System," in *The Interpretation of Cultures: Selected Essays* (New York: Basic Books, 1973), 87–125.

13. See, for examples, Talal Asad, *Genealogies of Religion: Discipline and Reasons of Power in Christianity and Islam* (Baltimore: Johns Hopkins University Press, 1993); Gerald James Larson, *India's Agony over Religion* (Albany: SUNY, 1995); Gauri Viswanathan, *Outside the Fold: Conversion, Modernity, and Belief* (Princeton, N.J.: Princeton University Press, 1998); and Tomoko Masuzawa, "The Question of Universality," Robert C. Lester Lecture, University of Colorado (Boulder: University of Colorado, 2000).

14. Some of this material appears in altered form in Paula M. Cooey, "Immigration, Exodus, and Exile: Academic Theology and Higher Education" in *Journal for Teaching Theology and Religion* 3, no. 3 (October 2000): 27–32.

15. For a classic example, see Zwingli's "Commentary on True and False Religion," in *The Protestant Reformation,* ed. Hans J. Hillerbrand (New York: Harper & Row, 1968), 108–21.

16. Geertz's often-used definition of religion as symbol system has come under attack precisely because it does not take into account how power configures within symbols systems, nor does it take into account the history of the concept religion itself. See, for example, Talal Asad, *Genealogies of Religion: Discipline and Reasons of Power in Christianity and Islam* (Baltimore: Johns Hopkins University Press, 1993). For a critique of the mystification of religion by scholars of religion, see Steven M. Wasserstrom, *Religion after Religion: Gerschom Scholem, Mircea Eliade, and Henry Corbin* (Princeton, N.J.: Princeton University Press, 1999).

17. See Richard A. Horsley, *The Liberation of Christmas: The Infancy Narratives in Social Context* (New York: Crossroad, 1989), 1–19.

18. See Larson, *India's Agony over Religion,* especially 1–44 and 178–225.

19. See Viswanathan, *Outside the Fold.*

20. There are two points worth observing here:

First, how the jurists perform against their own explicit intentions requires an extended deconstruction that is beyond the scope of this essay. I note in passing, however, that such a deconstruction would focus on sociopolitical analysis rather than psychological analysis. The question at the heart of the matter is this: What is it about the sociopolitical context that derails explicit individual and group intentions to the contrary? How is the culture so inscribed as to subvert explicit intentions?

Second, subsequent decisions following *Lynch v. Donnelly,* while in some ways clarifying, nevertheless continue this practice. See, for example, *Allegheny County v. ACLU of Pittsburgh* 492 U.S. 573 (1989). The Court determined that a Nativity scene, marked by a banner reading *"Gloria in Excelsis Deo!"* and placed on the grand staircase of the Allegheny County Courthouse, violated the establishment clause because it stood alone (without other clearly secular symbols). The Court further ruled that a second display, also on government property, one block away from the first, did not violate the establishment clause. The second display consisted of a menorah, placed next to a large Christmas tree, accompanied by a banner reading, "During this holiday season the city of Pittsburgh salutes liberty. Let these festive lights remind us that we are keepers of the flame of liberty and our legacy of freedom." The text and the placing of the Christmas tree apparently vitiated any conflict over the theological symbolism of the menorah, thus extending ceremonial deism to include in this instance a specifically Jewish symbol. To heap further irony upon irony, that the Court itself was the vehicle for emptying the first display's symbol of its political and economic meaning and the second display's symbols of their theological content remains masked throughout the discourse of the trial.

21. See for examples, Raymond E. Brown, *Birth of the Messiah: A Commentary on the Infancy Narratives in Matthew and Luke* (Garden City, N.Y.: Doubleday, 1977), and Horsley, *The Liberation of Christmas.*

22. Many theologians, among others, regard Matthew 5:1–7:27, the "Sermon on the Mount," to be a blueprint for God's rule on earth.

23. For example, some of the more liberal churches put on Christmas fairs where families purchase goods for the two-thirds world and domestic poor, such as sewing machines, tools, and livestock, given in the name of particular family members and friends. Instead of the usual gifts, said family and friends receive handmade ornaments and cards (made by church members), noting the purchase. Does this simply shift the grounds of consumerism or does this practice create a different understanding of gift?

Epilogue

Richard Horsley

Christmas evokes great anticipations for fulfilling experiences. Expectations are high for fun parties at the office and with groups of friends, special performances, and especially for that wonderful intimate time together as a family and for those gifts that will be under the tree on Christmas morning. Before long, however, nerves are frayed from the extra heavy traffic of the season, the long lines at the check-out registers, and pretending to be caught up in the "Christmas spirit." To add the extra activities necessary to participate in the prolonged five- or six-week Christmas festival onto already busy or overextended schedules raises the level of stress precariously high. Then, of course, things don't turn out nearly as nicely as expected. Many are downright relieved when it is all over and they can really get a "holiday" from the frenetic festival. Most feel seriously ambivalent about Christmas. Many suffer through it with considerable discontent and depression.

To complain about and criticize Christmas, however, is to risk being labeled as a "Scrooge" or a "Grinch." There is no holiday that Americans "buy into" more than the Christmas "Holidays." As Kathleen Sands observes in chapter 4 above, this is because Christmas is understood not as a religious festival—we have learned to criticize religion!—but as a "secular" festival. This has a depressing effect on our ability to criticize or to decline to participate in the various rituals of Christmas. Freedom of religion is one of those most cherished rights in the United States, guaranteed by the Bill of Rights. We have the right to choose or reject beliefs, to participate or not participate in holidays that are recognized as religious. But to opt out of gift giving and receiving, to decline invitations to parties, or simply to voice criticism is to risk social shame and "excommunication."

As noted in the essays above, however, the pretense that Christmas is "secular" serves to veil the surreptitious transfer of religious authority to secular behavior, particularly the sale of commodities. No less than the Supreme Court's justices argued that the all-important intent of Christmas, with its displays of Santa's village, snow men, and Nativity scenes, is to create a spirit of giving so that people will do more shopping. Yet, by participating in the consumption rituals of Christmas like shopping for gifts, most people do not realize that they are participating in the religion of consumer capitalism. They are being induced by the advertising media and the corporate sponsorship of festival performances and displays to serve the superhuman force(s) that determine their life, without making a conscious decision to do so.

But what if Americans wanted to assert their freedom of religion with regard to Christmas? They would be building on a long historical heritage of taking action to insist on fundamental rights. Although it meant destruction for Native American peoples, the European settlement of the Atlantic Seaboard was an attempt to assert freedom from political and religious tyranny. Similarly, the Declaration of Independence and the Revolutionary War asserted freedom from authoritarian political rule. The emphasis in the formation of the United States, however, was so heavily focused on political freedom that the founders and founding documents did not anticipate the possibility of future domination by economic power. Given the dramatic transformation of traditional agrarian society by the industrial revolution in the nineteenth century, and then the even more dramatic transformation from small local businesses into huge multinational corporations, accompanied by media advertising's channeling people's desire into gross consumption, new forms of domination have taken control of our lives. And they have done this is in ways that have become a new religion, as we can see by simple comparison with traditional religious practices. Since the new forms of religious domination are inseparable from the economic practices that they serve and legitimate, however, assertion of the freedom of religion almost necessarily involves assertion of economic freedom as well.

Those who may wish to assert their freedom of religion, their right not to believe and participate in the religion of consumer capitalism that has come to pervade the airwaves and the visual, spatial, and aural environment, cannot go it alone. American hyper-individualism, like the separation of the "secular" from the religious, is another illusion on which advertising and consumerism thrive. The illusion that the individual can exercise freedom to choose, as if there were no determining influences in one's life and the context and environment of individual life, enables the media to keep people atomized, without regular social and political association and susceptible to the centralized programming and advertising that creates in them the requisite "moods and motivation" that induce the desired patterns of consumption. The historic assertions of freedom were certainly not matters of individual dissent or refusal, but of collective action by associations and communities of people. Similarly, it is a modern illusion that religion is primarily a matter of individual belief. Rather practice of religion involves beliefs and rituals and celebrations shared with an association or community of other persons.

Those who may wish to assert their freedom of religion with regard to Christmas as the festival of consumer capitalism will have to sort out what they are affirming and what they are rejecting. Presumably most of us are very much in favor of festivity and celebration, but we want it to be our celebration. We want especially to choose what we are celebrating rather than allow huge corporations to sponsor various aspects of the holiday festival as a way of enticing us into a mood in which they can sell us a bill of goods that we neither really want nor need and that will not satisfy our deeper longings. Presumably also, most would affirm abundance. Yet we know that it is not ultimately very satisfying and is utterly unfair and unjust that the abundance is hoarded by a tiny fraction of the world's population and not shared particularly with millions of starving and undernourished people in the world. All indications are, moreover, that the world cannot sustain for very long the level of consumption driven by consumer capitalism and mystified, enhanced, and legitimated by the Christmas festival under the guise of gift-giving.

Similarly, declining to participate in consumer capitalist Christmas may be one of the best ways to cultivate the rich multi-cultural traditions often associated with the holidays. The capitalist commodification of culture in fact culturally impoverishes people and diminishes their social and familial life as well. It is not difficult to imagine what is lost when the only way a child hears a beloved story is from a cartoon version on "kid-vid" or a Christmas special, even if watched together with the parents. Hearing Christmas carols, cantatas, and concertos only on CD or TV deprives people of the personal and interpersonal enjoyment and satisfaction of making music themselves or hearing them performed live by a local musical group.

Creative resistance and alternatives to consumer capitalist Christmas have been around for some time. Some are well-established in certain areas, although most are simply local community and association's pursuits. A few groups have published ideas and a few organizations have mounted regular demonstrations.[1] Others have mounted compelling alternative performances and alternative rituals and festivals. In some cases even large-scale community-wide celebrations that involve tens of thousand of participants have become annual "traditions." The following is intended only as an illustrative review of some of the alternatives that we are aware of.

Parody and satire help us maintain our sanity. Less commercial and more "down-home" country music is usually good for poking fun at the dominant culture. Satire and parody help us not to take things that are supposedly merely "secular" too seriously. For the phony family values that Santa Claus has been used to evoke, we could sing along with the song about how

> Grandma got run over by a reindeer
> Walkin' home from our house Christmas Eve....
> You may say there's no such thing as Santa,
> But as for me and Grandpa, we believe!

Editorial cartoonists contribute every so often. One from early in the Christmas festival of 2000 presents an astute analysis of what's really happening in the festival of consumption, including its undermining of "family values." A little boy on Santa's lap says "I want lots of stuff that I don't need and that won't make me any happier, so my parents will plunge deeper into debt, be forced to work all the time, leaving me alone to play with guns and online porn." Another, showing a picture of parent and child at a check-out booth, explained the retailers' severe disappointment at the actual decline in anticipated retail sales during Christmas 2000 as due to people discovering the real reason for the season.

Christmas itself, especially the nostalgic "old-timey" Christmas of the Victorians and of the extensive "Enchanted Village" display in department stores and of the movies such as *White Christmas,* consists mostly of "invented tradition"—invented by those elite Knickerbockers in early-nineteenth-century New York City, by Hollywood, by multinational corporations, by Madison Avenue. How appropriate then for people to invent some traditions of their own or to revive and adapt some really old ones! It would be difficult to rival the age-old tradition of celebrating the Winter Solstice, for example, by watching through the longest night of the year (usually December 21), with candles burning, for the return of the life-giving sun. Many groups, usually relatively small gatherings of friends, are creating their own celebrations of the Solstice, such as neo-pagan wiccans who gather round a fire watching through the night for the rebirth of the sun or associations that have "winter parties" as a pointed substitute for "Christmas parties." On a larger scale, and now spreading from the Boston area to other large urban areas such as Portland and Puget Sound, is the creation of the "Christmas Revels." Beginning with the rival of old English customs such as mumming and Morris dancing and other carnival-like features, the "Revels" have offered performances based on carefully researched revival of traditional rituals and performances of a variety of peoples and areas. Another recent creation that has a bit of satire and a distinctive ethnic flavor is the performance of the Klesmer Nutcracker. In a bit of a spoof on the highly artistic and pricey performance of the Nutcracker ballet downtown, a band plays a gleeful adaptation of Tchaikowsky's "Nutcracker Suite" in a mainly Jewish neighborhood in the musical idiom of klesmer, reviving the traditional music of the performers' grandparents who immigrated from the Jewish ghettos of Eastern Europe, in connection with the American Jewish community's distinctive celebration of Hanukkah as an alternative to Christmas, ostensibly a Christian festival.

Most Christian denominations and groups have simply gone along with the dominant Christmas festival as it has developed. Even the die-hard New England churches of Puritan heritage eventually gave in. Judging from the results of attempts by the Knights of Columbus and others to "put Christ back in Christmas," such efforts only too easily become absorbed into the dominant festival, lending further legitimacy and blessing from "real" religion. Some churches are now considering the possibility of establishing a different time for the celebration of the birth and incarnation of Christ in order to separate it more clearly from the festival of consumption. Of course, that does not solve the problem of how to resist and create an alternative to the dominant festival from which they wish to dissociate the birth of Christ. One alternative established in Boston and now spreading to other cities is "Black Nativity," a performance in Gospel music and dance of the story of Jesus' birth as told by the poet Langston Hughes. One can easily imagine local church communities creating more complete multifaceted, prolonged, and highly participatory alternative festivals that reinforce in community drama, music, story-telling, meals, and rituals the alternative values and practice that such a community would decide to embody.

The cooperative exercise of freedom of religion, however, is unavoidably inseparable from the economic dimension, given the dominance of what has become consumer capitalist Christmas. Such resistance and alternative practice would thus presumably focus on consumption. In tens of thousands of cases, of course, individuals and families purposely make their own gifts, thus avoiding participation in the orgy of consumption, at least at this symbolic time. Others purposely buy gifts from local artisans and/or Mom and Pop stores in order both to support local economies and avoid the dominant economic system. More dramatically "taking it to the streets," particularly in up-scale shopping areas, one group has already begun demonstrations in shopping areas on "Buy Nothing Day," pressing the public to deliberately avoid consumption, at least symbolically, on what has become the biggest shopping day of the year, the day after Thanksgiving. One can imagine other creative alternatives that either avoid retailing and advertising altogether, or channel it into support of local economies.

Larger community alternatives are unusually difficult to organize, hence are relatively few. One that has drawn massive participation from the general public where it has been organized, suggesting that there is a widespread yearning out there for more genuine community-based celebration, is what is called "First Night." This is a most remarkable contrast to the extensive and frenetic and completely commercialized Christmas festival that precedes it. Advertising and retailing, except for restaurants and coffee shops, are absent. The streets of the central city are closed to traffic. Hundreds of thousands of people, many parents with small children, many entire families, and many groups of friends of all ages, come out to enjoy the ice-sculptures, the fire-works, the abundant activities and performances, and, of course, one another, as they celebrate the coming of the New Year. The opening grand parade features neighborhood and/or ethnic groups in low-cost ethnic or other creative costumes and street performances. Note the contrast to the nationally televised and corporately sponsored "Tournament of Roses Parade" the next morning. In between a "family fireworks" early in the evening for the children and the midnight fireworks for the late revellers, those who participate can take in their choice of hundreds of performances, ranging from classical, rock, and folk music to participatory theater and dancing in the many churches and other auditoriums that open their doors to the festivities. Such a festival, now in its twentieth year, offers hope that there is still a vital community spirit in a multicultural society quite apart from the dominant economy of consumption celebrated and mystified in the great American Christmas festival.

Note

1. For example, a group named "Alternatives" has published *To Celebrate Re-shaping Holidays and Rites of Passage* (Ellenwood, Ga.: Alternatives, 1987); *Whose Birthday Is It, Anyway?* (Ellenwood, Ga.: Alternatives, 1989).

Contributors

PAULA COOEY is Margaret W. Harmon Professor of Christian Theology and Culture at Macalester College.

RICHARD HORSLEY is Distinguished Professor of Liberal Arts and the Study of Religion at the University of Massachusetts Boston.

MAX A. MYERS is Canon Theologian at St. Paul's Cathedral, Buffalo, New York.

ELIZABETH PLECK is Associate Professor of History at the University of Illinois Urbana-Champaign.

KATHLEEN M. SANDS is Professor of Religion at the University of Massachusetts Boston.

A. P. SIMONDS is Associate Professor of Political Science at the University of Massachusetts Boston.

JAMES TRACY is Headmaster of Boston University Academy.

Index

advertising
  American values and, 15
  complaints about Christmas, 102–3
  example of, 84–85
  as faux religion, 103–4
  gender power relations and, 108n.33
  harmful effects of, 105–6
  of jewelry, 87
  and the lack of guilt about consumption, 16
  language of, 89–96
  other holidays and, 15–16
  range of influence of, 104–5
  Super Bowl and, 96–97
  of toys, 86–87
  turn-of-the-century, 14
  year-long business cycles and Christmas, 97–102
African Americans
  Christmas movies and, 51, 75–76
  Kwanzaa and, 22–25
  migration to the North by, 18n.2
  women, in the sixties, 32
  See also Black power; Kwanzaa
Agrippa I, 152
AIDS, 197
Akitu, 175, 176, 177, 178
alcohol, 3, 29, 44, 53
alienation from Christmas, 19, 20–21. *See also* anxiety about Christmas; holiday blues
Allegheny County v. ACLU of Pittsburgh, 218n.20
Allen v. Hickel, 27
American Civil Liberties Union, 27
American Jewish Committee, 27
American Jewish Congress, 27, 28
anti-Semitism, 43, 63, 74, 139
anxiety about Christmas, 10–11. *See also* alienation from Christmas; holiday blues
apocalyptic literature, 135
Archelaus, 148
Arnell, Peter, 87
Asian Americans, 76
Astaire, Fred, 43, 69, 80n.6
atheists, 27
Athronges, 133–34, 151

Augustus
  festival in honor of, 117, 119
  Greeks' worship of, 187n.12
  on Herod, 146
  imperial cult of, 120
  Jesus contrasted with, 116, 130, 135–36
  pax Romana of, 122
  tribute exacted by, 126
  See also Caesar

Babylon, 176, 177
Babylonian captivity, 213–14
Battle for Christmas, The (Nissenbaum), 2–5, 9, 40. *See also* Nissenbaum, Stephen
Bauer, David, 159n.1
Bell, Catherine, 56–57
Bellah, Robert, 200
Ben, Lisa, 70
Berlin, Irving, 43, 59, 60, 74, 75
Bernays, Edward, 107n.23
Bérubé, Allan, 65
Bethlehem, 127, 128, 130
birth narratives. *See* Jesus
Blackmun, Harry, 201, 203, 205, 211
Black nationalism, 22–24
"Black Nativity," 223
Black power, 22
Boorstin, Daniel, 92, 109n.47
brand names, 87
Breen, Joseph, 42
Brennan, William, 201, 203–5, 209, 210, 211
Brown, Norman O., 20
Brown, Raymond, 137n.29
Buddhism, 196
Burger, Warren, 201, 209, 210–11

Caesar
  census of, 125–29
  festivals for, 114–21
  Galilean and Judean resistance to, 123–25
  Jesus contrasted with, 121–22
  pax Romana of, 122–23
  See also Augustus
Caligula, 125
Camus, Albert, 20
capital, 183–85. *See also* capitalism; consumer capitalism